Introduction to Human Memory

Introduction to Modern Psychology

General Editor: Max Coltheart
Professor of Psychology, University of London

The Construction of Personality: An Introduction, Sarah Hampson
Clinical Psychopathology: An Introduction, E.M. Coles
Consistency in Cognitive Social Behaviour: An Introduction to Social Psychology,
    Camilla Mower White
Introduction to Human Memory, Vernon H. Gregg
Language Processing, Margaret Harris and Max Coltheart
Introduction to Physiological Psychology, Simon Green

Introduction to Human Memory

Vernon H. Gregg

Department of Psychology
Birkbeck College
University of London

Routledge & Kegan Paul
London, Boston and Henley

First published in 1986
by Routledge & Kegan Paul plc

14 Leicester Square, London WC2H 7PH, England

9 Park Street, Boston, Mass. 02108, USA and

Broadway House, Newtown Road,
Henley on Thames, Oxon RG9 1EN, England

Set in Baskerville, 11 on 12 pt
by Columns of Reading
and printed in Great Britain
by Robert Hartnoll (1985) Ltd
Bodmin, Cornwall

Library of Congress Cataloging in Publication Data

Gregg, Vernon H., 1949-
Introduction to human memory.
(Introductions to modern psychology)
Bibliography: p.
Includes indexes.
1. Memory. I. Title. II. Series.
BF371.G73   1986   153.1'2   85-11825

British Library CIP data also available

ISBN 0-7100-9687-9
ISBN 0-7102-0708-5 (pbk.)

For Danielle, Jonathan and Nicola

Contents

Figures

Preface

This book aims to acquaint the reader with a body of recent experimental findings and theoretical ideas concerning human memory. In writing it I have taken account of the questions my own students have persistently asked and the issues they have had difficulty grappling with.

While each chapter deals with an identifiable area of memory research I have taken care to build on what has been covered in earlier chapters with the aim of providing an integrated treatment of the subject. Throughout the book there is an emphasis on the way ideas about general and specific aspects of memory have developed over the recent past. I have tried to avoid expressing a strong commitment to any particular theoretical approach. Rather, I have attempted to help the reader appreciate the variety of approaches which characterizes memory research and adopt a critical attitude to them all.

A number of people have given me comments on this book at various stages of preparation and I thank them all. But I must give special acknowledgment to the advice and encouragement provided by John Gardiner of the City University, London, with whom I have had the privilege to carry out research over a number of years, and by my close friend Slater Newman of the State University of North Carolina.

Birkbeck College
University of London

Acknowledgments

The author gratefully acknowledges permission to include the following figures:

Figure 2.1   (From Sperling, 1960). Copyright (1960) by the American Psychological Association. Adapted by permission of the publisher and author.

Figure 2.2   (From Sperling 1967). Copyright (1967) by North-Holland Publishing Company. Adapted by permission of the publisher and author.

Figure 2.3   (From Sperling, 1963). Copyright by The Human Factors Society Inc. Adapted by permission of the publisher and author.

Figure 2.4   (From Posner *et al.*, 1969). Copyright (1969) by the American Psychological Society. Adapted by permission of the publisher and author.

Figure 3.2   (From Darwin *et al.*, 1972). Copyright (1972) by Academic Press Inc. Adapted by permission of the publisher and author.

Figure 3.4   (From Crowder and Morton, 1969). Copyright (1969) by Psychonomic Journals Inc. Adapted by permission of the publisher and author.

Figures 4.1 and 4.2   (From Waugh and Norman, 1965). Copyright (1965) American Psychological Association. Adapted by permission of the publisher and author.

Figure 4.3   (From Glanzer and Cunitz, 1966). Copyright Academic Press Inc. Adapted by permission of the publisher and author.

Figure 4.4   (From Craik, 1970, and Rundus, 1971). Copyright (1970) by Academic Press Inc. and (1971) American Psychological Association. Adapted by permission of the publishers and authors.

Figure 4.5   (From Atkinson and Shiffrin, 1971). Copyright (1971) by Scientific American Inc. Adapted by permission of the publisher.

Figure 6.2   (From Flexer and Tulving, 1978). Copyright (1978) American Psychological Association. Adapted by permission of the publisher and author.

Figure 8.1   (From Craik, 1977). Copyright Van Nostrand Reinhold Company. Adapted by permission of the publisher and author.

1 Introduction

Understanding memory

A conceptualization of memory

Even the most cursory examination of human behaviour reveals that current activities are inescapably linked to the past. Such knowledge of the physical world, of the properties of objects and substances, of machines and animals, that a person requires for a competent and safe existence must be acquired by experience. This experience may be direct contact with the environment or it may be the communication of facts by verbal or other means, but the cumulative effects of past experiences lie at the root of knowledge. This is true also for the social environment: the acquisition of language skills and social conventions all depend on experience, as do expectations about the behaviour of members of perceived social groups. In addition to such general knowledge, how people perceive themselves – their self image – depends on placing themselves in relation to what has happened in the past and what consequently may be expected to happen in the future. Equally, in addition to such general knowledge competent behaviour requires that specific past events exert their influences in the present. For example, it is essential that there is some 'keeping track' of what has happened: if the completion of particular tasks were not influential on future behaviour they might be repeated again and again! And imagine the difficulties if resolutions for future actions exerted no influence when the time to act came!

These observations, while superficial, show that coping with the present and planning for the future invariably involve drawing on past experience. There must, then, be some means, internal to the individual, of bridging the gap between the past and the present. Understanding that bridging forms the basis of memory research and of this book.

The cognitive approach

The study of human memory can be approached in any of a number of ways. Interest may, for example, be concentrated on those biochemical changes in neural pathways which accompany the acquisition, retention or forgetting of material. Alternatively, the specific neural structures in the brain which are necessary for particular remembering activities may be the subject of enquiry. But while it must be accepted that certain physical processes and structures are necessary for the proper functioning of memory, the psychology of memory need not be concerned with them at all. It is possible, for example, to gain a satisfactory understanding of why a person should strive to remember the contents of a psychology course, or why he should wish *not* to remember a particularly unpleasant experience, without resorting to physical mechanisms.

Yet another approach to understanding memory falls within the framework of what has become generally known as *cognitive psychology*. This is based on the assumption that observed patterns of behaviour, together with private subjective experiences, depend on unobservable 'mental' events involving mental mechanisms and processes. The fundamental aim of cognitive psychology is to identify these events and to determine lawful relationships amongst them, and between them and observed behaviours. In the preceding section it was made clear that the concept of memory has a crucial role to play in understanding behaviour, both overt and covert. Thus, cognitive psychology encourages, indeed demands, specific attention to the internal representations of past experiences and their utilization in mental activities. It emphasizes the interdependence of memory and other mental processes and so provides a broad and fertile framework within which the study of memory may be undertaken.

The cognitive approach is not new. As we shall see shortly in connection with memory specifically, concern with and speculation about the nature of mental processes can be traced back to the early Greeks with continuing interest up to modern times. In the latter part of the nineteenth century it was accepted that the aim of what had recently become the independent discipline of psychology was the analysis of mental processes such as sensation, perception and imagery. To this end it was common to employ the method of introspection in which subjects reported on their own conscious mental activities. But the shortcomings of this method quickly became apparent and it did not support the study of mental events for long. The method relies on the use of trained observers and the training may well bias what is observed and what is reported. Indeed, the very act of observation may well change the processes being observed. Other shortcomings include the private nature of the observations: different observers may give different reports of the same phenomenon but there is no way of checking this because the observations are not open to public scrutiny or replication. And, of course, not all mental processes need be conscious ones.

The limitation of introspection led to a loss of interest in what may aptly be termed 'mentalism' and helped pave the way for the growth of behaviourism particularly in America. Behaviourists from Watson (1913) to Skinner (e.g. 1963) have maintained that behaviour should be explained without reverting to hypothetical internal mechanisms either conscious or unconscious, and no matter whether they are based on subjective reports or other sources of evidence. Such mechanisms, according to the behaviourists, cannot be observed *directly*, are purely speculative, and so may be deceptive. Instead, explanations must be derived in terms of observable variables, e.g. amount of reinforcement, speed of response, retention interval, and so on. Behaviourists, then, have maintained that the mental activity which may or may not accompany behaviour is unimportant to any satisfactory understanding of that behaviour.

It is now generally accepted that there are a number of

fatal difficulties for classical behaviourism and its 'empty organism' approach. One of these difficulties stems from the fact that an identical physical stimulus may give rise to different responses on different occasions. To take a simple example imagine that you have always made a left turn at a particular road junction on your way home from college. One evening, though, having decided to visit a friend you turn right at this junction. Such a new response to an old stimulus cannot be understood without involving some internal goal or plan (see Miller, Galanter and Pribram, 1960). Likewise, the same response made to the same stimulus on different occasions may demand interpretation in terms of *intentions* as when striking someone is done accidentally rather than intentionally. Human behaviour is not stimulus-bound; it cannot be accounted for in terms of specific patterns of stimulus-response pairings experienced in the past. This point has been made clear by Chomsky (1959) in his attack on the behaviourist account of language behaviour (see Harris and Coltheart (1986).

While classical behaviourism has run into problems of the sort just mentioned it must not be forgotten that this approach was itself largely a response to the inadequacies of introspection and was bound to be influential so long as adequate paradigms for studying mental processes were lacking. Of course, there were those such as Freud, Piaget and Bartlett who, during the first half of this century, stressed the importance of inner processes and mechanisms for understanding behaviour. But over the last 30 years or so the cognitive approach has received a fresh impetus with the development of information-processing science and technology dealing with the internal workings of computers and other electrical and electronic systems. This area of scientific activity confirmed the reality of specific internal and directly unobservable processes capable of mapping *input* on to *output* in a variety of complex ways and consequently suggested new paradigms for the study of cognition. This new impetus to mentalism found elegant expression in a number of works including Broadbent's (1958) *Perception and Communication*, Miller, Galanter and Pribram's (1960) *Plans and the Structure of Behavior*, and Neisser's (1967) *Cognitive Psychology*. But why should developments in cognitive psychology and in memory theory in particular apparently be dependent on developments in other spheres of science? We turn to this question now.

Theories and models

Scientific endeavour involves discovering lawful relationships amongst phenomena, i.e. finding order in nature. Throughout past centuries there have been conflicting views on the necessary manner in which this goal must be achieved and it is worth noting that much of the debate has been amongst philosophers rather than practising scientists. On the one hand there have been those who believed that scientific progress can be achieved only by the method of *deduction*, that is, arguing from a 'given' set of axioms to predict certain phenomena which are then confirmed or disconfirmed by observation. In contrast, proponents of *induction* have argued that the necessary scientific method involves firstly the observation of phenomena and *then* the formulation of laws which comprehend those phenomena. The generally accepted view now, formed notably under the influence of writers such as C.S. Pierce and K.R. Popper (see, e.g., Popper, 1959), is that in practice neither induction nor deduction is sufficient to account for scientific progress, nor indeed are the two taken together. Clearly, deduction alone is not sufficient because it provides no source of the axioms from which deductions may be made. Induction, on the other hand, provides no guide to which phenomena should be observed, nor does it give any hint as to how a start may be made in seeking order amongst any observations which are made. And, if some law which comprehends a set of observations is arrived at it is always possible to find alternative laws which also comprehend them: induction simply cannot lead to 'truth' with any certainty.

The separate limitations of induction and deduction as accounts of scientific method are not overcome merely by combining the processes – even then there are gaps to be filled. It is perhaps best to illustrate this point with a specific example. Suppose that some subjects take part in a memory experiment. On each trial they are shown a consonant trigram (e.g. BNK) for 2 seconds and then required to count backwards by threes, aloud, from a given number. After an interval of counting (t seconds), a signal indicates that they must recall the consonants in the correct order. The consonants change from trial to trial, and so does the interval of counting. (Without the counting the subjects could rehearse the consonants and presumably would recall them correctly no matter how long the retention interval!) Imagine, now, that the points in Figure 1.1 represent the average performance of the subjects, expressed as the percentage of trigrams correctly recalled (P per cent), at various retention intervals (t seconds). Familiarity with mathematical functions should suggest that performance is related to the time elapsed by the formula:

$$P \alpha \frac{1}{(t+1)}$$

hence $P = \frac{k}{(t+1)}$ where k is a constant, in this case 100.

This formula, which was arrived at by induction, represents a *theory* and can now be used to deduce values of P for new values of t, and these could then be confirmed or disconfirmed by observations. So far so good. But suppose now that a new set of observations shows that the relationship $P = \frac{k}{(t+1)}$ only holds good for a limited range of t values, or is restricted to specific conditions involving consonant trigrams and backward counting. The theory itself does not suggest any way in which a modification should be made to account for these new observations. And, of course, neither induction nor deduction provide any account of the motivation to make the original observations: possibly some purely practical requirement impelled the study, or perhaps the investigation was simply 'playing games with nature'! P.B. Medawar deals with these problems in his book *Induction and Intuition in Scientific Thought* (Medawar, 1969).

As the title of his book suggests, Medawar argues that

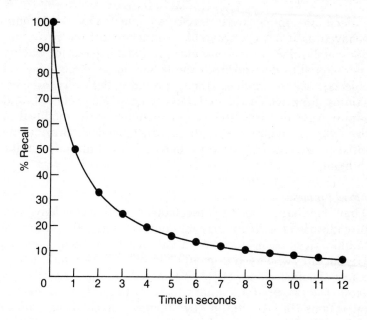

Figure 1.1:   *A fictitious forgetting curve*

intuition is an important ingredient of the scientific method: it is this which provides the source of ideas which induction and deduction, even when taken together, fail to suggest. But clearly intuition involves more than mere unaided guessing, so how are the ideas which form the starting point of the deductive process, or which suggest modifications of disconfirmed ideas, arrived at? As Braithwaite (1962) points out, very often an appeal is made to some area of nature where phenomena have been successfully understood, i.e. lawfully related. The laws from this area of science are then used as analogies for the laws governing those phenomena for which an understanding is sought. Braithwaite refers to such analogies by the term *as if models*, using the term *model* rather than *theory* when the range of phenomena which may be so understood is small. He argues that their use involves the assumption that the phenomena of interest are related *as if* they were produced by some principle or set of principles which are already understood. Thus early attempts to understand optics were based on the notion that light behaved as if it were wave-like (understood from investigations of liquids) or corpuscular (i.e. small particles having characteristics derived from the behaviour of large spherical objects). *As if* models, then, provide ideas, hypotheses, axioms, from which the deductive process may proceed, and supply ways in which theories or models may be modified in the light of further observations. Such models, Braithwaite insists, are an important ingredient of most scientific thinking.

Models of memory

That familiar, concrete mechanisms of technology can provide useful *as if* models for understanding the nature of 'mind' has been recognized at least as long ago as Hippocrates who lived from 460-375 BC (see Marshall, 1977). Later Thomas Reid (1719-96) stated in his *Essays on the Intellectual Powers of Man* that it is 'very natural to express the operations of the mind by images taken from things material'. This is certainly apparent in the development of models of memory. One of the earliest documented *as if* models of memory was that of Plato who likened the properties of human memory to those of wax tablets. Sensory images, he suggested, leave impressions on the mind just as a signet ring may leave an impression on wax: the persistence of the impressions is analogous to remembering while fading or effacement is analogous to forgetting. The wax tablet analogy survived over many centuries being utilized by, for example, Gratoroli in the sixteenth century, Harris in the eighteenth century, and William James at the turn of this century. Apart from the rather obvious analogy between the persistence and fading of impressions with retention and forgetting of memories the wax tablet model has other attractive features. For example, certain individual differences in memory ability can be understood in terms of the size of the wax tablet determining how many impressions can be retained, and the consistency of the wax determining the ease with which impressions can be made and their durability. According to several versions of this model recognition of an object or person as familiar, i.e. having been seen before, takes place by a process analogous to matching the current sensory image against an impression on the wax. Failure to find a matching impression leads to the experience of unfamiliarity. But, as Plato acknowledged, this model has a major shortcoming in that it provides no mechanism for *recalling* rather than *recognizing* what is in memory. To deal with this problem he resorted to another *as if* model based on an aviary. According to this model learning involves capturing ideas (birds) in memory (the cage), and recall involves retrieving particular birds from the cage. The model suggests that failure to recall does not necessarily mean that the required memory is not present but possibly that capturing it is difficult. Furthermore, just as similar birds flock together so do similar ideas and related memories may be erroneously recalled because of their proximity to the sought-after memory.

In the eighteenth century David Hartley (1705-57) capitalized on Isaac Newton's work on energy and motion to propose that memories are retained by the vibration of medullary particles. The activity of these particles, he proposed, is increased by sensory activation and gradually decays as energy is dissipated. (It is interesting to note that Hartley's model is remarkably similar to at least one recent model of word perception (Morton, 1969).) In the next century a number of writers drew on analogies with chemistry. Jules Luys (1829-95) turned to phosphorescence, the continuing luminosity of certain materials after the source of light has been removed, to make a simple analogy while John Stuart Mill (1806-73) proposed a more complex model based on 'mental chemistry'. One attractive feature of this latter model is its recognition of the dynamic nature of memory: just as chemical compounds (such as water) are quite different from the elements of which they are composed (hydrogen and oxygen), so the fusing of sensory elements creates new mental entities which are more than the sum of the parts. Later still, the property of photographic plates of responding to and retaining optical details was taken as the basis of memory models. Yet more recently both weathered signposts (Brown, 1964), electrical condensers (Shephard, 1961) and the hologram (Chopping, 1968; Eich, 1982) have provided *as if* models.

Among recent analogies those involving information processing systems, especially the electronic computer, have provided perhaps the most successful *as if* models of cognition broadly and of memory in particular. Indeed, so effective has been the exploitation of the computer analogy that the term 'cognitive psychology' is often taken to mean the modelling of mental processes based on such devices rather than in the sense of a general concern with mental events.

A basic computer incorporates an input system, a central processor, memory, and output generator. Typewriter keyboards, magnetic tapes, card readers, or even speech recognition devices may provide sources of input. But whatever the initial nature of the input it must be converted or *coded* into a form which the central processor can utilize. Once this has been done the information contained in the input can be operated on by the central processor according to the instructions already stored in the system as a whole. The results of these operations can then be recoded and used to provide output via typewriters or visual display units, or to control mechanical devices. It is also possible that the instructions stored in the computer are automatically adjusted so that future operations take account of the outcome of current operations.

It should be easy to appreciate that the storage of information is involved in several ways even in a basic computer. The rules for converting the input from its 'external' form (e.g. holes punched in cards) to the code used by the electronic central processor may be permanently embodied in the system. Other details, such as instructions about what to do with the information contained in the input when it arrives, may also be maintained permanently or changed as desired. In contrast, a number of very temporary holding devices or buffer stores are necessary to retain information while it is being dealt with. This is obviously necessary where there is a discrepancy in the speed with which successive operations are carried out, or when information from different sources must be combined. For example, reading items from punched cards may be slower than the rate at which the central processor can deal with them. So each item must be assembled, the first part being held in store until later parts have been read and coded. Indeed, a batch of items may have to be held until they are all ready to be passed on to the central processor. Similarly, the results of processing may be produced faster than the output devices can deal with them and, again, one or more buffer stores will be necessary to hold information until it has been cleared.

The *as if* model of human memory provided by the computer is compelling for a number of reasons. Paramount amongst them, perhaps, is the mere fact that computers accept information from the outside world, store it, manipulate it, and respond to it on the basis of information acquired previously. As Neisser states when discussing the impact of the computer analogy on psychological theory, 'whether they do these things just like people was less important than that they do them at all. The coming of the computer provided a much-needed reassurance that cognitive processes were real: that they could be studied and perhaps understood' (Neisser, 1976, pp. 5-6). But, as Neisser made clear, the computer analogy has been attractive to psychologists for a number of other reasons. One of the attractions stems from the distinction between the structure of the computer and the instructions which govern the flow of information around that structure. Turning back briefly to the models of memory discussed earlier it is clear that any comprehensive model of human memory must be more complex than a wax tablet, photographic plate or set of vibrating particles. These models seem to go little further than acknowledging that there is some medium which accepts and retains experience (Gomulicki, 1953). In essence, they are extremely simplistic, offering little by way of the required detail and flexibility necessary to account for the wide range of memory phenomena. In these respects the computer analogy is very advantageous. The structure of a computer, the *hardware*, can be made extremely complex, and the programs which govern the flow of information around the hardware can be not only complex but flexible and adaptable.

Another advantage of the computer analogy is that in

general the workings of computer systems are orderly, and are *understood*, in the sense used by Braithwaite: in principle it is possible to map an input event on to an output event by a sequence of causally linked internal events. This is important because using the computer analogy encourages a disciplined approach to mental causality. Also, perhaps less obviously, the analogy provides the student of cognition with a rich set of concepts and a vocabulary with which to refer to them. Thus, terms such as *memory store, central processor, slave systems, recoding, output buffers, storage capacity,* have found a place in the vocabulary of students of memory (sometimes even of those who do not utilize the computer analogy). Despite the advantages of the computer analogy there are some dangers associated with it. It is possible to take the analogy too far. One warning signal is the fact that computers can do some things much better than can human beings. For example, storing and retrieving vast arrays of numbers, and complex calculations, can be done more effectively by computer. This suggests that those things they do equally well may be achieved in different ways. Another problem arises from the nature of computer hardware which has a fixed architecture: there are fixed routes of information flow and fixed capacities for each store. In principle there is no reason why the human memory system should not also be considered to have an invariate structure with the flexibility stemming from the software it employs. But, apart from the problem of accommodating ontogenetic growth in the human system there are fundamental difficulties with the practical assessment of these characteristics. As Craik and Lockhart (1972) noted in their critique of computer models, there are many different values placed on the capacities of one hypothesized store by different researchers. This situation does not arise merely because the measuring techniques differ in their 'powers of resolution', but rather because it is difficult or impossible to know what software the subject might be employing at a particular time. Thus, the distinction between the hardware and software of the model cannot be kept sharp as the computer analogy strictly requires. Nevertheless, this analogy has been extremely influential as will be apparent throughout this book.

Experimental methods

Isolating memory

The experimental investigation of human memory was initiated by a German, Hermann Ebbinghaus, who conducted a study extending over the years 1879 and 1880 and published his results in a monograph entitled *Memory* in 1885. Ebbinghaus had realized that very little was known about memory at that time and, having become familiar with Fechner's application of experimental methods to the study of perception, he saw the value of applying such methods, borrowed from the natural sciences, to the study of memory. He identified the difficulties of such an enterprise as being how 'to keep approximately constant the bewildering mass of causal conditions which, insofar as they are of mental nature, almost completely elude our control, and which, moreover, are subject to endless and incessant change', and how to 'measure numerically the mental processes which flit by so quickly, and which on introspection are so hard to analyse' (1913, pp. 7-8).

Ebbinghaus tackled the first of these difficulties by testing himself under strictly standardized conditions. To this end he attempted to remove the influence of previous learning by devising and employing the *nonsense syllable*, that is, a consonant-vowel-consonant unit which is not a word (e.g. *Wux*). He constructed a large pool of these nonsense syllables and divided them into lists of different lengths which he read out aloud at a constant rate of 150 per minute. In addition, he always tested at the same time of day, stopped when he felt fatigued, and had a 'warm-up' on each day to get himself up to his previous general level of performance. Furthermore, he tried to avoid mnemonic 'tricks' and any meaningful associations suggested by the syllables.

As his measure of performance Ebbinghaus counted how many repetitions of a list it took for him to be able to recite it without error. In this way he could compare the learning difficulty of lists of different length. To assess retention he employed the *method of savings*: the number of trials taken to relearn a list after an interval relative to the number of trials taken for the initial learning indicated how much learning had been retained. In addition, it was possible to use the method of savings to assess the effect of different numbers of repetitions of a list on retention 24 hours later. The brilliance of this method just has to be appreciated! Not only does it provide an empirical measure of memory but it is very sensitive and so capable of revealing influences of previous learning which are not detectable when more discrete measures, such as counting the number of items recalled on a single test trial, are employed (the use of such discrete measures reveals nothing about degrees of learning which might be present with other items but which are not sufficient to produce overt recall of them).

Ebbinghaus deliberately avoided the natural complexity of memory in order to demonstrate that it could be studied objectively. This was important at a time when such a possibility was regarded with scepticism, but his approach faces the criticism that his results have little *external validity*. That is, they are not obtained outside his narrow range of conditions involving fast presentation rates and a highly dedicated and practised subject determined to avoid the use of mnemonic 'tricks' and any meaningful associations suggested by the 'nonsense' syllables. F.C. Bartlett voiced this criticism in his book *Remembering* (1932), maintaining that by attempting to suppress the natural 'search after meaning' Ebbinghaus had avoided the very essence of human memory. Bartlett reported a number of experiments involving memory for *meaningful* material such as stories, passages of prose, and pictures. One of his stories, 'The war of the ghosts', was derived from an Eskimo folk tale and contained a number of elements, such as actions (e.g. hunting for seals) and supernatural ideas which were not familiar to the English subjects. When, after a single presentation, this story was reproduced on successive occasions a number of gross errors appeared. The reproductions were much abbreviated – details were omitted, as were whole elements such as the supernatural ideas which did not fit with the subjects' expectations about the story. More dramatically, the contents were distorted so as to make them more compatible with the subjects' own cultural experiences. Bartlett concluded that remembering is a *schematic* process, that is, people interpret stimuli by means of a set of schemata or plans of the world based on past experience. When the material is not consistent with these schemata it is still interpreted in terms of them. What is retained, then, is a schematized version of the original material and this is used at recall in an attempt to reconstruct the original: both learning and recalling are active processes.

A broad look at modern memory theory and experimentation shows how widespread is Bartlett's influence: this is apparent in the general acceptance that a person's knowledge of the world, and indeed of his own mental processes, plays an intimate part in learning and remembering – that it is simply not possible to isolate the memory system from the rest of cognition. Nevertheless, the methods introduced by Ebbinghaus, which dominated the study of memory for 60 years or so from 1885, may still be seen as influential whenever objective, empirical means of assessing memory are employed, and whenever there is a attempt to control the conditions of learning and testing. Indeed, it is perhaps a testament to Ebbinghaus's influence that now and again various authors see fit to remind others that it is not possible to 'decouple' memory from other mental functions (e.g. Reitman, 1970). We shall touch on this point again shortly in this chapter but first some basic procedures used in memory research are described.

Basic test procedures

There are two major classes of empirical methods used to assess memory, namely, recall and recognition. The precise ways in which these classes should be distinguished has been a matter of intense debate which will be dealt with in Chapter 6. Here, though, some description and discussion of certain aspects of the procedures will be helpful in understanding what follows throughout the book.

A typical *recall* procedure involves a presentation phase in which the subject is presented with a set of to-be-remembered items, and a recall phase in which he must report as many of those items as possible. In *free* recall there are no constraints on the order in which the items may be reported and performance is assessed simply by counting the number of to-be-remembered items recalled. In *serial* recall the items must be recalled in the order of presentation; performance may be assessed by the number of items recalled in the correct position in the sequence or by the greatest number of items that can be reliably recalled. This latter measure is known as the *memory span* and has long been used as a standard index of immediate-memory ability. Serial recall involves two components – recalling the items and sequencing them correctly. It is possible to reduce the demands of *item recall* by drawing the items from a small population completely known to the subject. Thus, presenting each of the digits 0 to 9 in a different random order on every trial effectively creates a test of memory for serial order alone.

Cued recall refers to situations in which specific cues are provided to direct or aid recall. The subject could be cued with 'recall the vegetable names in the list', 'What was the list item rhyming with plough?', or 'what letter was paired with X?', and because cues have a directing function cued recall is often superior to uncued recall. It is important to note that in one sense all recall is cued: in a typical free recall task the cue is really something like 'the list you have just seen'. But so-called *cued recall* involves more specific cues about what should be recalled and the distinction between cued and uncued recall remains an important one.

The cues provided in a *recognition* test are the actual items themselves. There are several versions of the recognition paradigm, but typically they involve presenting a list containing the to-be-remembered or *old* items. In the subsequent test old items are mixed with *distractors* or *new* items which were not seen in the presentation list and the subject is required to work through the test items deciding which are the old ones. Intuitively recognition, with its highly specific cues – the items themselves – seems an easier task than recall. But several aspects of the recognition test, notably the nature of the new items, are crucial in determining the level of performance. When the new items are similar to the old ones, e.g. faces of similar appearance, or words with related meanings, discrimination between them on the basis of list membership tends to be difficult.

Indeed, the occurrence of such confusion may be used to explore the basis of remembering: if the presence of *new* words sounding similar to *old* ones has no detrimental effect on recognizing the *old* words while the presence of semantically similar *new* words does it would suggest that semantic but not acoustic features of words play a part in remembering lists of words.

The relative numbers of new and old items in a test may influence the proportion of targets recognized by biasing the subject's responses. If the subject is rational and knows, or merely believes, there are relatively few old items he will be more reluctant to respond 'old' than if there are relatively many, other things being equal. And of course, some old items will be correctly classified even if the subject is guessing the whole time, e.g. if half the test items are *old* it is possible that 50 per cent of them (or more!) will be correctly recognized when the subject is simply responding at random. Thus, for at least two reasons, the number of old items correctly responded to as 'old' is not an adequate indication of the underlying state of memory. There are several means of correcting recognition scores to take account of such possibilities and two of them based on theories developed in the context of studies on perception – the high threshold theory and the signal detection theory – are described in the Appendix.

The problem of guessing can occur in recall, but it is unlikely to be a serious matter when the list items are drawn randomly from a large population such as all English words. However, when subjects realize that items come from a small population such as *domestic animals*, recall scores can be enhanced by simply generating exemplars of the category and uncritically responding with them. Here, too, it is possible to take some account of such a possibility by, for example, examining the number of *intrusions* appearing in the recall protocols, and treating them somewhat similarly to the false alarms that occur in recognition. Indeed, when the to-be-remembered items are drawn from a well-defined population that is familiar to the subjects free recall may be accomplished by simply carrying out an 'internal' recognition test on each item in turn. That would, in principle, be identical to the situation in which the whole population was presented by the experimenter as *old* and *new* items in a recognition test. Nevertheless, in such situations recall and recognition scores do not always correspond, as Davis, Sutherland and Judd (1961) showed. In one part of their study they presented a list of two-digit numbers drawn randomly from the population 10-99. Free recall was superior to recognition when all 90 numbers were presented at test and it is not difficult to identify some possible reason for this discrepancy. For example, in free recall a subject may respond with items in any order he wishes. If he believes he can maximize his score by recalling items he knows are best retained in memory he is free to do so. In contrast, a recognition test prescribes the order in which items must be dealt with and forces consideration of distractor items, and both of these procedural details can interfere with items that would be successfully *recalled*.

Finally in this section we turn briefly to the use of reaction times. The time taken to complete recall and recognition can provide important evidence about the way in which information is stored in memory and how it is utilized. This is especially true where subjects do not normally make errors as when they are required to remember a single letter or digit, or when asked questions about general knowledge such as 'Do canaries have wings?'. In such circumstances, where accuracy of performance provides no clues about underlying cognitive processes, reaction time techniques can sometimes do so. The basic logic behind their use is fairly straight-forward and involves the assumption that if stimulus and response factors are held constant changes in the number and difficulty of cognitive operations will be reflected in the reaction times. (Legge and Barber, 1976, give a very readable introduction to this topic while Sternberg, 1975, provides an excellent account of the application of reaction time techniques to the study of memory.)

One problem with the use of reaction time as the dependent variable arises from what is known as the *speed-error trade-off*. This refers to the relation between speed and errors – if responses are made more and more rapidly so the number of errors will increase as necessary cognitive processes are only partially completed or missed out altogether. While there are a number of ways of taking account of the proportion of erroneous responses (see, e.g., Pachella, 1974) many researchers are content merely to accept the observed reaction times as a means of assessing cognitive processes provided small and similar error rates occur in all experimental conditions. (It is necessary to insist on at least some errors as a check that subjects are working at close to the limits of their capabilities.)

Controlling and monitoring

On one occasion when the author was travelling by train a woman fell from a carriage door and was killed. In order to identify the body the police asked passengers to describe the person who had occupied a seat with unattended luggage beside it. No one, of course, had expected to be questioned on such a matter but all the nearby travellers agreed the occupant of the seat had been a woman, and there was general agreement about her age and the colour of her hair. In contrast, there was virtually no agreement on the style and colour of her clothes. Everyone was relieved at being able to assess their memory performance when the woman, who had been enjoying a meal in the dining car, returned to her seat. The victim had come from another part of the train. Interestingly, and perhaps not typically in such circumstances, the agreed description offered by the other passengers did bear some resemblance to the woman's appearance. While no one had paid attention to her with the intention of remembering her description some details had been retained.

It is likely that a considerable amount of learning takes place on an *incidental* basis, that is, without any intention to remember. This seems especially true in early childhood when planful behaviour has not yet developed. But that is not to suggest that incidental learning takes place without attention to the material – indeed, there are good grounds for believing that the way in which the material is attended to, rather than intention to remember *per se*, is crucial for what is remembered (e.g. Hyde and Jenkins, 1973). Nevertheless, to the extent that learning takes place without any intention to learn, some processes in memory must operate *automatically*. The idea of automatic processes has been incorporated into a number of models of human performance (e.g. Posner and Snyder, 1975; Shiffrin and Schneider, 1977) and is discussed in detail by Hasher and Zacks (1979) specifically in relation to memory. Essentially, automatic processes occur without intention, without necessarily giving rise to awareness, and without interfering with other cognitive activities. Chapter 5 deals with what can be remembered in the absence of any intention to learn and the nature of the processes underlying any such learning.

In contrast to circumstances in which subjects have no expectation of a memory test and where any learning may be attributable to automatic processes, many laboratory studies include detailed forewarnings of impending tests and provide practice to familiarize subjects with the task and materials. What cognitive activities occur in such circumstances? There is much evidence showing that, in addition to any 'effort after meaning' as demonstrated by Bartlett (1932), subjects exercise deliberate control over their memory systems in response to the particular conditions in which the presentation of material, retention and testing occur. The processes involved in such deliberate control have been referred to by Hasher and Zacks as *effortful* processes because, in addition to being deliberate, they draw on the overall capacity of the cognitive system and so divert resources from any other ongoing activity. Such effortful processes correspond to the 'accessible controlled processes' of Shiffrin and Schneider (1977) and the 'strategies' of Posner and Snyder (1975). It is by this latter term that such processes will be referred to here. Just what these strategies may be under various specific conditions is discussed in later chapters. For the present, therefore, it will suffice to offer merely some evidence to demonstrate that subjects do exert control over memory processes in response to what they see as the demands made upon them by the task at hand.

A number of studies have been concerned with subjects' expectations about the type of test they will receive and the effects these have on the ways they go about storing to-be-remembered material. In some of these studies it was found that free recall performance was higher when a free recall test rather than a recognition test was expected, while recognition performance was superior when recognition rather than recall was expected (e.g. Carey and Lockhart, 1973; Tversky, 1973). This interaction between expectations held during presentation and the actual type of test indicates that subjects appreciate that different ways of storing to-be-remembered items favour different types of test and that they control storage processes accordingly (see Tversky, 1973; Balota and Neely, 1980). It seems, then, that people know something about the workings of their memory. Flavell (e.g. 1981; Flavell and Wellman, 1977) has studied this aspect of cognition, especially with children, and refers to it as *metamemory*. According to Flavell normal adult subjects are sensitive to the need to exert deliberate control over memory processes in certain situations. Also, they realize that certain variables are important to memory performance. That is, for example, they have some appreciation of their own strengths and weaknesses (they might know they are good at remembering faces but poor at names), that certain types of material are generally more difficult to remember than others (nonsense syllables are more difficult than words), that long lists of items are more difficult than short ones and, the point made already, that particular strategies for learning and remembering are best for particular tasks.

Appealing though the concept of metamemory may be, there are a number of problems still to be dealt with. In their review paper Cavanaugh and Perlmutter (1982) criticize studies of metamemory because of the over-reliance on subjects' verbal reports of what they know about their memory. It is possible, for example, that such reports may reflect what a subject feels his memory should be rather than what he believes it to be in fact. This is especially likely when he knows that no test of performance will actually be given or if he perceives his self-assessment as being very revealing about his personal ability irrespective of any test which may come later. Thus, when asked how many trials he will require to completely learn a set of items he may 'fake good' and give an unwarranted, low, estimate. It is perhaps not surprising, therefore, that correlations between assessments of metamemory and actual performance have, on the whole, been rather low. Nevertheless, as Cavanaugh and Perlmutter point out, this situation does not necessarily undermine the central idea of metamemory but it does show the need for more satisfactory, objective methods of assessing subjects' knowledge about their memory.

Another criticism that Cavanaugh and Perlmutter level against the prevalent concept of metamemory is the lack of a clear distinction between knowledge about the workings of memory and the *executive* that utilizes such knowledge to 'orchestrate' the memory system. Without such a clear distinction it is not possible to decide whether poor performance is due to the poor utilization of well-articulated memory knowledge or to the efficient use of impoverished knowledge.

One function often classified under metamemory but which may be attributed instead to the executive was studied by Hart (1965) who referred to it as *memory monitoring*. Hart's technique involved asking questions such as 'What sea does West Pakistan border?' Most of the subjects were able to give answers to some of the questions but not to others. Where answers were not forthcoming the subjects were required to rate on a six-point scale how certain they were that they really did or did not know them. Following that a recognition test was given in which each of the correct answers to the failed questions had to be picked out from four alternatives. It was found that where subjects expressed a strong feeling that they did not know the answers they recognized only 30 per cent of them correctly (chance level was 25 per cent). In contrast, recognition was 78 per cent correct for those answers for which there had been a strong feeling that they were known. Subjects, then, were able to assess when particular items were stored in memory even though they did not know what they were. But how could such an apparently paradoxical situation come about? One explanation is provided by the results of a study conducted by Brown and McNeill (1966). They investigated another feeling-of-knowing condition commonly experienced and referred to as the 'tip-of-the-tongue' (TOT) feeling. They gave subjects dictionary definitions of rare words and asked them to supply the word so defined. When subjects reported that a word was on the tip of the tongue, i.e. they 'knew' the word but its name tantalizingly escaped them, they were asked to give the initial letter, the number of syllables, words sounding similar to it, and so on. It was clear from their ability to provide such details that the subjects had access to several features of the word even though the name escaped them.

While Brown and McNeill's study has been criticized and refined (see, e.g., Koriat and Lieblich, 1974) it provides a plausible account of the paradox created by the feeling-of-knowing phenomenon by emphasizing that the name of a word is only one of its many features held in memory and that some of those features may be retrieved when the sought-after name cannot be. Presumably the strength of the feeling-of-knowing depends on the number and nature of the features retrieved. Whatever the explanation it is easy to see that such monitoring of memory content could be useful by indicating whether or not further efforts at remembering are likely to be worthwhile. However, let us return to the point raised earlier concerning the classification of memory monitoring under executive functions or metamemory. Taking into account Cavanaugh and Perlmutter's distinction between these two classes, it seems best to place under metamemory the subjects' knowledge that the feeling-of-knowing state does indicate the availability of items in memory and hence that further efforts may or may not be worthwhile. The processes of monitoring and deciding what to do on the basis of the information so obtained are best seen as executive functions.

Episodic and semantic memory
Commenting on the other papers published with his own in the book *Organization of Memory* Tulving (1972) noted that they could be placed into two broad groups. One group of papers dealt with subjects' ability to remember which stimuli had been presented during the experimental session. The other group was concerned specifically with knowledge about verbal symbols (i.e. their meanings and inter-relationships) that the subjects brought with them to the laboratory. On the basis of this broad distinction between paradigms

Tulving proposed the further, more fundamental distinction between what he termed *episodic memory* and *semantic memory*.

According to Tulving episodic memory is concerned with autobiographical information, that is, it contains a record of the individual's personal experiences. Thus, for example, reference would be made to the contents of episodic memory to answer questions such as 'Did you post the letter I gave you this morning?', or 'Where did you spend your holiday last year?' Of course, personal experiences are not limited to externally observable events but include private events such as dreams, thinking through problems, and emotional experiences: these experiences, also, may be represented in the episodic record. Episodic memory, then, stores representations of the individual's experiences according to their temporal and contextual relations to those of other events. In order to remember where last year's holiday was spent the appropriate region of the episodic record must be consulted. The same is true for experimental paradigms in which the subject is required to recall or recognize those stimuli presented during the experimental session: each presentation represents an episode in the subject's personal experience.

In contrast to episodic memory Tulving proposed that semantic memory contains information necessary for the use of language. 'It is a mental thesaurus, organized knowledge a person possesses about words and other verbal symbols, their meaning and referents, about relations among them and about rules, formulas, and algorithms for the manipulation of these symbols, concepts and relations' (Tulving, 1972, p. 380). Thus, semantic memory must be consulted in order to answer questions such as 'Are whales mammals?', 'What is the chemical formula for water?', 'Which month follows July in the calendar?' and 'Which is the stronger association, between *table* and *chair* or between *table* and *nose*?' And, of course, semantic memory is involved in the understanding of any verbal material used in tasks of episodic memory. Hence, the results of consulting semantic memory may influence what is registered in episodic memory. As might be expected, given the complexity of human knowledge and its utilization, studies of semantic memory employ a wide variety of paradigms. These include assessing the numbers and patterns of word associations (e.g. Kiss, 1975; Noble, 1963), the use of the semantic differential to assess conative meanings of words (see, e.g. Osgood, 1953), and the analysis of reaction times to questions such as 'Is a canary a bird?' (e.g. Collins and Quillian, 1969; Smith, Shoben and Rips, 1974). Also, of course, studies of language use, its development and pathology (see Harris and Coltheart (1986) fall within the broad domain of semantic memory.

Tulving's classification of memory paradigms and the phenomena they deal with is essentially based on memory content, that is, whether or not there is any *autobiographical reference*. Now it may be asked, 'What is the utility of such a classification? Why not merely accept a common type of memory for autobiographical and personally ahistorical knowledge?' Well, any new classification of phenomena may lead to new ways of looking at issues and generating new ideas about problems. It could emerge that different *functional* rules govern the various classes. Alternatively, it may turn out that the classes are functionally similar, in which case a general principle may be discovered. While introducing the distinction between episodic and semantic memory Tulving suggested some ways in which they do appear to differ other than in terms of their content. Episodic memory is prone to forgetting but semantic memory is much less so: subjects often forget that a particular word was presented in a list but rarely forget the meaning of it. Also, amongst other differences, there seem to be different consequences of retrieving information from the two memories: the act of recalling a word from a list may itself be registered in episodic memory while recalling, for example, that a collie is a dog seems to leave the content of semantic memory unaffected. Nevertheless, Tulving made it clear that his distinction between episodic and semantic memory was offered as no more than a *potentially* useful one. Subsequently, though, the functional differences between the two types of memory have been formalized by a number of people including, as we shall see in Chapter 6, Tulving himself (Tulving, 1976). This has had the consequence that the adequacy of the distinction has been questioned on grounds that include the logical one that all personal knowledge is ultimately derived from experiences. Empirical grounds for questioning the distinction include findings that the involvement of items in preceding episodes influences performance on tests of semantic memory, and that certain experimental variables have similar influences on episodic and semantic memory (see, e.g., Anderson and Ross, 1980). Nevertheless, it would be wrong to treat such arguments against the episodic-semantic distinction as concluding the matter because evidence favouring the distinction also continues to accumulate (e.g. Jacoby and Dallas, 1981). However, it is not intended to resolve the matter here (it is discussed again in Chapter 6). Rather, the purpose of introducing Tulving's notions of episodic and semantic memory is to orientate the reader because most of what appears in the following chapters is concerned with episodic memory.

Organization of chapters

The preceding sections of this chapter cover some important theoretical and empirical aspects of memory research and provide a general introduction to the remaining chapters. These chapters are concerned mainly, but not exclusively, with episodic memory, that is, as we have just noted, with storing and utilizing the representations of particular experiences.

Chapter 2 deals with visual memory. It covers issues which include the amount of visual detail that can be retained about pictures and faces, the possibility of several visual memory stores, and the nature and function of mental imagery. A related set of issues concerning auditory memory is dealt with in Chapter 3 which includes special consideration of differences in memory for items presented auditorily and items presented visually.

Throughout Chapters 2 to 6 there is an attempt to show something of the way in which current ideas have developed, at least over the recent past. This is especially true in Chapter 4 which concentrates attention on the short-term retention of verbal items. This chapter has as its starting point the idea that performance on tests of immediate memory consists of two components – some items are retrieved from a small-capacity *short-term store* which is very susceptible to interference, and others come from a large-capacity, more durable *long-term store*. The development of ideas about the nature and functions of the short-term store is traced from its original conceptualization in the early 1960s to recent ideas according to which it is part of a complex system with a part to play in cognition generally.

The short-term store is often assigned a role in *encoding*, or establishing, material in more permanent storage. Some of the strategies subjects deliberately employ to this end when attempting to learn lists of words in the laboratory are discussed in Chapter 5. This chapter, which deals with encoding generally, also looks at some circumstances in which learning takes place without intention on the part of the subject and some theoretical implications of them. Chapter 6 discusses some accounts of how items in memory are retrieved and some limitations in the processes responsible. Particularly important here are comparisons of recall and recognition performance and the relation between the way items are encoded in memory and the circumstances under which they can be retrieved.

It may already have occurred to the reader that the organization of Chapters 2 to 6 owes much to the information processing analogy of memory. The sequence of topics corresponds with the idea that stimuli are processed through a fixed series of stages beginning with sensory features and progressing to greater degrees of abstraction and durability of memory representations. However, memory models involving a fixed serial ordering of processing stages are not easy to defend as will become clear early in Chapter 2! And the organization of chapters must be seen as owing something to convenience in addition to any belief that it reflects in some rather loose and general manner the organization of human memory.

Emphasis on the distinction between automatic and effortful processes recurs throughout Chapters 2 to 6 and is pertinent to the treatment of forgetting in Chapter 7. This deals with psychodynamic causes of forgetting, the effect of instructions to forget certain items under normal laboratory

2 Visual memory

In 1922 G.W. Allport gave a test of visual memory to sixty children aged about 11 years. He asked each child to spend just over half a minute studying a complex picture depicting people, houses and other details. The picture was then removed and the child asked to describe it. A number of the children were able to give extremely detailed descriptions, some even being able to spell out letter by letter the unfamiliar word *Gartenwirtschaft* written on a building in the picture, and to do so backwards as well as forwards. These particular children reported that they were able to project a detailed image of the picture on to the grey surface and 'look' at it as if it were the original stimulus. There can be little doubt that the children's descriptions of these so-called *eidetic images* were correct, given their level of recall performance. According to Haber and Haber (1964) about 10 per cent of 11-year-olds possess the ability to retain and utilize eidetic images and this ability usually declines rapidly over the following few years.

An impressive demonstration of eidetic imagery was made by Stromeyer and Psotka (1970) using a random dot stereogram. This consists of two dot patterns each of which alone is entirely meaningless. But, when viewed stereo-scopically, one being presented to the left eye and the other simultaneously to the right, the perceptual fusion of the two produces a meaningful pattern. Stromeyer and Psotka tested an eidetic subject by letting her inspect one pattern with the left eye for 3 minutes and then showing the other pattern to the right eye after a delay. She was able to report the meaningful pattern when up to 24 hours separated the two presentations. Since the first presentation was meaningless on its own it could not be described verbally nor interpreted semantically. Hence, it seems the successful report of the complete pattern must have been based on visual information held in memory. Stromeyer and Psotka's subject appears to have a uniquely detailed eidetic ability but, perhaps reassuringly in some respects, Wallace (1978) obtained evidence for the recovery of similar, albeit less persistent, eidetic ability in a small group of subjects when hypnotism was used to regress them to childhood.

Normally it is not possible to so clearly attribute performance solely to the persistence of detailed visual traces. Recognition and recall of visual stimuli are usually based on a number of information sources, including verbal memory. Thus a German speaker looking at Allport's picture may be able to recall correctly the word *Gartenwirtschaft* by retaining in some non-visual form knowledge that an inn was present and not by reading the word from a mental image. Likewise, it is possible that a witness to a crime may identify a criminal by the emotional qualities of his face rather than by comparing him with a detailed visual image constructed from memory. In this chapter we shall consider the problems of separating the contributions of visual and non-visual traces to memory for visual stimuli, and how much visual detail can be retained and for how long. The starting point is the study of *iconic memory* and the way this short-lived store may be considered to hold visual information just long enough for it to be recoded into more permanent visual and verbal codes.

Iconic memory

When a visual display containing a number of letters, say 12 of them, is presented for a brief period of about 50 milliseconds subjects are able to report only about 4 or 5 of them. Obviously it is not possible to *respond* with 4 letters during the short time the display is present so one or more memory stores must bridge the interval between the offset of the display and the last letter reported. George Sperling became interested in the limit on the recall of letters in these circumstances and sought to determine if it arises from the rate at which items can be read from the display and entered into memory, or if some crucial memory store is limited in durability or the number of items it can hold.

Sperling's experiments

When Sperling (1960) presented visual arrays containing 12 letters his subjects reported they could 'see' the *whole* display for a brief period after the display had terminated. Such reports suggested that all the items were represented in memory and that the ability to report no more than about 5 of them arose neither from the rate at which they could be read from the display into memory nor from the capacity of the memory store. Rather, the limit seemed to have stemmed from the rate at which items could be *retrieved* from a literal or *iconic* store before the traces decayed. Sperling set about testing this idea experimentally. He argued that if all the array is represented in the iconic store at the offset of the display the subjects should be able to report any part of it provided no more than 4 or 5 items are required. He realized that by assessing performance in a small sample of the items it would be possible to estimate the total number of items available in the store. His technique is adequately illustrated by one set of conditions which he employed.

Subjects were presented with an array containing 3 rows of 4 randomly selected letters and lasting 50 milliseconds. In the *whole report* condition they were required to report as many letters as possible and, as with earlier experiments, 4 or 5 letters were reported on average. In the *partial report* condition recall of only one row was required this being indicated by one of 3 auditory cues. If the cue was presented *immediately* the display terminated an average of about 3 of the 4 letters were recalled no matter which row was cued. Since the cueing was unpredictable it is possible to conclude that 75 per cent of letters in *all* rows were recallable on each trial, i.e. $3 \times 3 = 9$ letters out of 12 rather than the 4 or 5 indicated by whole report. Furthermore, since it takes time to identify the cue and start reading letters from the iconic store, this value is likely to underestimate the store's capacity. Sperling's results, then, indicate that performance is not limited by the *capacity* of iconic memory; the whole display seems to be briefly represented in memory, as the reports of his earlier subjects had suggested.

Effects of cue delay

While the superiority of partial over whole report is consistent with the presence of a short-lived visual store capable of holding an entire display it is not conclusive evidence. It is possible to argue, as Holding (1975) has done, that the partial report superiority arises for two main reasons, neither depending on iconic storage. First, if the cues are not truly randomized subjects can predict at better than chance level which row will be cued (experimenters often ensure that each cue is tested equally often, for example). Second, more items must be recalled in whole report than partial report and the act of recalling could produce interference which is most damaging to whole report, therefore. Importantly, both these effects could conceivably take place in a verbal memory system which has no iconic store.

   Coltheart (1975) points out that if Holding's arguments are valid then slightly delaying the onset of the cue will not affect performance because such a manipulation will influence neither the subject's ability to predict the cue nor the interfering effect of recall. If, on the other hand, the visual information is held as a rapidly decaying iconic trace then performance will be affected by cue delay. Fortunately Sperling (1960) anticipated this controversy and included various cue delays in his experiments. The effect of increasing cue delay was to systematically reduce the advantage of partial report over whole report so that it virtually disappeared at delays of about half a second and more. This effect is shown in Figure 2.1. Clearly, then, the finding that even small cue delays reduce the partial report superiority cannot be explained adequately by cue anticipation or output interference.

   The effect of cue delay is certainly consistent with the idea that the partial report superiority arises from a store which

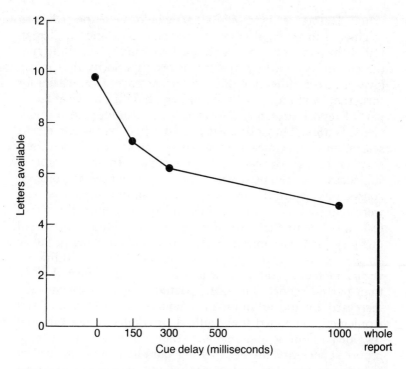

Figure 2.1: *Estimated letter availability as a function of cue delay (adapted from Sperling, 1960)*

holds information only briefly. But, *on its own*, this effect does not force the conclusion that the store is iconic, i.e. has a visual format. There are, however, a number of findings which more directly indicate that the basis of the partial report superiority is indeed iconic. One of these findings has already been mentioned, namely, the effectiveness of cues for position in the visual array. Another was made by Averbach and Sperling (1961). They found that the illumination of the visual fields preceding and following the stimulus array affects the duration of the partial report superiority: with bright fields the superiority is lost after cue delays of less than 500 milliseconds but with dark fields this delay is extended somewhat.

The dependence of partial report superiority on purely

visual factors is precisely what would be expected if it originated in a visual store. However, Sakitt and Appleman (1978) have argued that it would be wrong to conclude that the cue delay at which partial report superiority disappears gives a direct indication of iconic persistence. One reason for this, they maintain, is their finding that the curve relating partial report superiority to cue delay is influenced by non-visual factors. They obtained partial report and whole report scores, and hence measures of partial report superiority, for a number of cue delays up to 5 seconds. In one condition subjects were presented with auditory sequences of words or consonants before the test of visual memory commenced and were required to maintain them in memory until the visual test was completed. In the second condition no verbal memory load was imposed. It was found that performance on the test of visual memory was reduced by the additional verbal memory load with whole report being affected more than partial report. Thus, the partial report superiority was increased by the addition of a non-visual task. Sakitt and Appleman concluded that while their results do not threaten the idea of an iconic memory they do show that partial report superiority in the Sperling paradigm may not reflect only iconic memory and so should not be taken as a direct indication of its characteristics.

Sperling's model
The fact that subjects are able to report 4 or 5 letters from a brief visual display even though iconic traces may be useful for less than half a second presents something of a puzzle. Clearly, items must be extracted from the icon at a much higher rate than subjects can report them to the experimenter. So, what happens to the information between the icon and response? Sperling (1967) summarized the steps he took to deal with this puzzle and the essential points of his solution are shown in Figure 2.2.

According to Sperling's model, visual stimulus information is entered into the *icon* at a very fast rate. The scan mechanism then rapidly extracts information from the icon as directed by partial report or whole report instructions and passes it to the *recognition buffer*. Here it is recognized, i.e. the

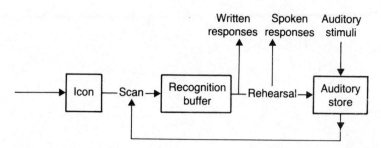

Figure 2.2: *Sperling's model for visual memory tasks (adapted from Sperling, 1967)*

appropriate instructions for motor responses are set up, and once this has been done the item can then be written down, spoken, or rehearsed.

Sperling (1963) investigated the rate at which the scan can extract items from the icon by manipulating the life of the iconic traces. He achieved this by following the stimulus array by a second stimulus consisting of jumbled letter fragments. Since the effect of this *mask* is to render the information in the icon useless it is possible to manipulate the time available for the scan to retrieve items from it by varying the time between the onset of the target array and the mask. The results are depicted in Figure 2.3 where it can be seen that over the first 50 milliseconds one more item becomes available for response with every additional 10 milliseconds the mask is delayed. Clearly, items cannot be reported, nor even rehearsed, at this rate (100 items per second), so the recognition buffer is required to hold information until it has been utilized by the response mechanism. Presumably, then, the limit of 4 or 5 items in whole report largely reflects the capacity of the recognition buffer to hold the instructions for producing responses.

Central and peripheral processes
Sperling's model is a functional model, that is it deals with the functions the memory system must fulfil. While it necessarily describes the sequences in which the functions may occur it does not relate them to physiological and

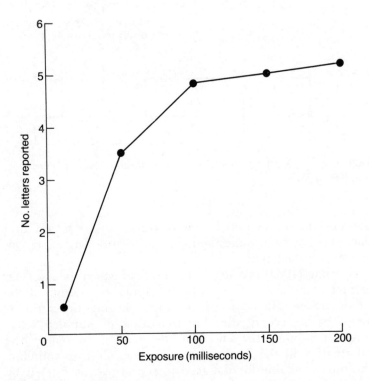

Figure 2.3: *Number of letters reported as a function of exposure duration (adapted from Sperling, 1963)*

neurological processes. In contrast, some theorists have attributed iconic memory to specific processes occurring in the retina (e.g. Sakitt, 1975). Yet another approach is represented by that of Turvey (1973) who has been able to capitalize on the physiology of the visual system to distinguish between central and peripheral processes while retaining a largely cognitive orientation.

Turvey's work was based on the masking technique which, as made clear earlier, involves the presentation of a visual stimulus which interferes with the processing of the target items. Turvey (1973) followed up earlier work which showed a difference in masking effects when target and mask were presented to the same eye (monoptic presentation) rather than to different eyes (dichoptic presentation). He investigated subjects' ability to report displays of one or more visual letters when they were followed by one of two types of mask, *non-figural* (random dots or simply a uniform bright field), and *patterned* (fragments of letters arranged randomly). This research showed that non-figural masks affect report of the letters if presented monoptically whereas pattern masks affect performance when presented either monoptically or dichoptically. This situation suggests two different masking processes, one taking place before inputs from both eyes are combined, and the other being more centrally placed than this. The distinction between the two masking processes is reinforced by other findings. For example, the disruptive effects of non-figural masks are determined by both the light energy in the target (duration × intensity) and the target-mask interval, whereas the effects of dichoptically presented figural masks are largely independent of target energy. In terms of Sperling's model Turvey's findings suggest that monoptic, non-figural masks affect the icon while patterned masks have their effects closer to the more central recognition buffer.

Sakitt (1976) has been more definite about the locus of iconic storage. She identified it with receptor processes in retinal cells and hence considered it to be a type of after-image as commonly experienced after steadily fixating a visual stimulus; when a white surface is subsequently fixated the stimulus shape is still perceived but in the complementary colour. Put crudely, Sakitt considered the icon to be a weak form of after-image. Coltheart (1980) gives an excellent review of Sakitt's complex theory and makes a number of counter-arguments. Amongst them is one based on the fact that after-images are static, i.e. they do not contain information about any movement of the stimulus. However, according to Treisman, Russell and Green (1975) iconic memory may contain such information. They presented brief arrays consisting of 6 items each being a dot rotating clockwise or anticlockwise, and required subjects to report the direction in which they moved under whole report or partial report conditions. The results showed a partial report superiority which declined with cue delay. Following the logic outlined earlier, it is possible to conclude that iconic memory underlay the partial report superiority and that it contains information about movement. It is difficult to reconcile these findings with the view that iconic memory is a form of after-image, therefore.

Nature of iconic memory: further evidence

Sperling placed the iconic store prior to the point at which stimulus information is categorized into verbal units. The point of categorization is theoretically important because all those processes which depend on semantic knowledge cannot be utilized until it is reached. We have already encountered evidence showing that physical features of the stimulus are more or less directly represented in the iconic trace but this does not rule out the possibility that post-categorical features are also represented in the iconic store along with visual features. Sperlin appreciated this problem and dealt with it by requiring partial report on a post-categorical basis. Subjects were presented with arrays containing both letters and digits randomly arranged and were cued to recall either letters *or* digits (partial report), or both letters *and* digits (whole report). Like a number of later investigators (e.g. Von Wright, 1968) Sperling found that partial report was no better than whole report and was able to conclude that the items cannot be selected by the scan on the basis of the letter-digit distinction. In that case selection has to await categorizaton in the recognition buffer.

It has been shown recently that a partial report superiority can indeed be obtained with categorical cues if the conditions are right. Merikle (1980) realized that in both the Sperling and Von Wright studies subjects always knew beforehand whether a trial involved whole or partial report. Thus the stimulus array itself was effectively the recall cue for whole report whereas uncertainty about what should be recalled remained until the cue was presented in the partial report conditions. Merikle ensured that the subjects did not know in advance whether a trial involved whole or partial report and equated the cue delays for these two conditions. The findings were quite clear. There was a partial report advantage for category cues and although it was not as large as for spatial cues it did decline over cue delays of up to 900 milliseconds in much the same way.

Merikle's results argue against the strictly serial arrangement of processing stages in Sperling's model by showing that either categorical information is stored with spatial information in the icon or is held in a separate, parallel store. As Coltheart (1980) notes, there are several studies which have shown that subjects asked to report items from a particular location rarely make errors involving items not present somewhere in the display, and this is true whatever the cue delay. It appears, then, that any decline in the partial report superiority with increasing cue delay is due to loss of *spatial*, not identity, information. This, in turn, suggests that categorical features of the display are rapidly represented in a store parallel to that containing visual features rather than having to be derived from information read from the visual store. And, of course, evidence that movement is represented in the visual store (as was noted above) requires a conceptualization of the icon somewhat different from the original idea put forward by Sperling.

Visual and verbal codes in short-term memory

Despite the complications to Sperling's model introduced by recent findings there seems to be agreement on the existence of some form of short-lived visual store which is subject to rapid loss of information and to masking. But does the representation of visual features of the stimulus end with the loss of information from this store? Or, is it possible for some more durable, if less capacious visual trace to be established so that knowledge of an item's name and appearance may co-exist over relatively long periods? This possibility was investigated by M. Posner in an elegant series of experiments.

Pattern and name matching
Posner's basic paradigm is conveniently described in Posner, Boies, Eichelman and Taylor (1969). Two stimuli are presented simultaneously side-by-side and subjects required

to indicate whether they are letters with the same name or not by pushing one of two keys. For example, AA and Aa both require *same* responses, and AB and Ab required *different* responses. Obviously this task is trivial if subjects can respond at leisure but if responses are made as rapidly as possible while maintaining accuracy reaction times may be taken to reflect the number and difficulty of the cognitive operations involved.

Posner *et al.* reported that *same* responses were over 80 milliseconds faster for the physical identity condition (AA) than for the physical mismatch condition (Aa). This difference can be attributed to the need to carry out the time-consuming process of naming the letters and comparing these names in the Aa condition whereas direct matching of physical features will suffice in the AA condition. This reasoning implies that provided visual information about both stimuli is available the AA condition will give faster responses than the Aa condition, and this should be true whether the information is held in memory or contained in the display. The advantage of AA over Aa, then, offers a means of studying the persistence of visual information in memory.

Figure 2.4, based on Posner *et al.* (1969), shows the effects of delaying the second stimulus relative to the first. These results show that as the delay is increased so the advantage of AA over Aa is reduced. This suggests that with increasing delay there is less visual information held in memory and the decision in the AA condition must be based increasingly on matching names rather than visual features. It should be noted that the curve shown in Figure 2.4 possibly does not give a true indication of visual trace decay because the name code of the first letter is presumably becoming increasingly available during the inter-item interval. Hence it may become more effective for the subject to opt for a name-code comparison for the AA condition before the visual code has decayed entirely. Thus the persistence of visual information may be underestimated by this procedure.

We began this section by suggesting that visual information is not lost even though iconic memory has decayed. But what evidence is there that Posner's matching task does not

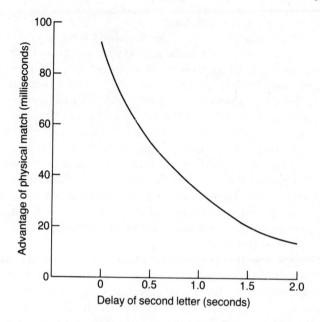

Figure 2.4: *Advantage of physical matches over name matches (adapted from Posner* et al., *1969)*

involve iconic memory? There are two pieces of evidence which are consistent with this position. First, the AA advantage over Aa persists longer than could be maintained by iconic persistence. Second, Posner *et al.* (1969) reported that the AA advantage persisted when the inter-stimulus interval was filled with the type of visual mask known to disrupt iconic memory.

Persistence of visual codes: further evidence
The persistence of visual codes in short-term memory has been studied by W. Phillips whose findings concur with and extend those of Posner (see Phillips, 1983). One of Phillips's experiments (Phillips and Christie, 1977) involved recognition memory for 4 × 4 matrices in which randomly selected cells were brighter than the others. A sequence of such

matrices was presented and, after a short delay, were followed by a sequence of probes. Subjects were instructed to indicate whether or not each probe was identical to one of the matrices in the presentation sequence. Phillips and Christie found that recognition performance was above chance for all positions but substantially higher for the last item presented than for others. In addition, this 'recency effect' persisted when a visual mask followed the final matrix. Phillips believes that these results show a non-iconic visual store capable of holding one stimulus item and persisting for several seconds. Presumably this store is identifiable as that demonstrated by Posner. In addition there is a visual store capable of holding pictorial information in less detail but being more durable and responsible for recognition of items from earlier serial positions.

Evidence for the persistence of visual codes over much longer periods of time than either Posner or Phillips and Christie employed has been provided by Hintzman and Summers (1973). They presented words in upper- or lower-case type and tested for recognition by showing them in the same or different case. The first important finding was that subjects could reliably *recall* the case in which items had been presented after presentation-test intervals of up to 3 minutes. This suggests that visual details were retained for this period but this is not a necessary conclusion because some quite abstract 'tag' may have been stored with the verbal representation of each word. Hintzman and Summers acknowledged this possibility but argued against it on the grounds that recognition of the presented items from amongst distractors was higher when the same case was used at presentation and test than when the case differed. It is difficult to explain this result without accepting that visual features of the stimuli are, to some extent at least, represented in memory and contribute to the recognition process (see, too, Kirsner, 1973). While there has been disagreement over the manner in which sensory features of verbal items are represented in memory (e.g. Light and Berger, 1976) it is widely accepted that these features are important in the retention of those items (see Kolers and Ostry, 1974; Nelson, 1979).

Generation of visual codes

It is worth returning to briefly reconsider Posner's letter matching task, and to distinguish between visual codes which are set up as a more-or-less direct consequence of stimulus presentation and those which are generated from internal sources.

Posner *et al.* (1969) studied conditions in which the first letter of the pair to be matched was presented *auditorily* and the second letter presented visually. In these circumstances of course, no visual trace can be derived directly from the stimulus. Nevertheless, when an auditory 'Capital A', for example, was the first stimulus *same* responses were faster when the second *visual* stimulus was 'A' rather than 'a'. This was especially true when subjects were practised and the interval between stimuli was longer than about 1 second. Taken together these findings indicate that, given sufficient time, visual codes may be constructed from long-term visual storage, held in short-term visual storage, and utilized to perform the matching task.

Other studies that reveal the ability to generate and maintain visual codes include those of Parks, Kroll, Salzberg and Parkinson (1972) and Tversky (1969). Parks *et al.* found that visual codes of letters can be maintained for as long as 8 seconds in anticipation of matching and Tversky extended the findings of voluntary control over visual codes to schematic faces. She required subjects to learn the names associated with a number of faces and then perform matching on the basis of the names. They were encouraged to maintain a visual code or a name code by manipulation of the likelihood that the second stimulus would be a face rather than a name. Irrespective of whether the first stimulus was a face or a name, *same* responses were faster when the second stimulus corresponded with the subject's expectations. Thus, they could apparently generate a visual code for direct matching of physical features.

Pictures and faces

The normal ability to recognize familiar faces and photographs of long-past holidays, and to recall visual details of past incidents, suggests that visual memory contains vast amounts of information. But just how much detail can visual memory hold and how much is memory for visual experiences influenced by other factors such as verbal processes? This section deals with these issues in relation to memory for pictures and faces.

Memory for pictures

A number of findings *appear* to show that visual memory has a large capacity for storing detailed information. For example, Shepard (1967) presented 600 pictures of common objects and tested 68 of them in a forced-choice test by pairing each with a distractor picture also of a common object. When testing was carried out immediately after the presentation sequence 96 per cent of the targets were recognized (chance level being 50 per cent). A week later performance was still as high as 87 per cent. Standing, Conezio and Haber (1970) used a similar procedure but presented 2560 colour slides of the type taken on holidays and sampled retention by testing 280 of them. Even with this large number of items performance on the forced-choice recognition test was about 90 per cent after an interval of several days. These levels of recognition performance may seem impressive but can it be concluded from them that detailed, photograph-like representations of complex stimuli can be retained in memory? One reason for not taking the results entirely at their face value stems from the nature of the tests employed. In a forced-choice recognition test it is possible that memory for one small detail of a target picture may be sufficient to distinguish it from the accompanying distractor. Thus, high levels of recognition for detailed pictures may not require the detailed visual storage which intuition suggests. In addition, interpretation of the picture may lead to retention of thematic or verbal information upon which performance may be based.

The method of Shepard and Chipman (1970) is able to demonstrate something of the detail contained in visual memory by using circumstances where verbal and partial information are unlikely to be influential. They selected 15 states of the United States and constructed a set of cards with every pair-wise combination of the names printed one on each card. The subjects, who were American, were asked to order the cards according to how similar are the shapes of the states represented on them. The data was analysed by a multidimensional scaling program which revealed four main groupings: straight-bordered and rectangular (typified by Oregon), vertically elongated and irregular (e.g. Illinois), small with ragged borders (e.g. West Virginia), and those with a 'handle' (e.g. Florida). These groupings again emerged when the judgments of pair-similarity were made with the cards displaying the shapes instead of the names of the states. Although these results do not establish that there were detailed, photographic-like representations of the states in the subjects memories they do, at the very least, show that the relationships between the real-world shapes of the states and the relationships between their representations in memory were very similar. Shepard and Chipman referred to this level of similarity between the real-world and internal representations as '*second-order isomorphism*' (the two entities cannot be truly isomorphic because that would require that they are identical).

A different approach to that of Shepard and Chipman has been adopted by J.M. Mandler in her studies of memory for pictures (Mandler and Johnson, 1976; Mandler and Ritchey, 1977). Her starting point was the question, 'Just what do people remember about pictures of scenes?' Rather than looking at overall levels of recognition performance, as had Shepard and Haber, she set about trying to identify how well various aspects of complex pictures are remembered. Her expectations were that aspects which convey the central meaning of a picture would be better retained than more superficial details. In a complex picture of a street scene, for example, the inclusion of a car and its spatial relations to buildings and pedestrians are more central to the picture's theme than any detailed description of the car (e.g. whether it is a saloon or estate). Furthermore, memory for superficial aspects were expected to be little affected by randomly arranging the objects on the picture whereas memory for aspects normally conveying thematic information should be severely disrupted by such a procedure.

The basic paradigm employed by Mandler is based on the reasoning that if a particular aspect of a picture is progressively forgotten then it should become increasingly difficult to discriminate between the original picture and distractors which differ from it only in that aspect. In one study (Mandler and Ritchey, 1977) subjects were presented with drawings depicting eight objects which might be found in a typical scene. The pictures differed in *organization* in that some of them had the objects arranged as they might be in the real world whereas in others they were arranged randomly over the picture. After intervals ranging from 5 minutes to 4 months subjects were required to recognize the original target pictures which were accompanied by distractors each of which was created by changing one of its aspects. The types of change fell into four categories. Two of these categories involved aspects central to the theme of the picture, namely, *inventory information* (replacing an object with one from a different class), and *spatial relations* (moving objects in relation to one another). The other two categories of change involved superficial aspects, namely, *descriptive information* (replacing an object with a visually different object from the same class), and *spatial composition* (changing the patterns of filled and unfilled spaces by moving, adding or deleting objects). Importantly, the changes were all made so as not to alter the organized or random nature of the pictures. The results were in line with the original expectations and showed that high organization improved memory for inventory information and spatial relations but not for descriptive information and spatial composition. In addition, inventory information and spatial relations were relatively well retained after 4 months while descriptive information and spatial composition showed rapid forgetting. These findings suggest that memory for pictures is best when an overall interpretation is possible in terms of a *scene schema*, or set of expectations based on the real world. This schema may be retained over long periods and contains an inventory of objects and their locations relative to each other. Retention of details not central to the picture's theme is very much less durable and is not influenced by the meaningfulness of the picture. Mandler's studies, then, are important because they show that it is possible to separate out memory for different aspects of pictorial stimuli, and they provide data concerning a number of these aspects.

The idea of a picture schema was employed many years ago by Woodworth (1938) to explain verbal influences on memory for simple line drawings. Carmichael, Hogan and Walters (1932) had presented subjects with a number of ambiguous visual forms and accompanied each by a name suggesting a particular interpretation. For example, two circles joined by a straight line was accompanied by the label *eyeglasses* or *dumbbells*. When the subjects were asked to reproduce the forms the drawings were distorted towards the shape suggested by the label, e.g. the joining line was arched upwards or thickened in the case of eyeglasses and dumbbells respectively. Such distortions could not be due to *automatic* changes in visual traces as the Gestalt psychologists had maintained because the labels would have had no specific effects in that case. Instead, Woodworth proposed that each stimulus was incorporated into a schema (the idea was borrowed from Bartlett) and subjects remembered this schema together with a correction necessary to produce the stimulus. The tendency to reproduce the labelled objects were interpreted as showing that subjects do indeed remember the schema but forget the correction.

Mandler's account of her own results is somewhat similar to Woodworth's in that she concluded that thematic aspects of pictures are retained better than surface details. However, Woodworth was emphasizing the possibility of accounting for the Carmichael *et al.* findings without resorting to the retention of visual traces at all, but in the light of what has been discussed in this chapter already this extreme position seems unwarranted. Nevertheless, it does seem safe to conclude that the level of visual detail stored in memory over any substantial period is normally quite small. The study by Nelson, Metzler and Reed (1974) illustrates this point. They found that recognition of detailed photographs as having been seen before was no better than for corresponding line drawings depicting merely the theme of the picture. But, the simple line drawings were recognized better than verbal descriptions of the scene.

Memory for faces

In seeking to establish the guilt of a suspect it has been widespread and legally established practice to require witnesses to recognize the person from amongst a number of others. Unfortunately, despite recognized safeguards for the accused such parades are full of hazards (see Yarmey, 1979). It is possible, for example, that the witness has seen the accused person somewhere other than the scene of the crime and identified him solely on this basis of familiarity. The previous occasion could have been the inspection of 'mug shots' in an initial attempt to identify the criminal or even while shopping in a local supermarket! Even where such biases do not exist eyewitness testimony can be extremely unreliable as an investigation by Buckhout (1974) shows. For this study a New York television company showed a film of a specially staged purse-snatching incident in which the assailant's face was in full view for several seconds. A line-up of the assailant and five other men of broadly similar appearance was then shown and viewers were invited to send in their decision about which of them was the assailant. The replies showed a chance level of responding – all the men in the line-up attracted about the same number of accusations. It would, of course, be of little comfort to an innocent suspect who was wrongly identified by a witness that the chances of it happening are only 1 in 6 or even 1 in 10 if the more traditional line-up were used! Unfortunately, as we have already noted, a number of factors may actually load the dice against the accused. One further source of bias which is particularly interesting is suggested by the recent work of Solso and McCarthy (1981). Their results show there is a real possibility that a suspect who generally appears unlike any of several criminals witnessed at a crime but who has a mouth similar to one of them, eyes like another, a nose like a third, and hair like a fourth stands a greater chance of being identified than any of the real criminals. It is reassuring in view of such reservations that, in Britain at least, identification by witnesses is no longer accepted as the sole source of incriminating evidence.

Numerous experimental studies of 'facial episodes' have been motivated by practical or theoretical considerations and, in contrast to Buckhout's study mentioned above, have generally shown performance well above chance levels. One method commonly used to investigate the basis of facial memory involves changing or concealing specific features between presentation and test and noting the effects on performance. In general, the use of such manipulations reveals that upper features such as eyes and hair are more important than lower features such as chin and mouth, although the mouth is more important than the nose (see Davies, Ellis and Shepherd, 1977; McKelvie, 1983). It is possible that eyes and hair are physically more complex and distinctive than chins and mouths, and this, in turn suggests the possibility that recognition of a face as familiar is achieved by matching the stimulus against a 'template' held in memory. However, there is evidence that argues against the idea that facial recognition can be accounted for solely by the matching of independent visual features, and some of it comes from investigations into the effectiveness of aids to the *recall* of faces.

Recall of faces by drawing or by verbal description is generally poor. This is accounted for in part, at least, by limitations in artistic and verbal skills because peformance of both skills is poor when the face is actually present and no demand is made on memory. To circumvent this problem many police forces use the photofit kit or some similar device which reduces the task of recall to a series of recognition tests. The kit contains a range of basic facial features (eyes, forehead and hairline, nose, mouth, and chin) from which faces may be constructed. Although this technique has been widely used the photofit constructions of one person are often not recognizable as the original by someone else even when they are constructed with the face actually present (Ellis, Shepherd and Davies, 1975). Surely, if it were possible to recognize each feature in isolation in the kit the face would be easily constructed. It is unlikely, therefore, that recognition memory for a whole face depends to any great extent on matching individual features of the test item with those held in memory. Nevertheless, it would be wrong to conclude that isolated features cannot be recognized at all (see Matthews, 1978; Seamon, Stolz, Bass and Chatinover, 1978).

Other evidence that recognition is not achieved simply by recognizing individual visual features comes from studies which vary the contexts in which the face is studied and tested. In one such experiment by Winograd and Rivers-Bulkeley (1977) target faces were studied in conjunction with a second face. Replacing or removing the accompanying face at the recognition test led to a decrement in recognition performance. We shall discover in Chapter 6 that such context effects have fundamental theoretical implications, but for the moment we need only note that context changes should have no effect if recognition is achieved by directly comparing visual features of the test face with those held in memory.

An alternative to the explanation based on recognizing individual physical features emphasizes that the face is a social object. The observer's interpretation of the face as a whole, or his emotional responses to it, are assumed to be represented in memory. According to this view, the finding that the eyes contribute greatly to recognition performance may be explained by the emotional responses they elicit rather than by the physical details they contain *per se*.

Some studies concerned with demonstrating the importance of social and semantic aspects of faces, as opposed to physical features, have attempted to manipulate the former aspects while keeping the latter aspects constant. In one such study Yin (1968) showed that inverting pictures of faces reduced recognition more than did inverting other complex stimuli such as pictures of aeroplanes and horses. Certainly, these results are consistent with the view that inversion reduces the perception of semantic-social aspects of faces as Yin claimed. But this interpretation must be accepted with caution because there is other evidence that when faces and non-face stimuli are equated for physical complexity the effects of inversion on recognition do not differ (Rock, 1974). Nevertheless, the importance of social and semantic aspects probably underlies findings that recognition memory is poor when photographic negatives are used as stimuli (e.g. Galper, 1970). Indeed, it is easy for the reader to confirm for himself the difficulty of identifying even a very familiar person from a photographic negative even though there is no loss of visual detail relative to a normal photograph.

A different approach to uncovering those aspects of facial stimuli that are critical to later recognition is illustrated by the study of Patterson and Baddeley (1977). In this study subjects were asked to rate a number of faces on either physical features or aspects of personality. Physical ratings were made on size of nose, thickness of lips, distance between the eyes and length of face. Personality judgments were made on dimensions of nice-nasty, reliable-unreliable, intelligent-dull, and lively-stolid. Performance on a subsequent test revealed better recognition when the rating was on personality rather than physical features. It is interesting to note that subjects may remember the context in which the face was encountered better when rating personality than when assessing physical features. Daw and Parkin (1981) who have produced this result suggest that the environment in which the face is photographed is involved in assessing personality but not physical features, and this view is supported by findings that labelling faces with occupations influences later recognition (Klatzky, Martin and Kane, 1982).

The evidence on memory for faces points to the greater importance of semantic-emotional aspects rather than individual visual features as the basis for remembering. It should be realized that this section has dealt with memory for faces which were unfamiliar to subjects before they were encountered in an experiment and that different principles may underlay the identification of celebrities or acquaintances (see, e.g., Bruce, 1982).

Visual imagery

We began this chapter by describing some examples of eidetic imagery, i.e. the ability of certain subjects to demonstrate the retention of detailed visual information. The term 'mental imagery' is generally taken to have connotations of sensory-like experiences generated from within. Thus, *eidetic imagery* is an apt label because it reflects not only the retention of visual detail (*eidetic* is derived from the Greek word meaning *form*) but also subjects' reports that experienced 'mental pictures' are used to facilitate recall. Now, a number of theorists have stressed the need to distinguish between 'an image' and 'having an image'; between representations in memory and the experience of those representations (see, e.g., Kosslyn, Pinker, Smith and Schwartz, 1981). So far throughout this chapter this need has been satisfied by largely avoiding the use of the term visual *imagery* and using instead terms such as visual *codes*. This has been possible because it is not necessary to consider whether subjects have conscious, visual-like experiences when explaining, for example, the findings of Posner and Tversky with letter- and face-matching tasks, or the results of Shepard and Mandler with their picture-recognition paradigms. Nevertheless, visual imagery is subjectively very compelling and this section discusses some explorations of the 'imaginal medium' which is suggested by subjective reports.

Subjective aspects of imagery
In 1880 Sir Francis Galton published his book *Statistics of Mental Imagery* in which he reported a survey of the abilities of 100 eminent men to form mental images. The responses to his questions, which were simply descriptive, ranged from the reported ability to form sharp detailed images of a scene, such as the morning's breakfast table, to an inability to form any image at all. Later, Galton's method of enquiry was developed by Betts (1909) into the 'Questionnaire upon Mental Imagery' (QMI). This formally assessed detailed aspects of imagery by requiring subjects to give ratings of vividness and clarity for some 150 items involving the different sensory modes, e.g. the sun sinking below the horizon, and the taste of salt. A shortened form of the QMI was developed by Sheehan (1967) and this has been extensively used in recent times to assess the ability to experience imagery. An even shorter questionnaire concerned only with visual imagery, the 'Vividness of Visual Imagery Qustionnaire' (VVIQ), has been developed by Marks (1973), and like the QMI confirms Galton's general finding of a wide range of reported abilities to experience imagery.

To some extent the *clarity* of visual imagery reported by individuals and assessed by the QMI and VVIQ is independent of reported ability to *manipulate* particular images. Some people report clear visual images but are unable to control them while others report they can make them move, change the colour of objects depicted in them, or distort components of the image into novel shapes. Amongst the questionnaires which assess this control of visual imagery is one developed by Rosemary Gordon which asks subjects to rate how readily they can manipulate certain images such as their car turned upside down and then being crushed. A. Richardson (1969), who describes this test in detail, has found amongst other things that scores correlate positively with the benefit athletes can derive from the 'mental practice' of motor skills. Another interesting observation made by Richardson illustrates the need to distinguish between the subjective clarity of images and control over them. One basketball player reported he could quite clearly image himself preparing to shoot but could not prevent the ball sticking to the ground when he bounced it!

There are numerous situations in which the use of imagery to solve problems is reported by subjects, and where imagery intuitively seems the most effective, if not the only means of doing so without external aids. For example, many subjects apparently use imagery to solve problems such as 'If Mary is shorter than Jane, and Ann is taller than Mary, who is the tallest of the three?' (see Huttenlocher, 1968). Also, when asked 'How many windows are there in your house?' the only ready way to obtain the answer seems to be to visualize the house and count the windows in the image. It is difficult, also to conceive of ways in which some of the problems employed by Guilford (1967) can be solved without resort to visual imagery. Guilford sought to identify specific cognitive abilities and so reveal the structure of intellect. One of his tests is a paper-cutting task in which subjects are given diagrams showing how a piece of paper is folded several times and small pieces then cut out. The pattern of holes which would result if the paper were opened out must then be identified from a number of alternatives. Presumably the most obvious way of dealing with this problem is to bring about an imaginal unfolding of the paper and hence Guilford's labelling of the ability tapped by the test as 'cognition of figural transformations'. Indeed, so compelling is the impression that tests such as this depend on the use of imagery for completion that they are often regarded as the most appropriate means of assessing imagery ability.

Despite the intuitive appeal of imagery as a means of dealing with certain problems the correlations between subjective assessments of imagery ability and objective performance on tests which should benefit from its use are not always high. There are a number of possible reasons for these discrepancies and some of them serve to highlight the difficulties inherent in the investigation of cognitive processes by introspective reports. It is possible, for example, that responses to questionnaires do not reflect only a straight-forward assessment of image clarity and control but are influenced by what subjects believe to be socially desirable. As J.T.E. Richardson (1980, Chapter 9) notes, there is evidence that scores on introspective questionnaires are related to the extent to which the individuals are dependent on recognition and approval by others as measured by the Marlowe-Crowne Social Desirability Scale. Also, informing subjects that high imagery ability is associated with intelligent, creative people has led to higher self-ratings than has telling them that it is associated with dull, uncreative people. In addition, of course, it is not possible to gain public access to the imaginal experience and so determine just how each individual maps this on to the rating scales of the questionnaire. Such considerations suggest that subjective reports of imagery should have little part to play in constructing models of cognition and, indeed, there is no necessity that they should. As we have already noted, it is possible to infer the use and properties of visual *codes* in memory without equating such codes with imaginal exper-ience or paying any attention whatever to subjects' reports of such experience. Nevertheless, subjective reports show the reality of imagery as an experience and its very existence invites exploration of its nature and function.

Imagery and perception

One of the obvious characteristics of imagery experience is its similarity to the experience of perceiving external stimuli. This is graphically illustrated by hallucinations. When these occur there is difficulty separating internal imagery from external reality and behaviour may be inappropriately dictated by the former. Such symptoms are one of the main indicators of psychosis but normal people can be misled as to the source of their experiences as an early experiment by Perky (1910) demonstrated. Perky told subjects to look at a screen, imagine a coloured object (such as a banana) projected on to it, and report what they 'saw'. The crucial aspect of this experiment was that, unknown to the subjects, slightly blurred pictures of the objects were projected on to the screen at various levels of intensity. Almost all the subjects reported 'projected' images of the objects but only when the experimenter-projected pictures were above a previously determined perceptual threshold. Thus they confused external reality with internal imagining.

More recently Segal and Fusella (1970) used a different technique to explore the relations between perception and imagery. They requested subjects to detect faint visual or auditory signals whilst maintaining visual or auditory images. Their main findings were that auditory detection suffered more from auditory than visual imagery while visual detection was poorest when visual imagery was maintained. This modality-specific pattern of interference, of course, rules out the possibility that imagery merely diverted attention away from external stimuli generally. Rather, imagery and perceptual activities seem to compete for resources at a level where stimulus modality is still represented.

One striking piece of evidence that indicates common processes in imagery and perception came from an experiment reported by Kosslyn *et al.* (1981). This was based on the established finding that visual acuity is better for vertical stripes than for oblique stripes: the distance from the looker at which the stripes appear to blur is shorter when they are oblique than when vertical. Kosslyn *et al.* report that the effect occurs with imaginary stripes! This is not an isolated finding as the paper by Fincke (1980) shows. Here a number of results are described indicating comparable similarities between imaging and the perception of external objects.

Isomorphism

As we have already noted many subjects believe they use imagery to perform tasks such as Guildford's paper-folding exercise. We have also noted the weak scientific value of such reports. Nevertheless, a large body of research has been motivated by the belief that imagery is essentially a 'working medium' which may be used in the performance of various tasks, and by the belief that it can be explored by methods that are scientifically acceptable. Amongst the main advocates of these views are Allan Paivio in Canada, and Roger Shepard and Stephen Kosslyn in the USA. Paivio's massive contribution to imagery research, especially its role in remembering verbal material, is touched on in Chapter 5. Shepard and Kosslyn, also, have sought to show the reality of imagery and to cast light on its nature and it will be helpful to summarize their approach before describing some of their work. In essence, they determine relations between task variables and observed performance and examine them against expectations based on the assumptions that imagery *is* employed by the subjects and that it has certain visual-spatial properties.

In one of Shepard's studies (Cooper and Shepard, 1973) subjects were presented with single letters in normal or mirror image orientations (e.g. R or Я) and required to indicate the orientation by pressing one of two keys as quickly as possible. This is a trivial task when the stimulus is upright, hence the important aspect of the experiment was the rotation of the stimulus clockwise or anticlockwise, e.g. ⍅, Я, ⍆, Я. The results took the form of an orderly increase in reaction time with departure of the stimulus from the upright and were consistent with the notion that the task was completed by rotating an image of the stimulus clockwise or anticlockwise into the vertical, whichever was the shorter.

Subjects in another condition were given advanced warning by an upright letter presented for 2 seconds. This was followed by an arrow indicating the angle at which the second presentation of that letter would occur. Again the task was to decide if the second stimulus was a rotation of the normal letter or a mirror image. Reaction times were very fast and very similar across all angles of rotation suggesting that it was possible to generate an image of the first letter, rotate it to the prescribed angle and, when the second stimulus appeared, make a direct visual comparison.

Cooper and Shepard's results are entirely in keeping with the use of imagery to perform their task and suggest that mental rotation bears a close relationship to the rotation of physical objects. They referred to this relationship as *second-order isomorphic*, a term we have already encountered in connection with Shepard and Chipman's study of similarity judgments on the shape of states. This relationship, in turn, is consistent with the view that images depict information in a visual-spatial medium and this is supported by a number of other studies. In one such study Kosslyn, Ball and Reisser (1978) had subjects first learn to draw a simple map of an island containing 7 objects (e.g. a hut, a tree, etc.). They were then asked to imagine the map, mentally focus on one of the objects and, on hearing its name, 'scan' to another object pressing a response key when the target was reached. The results showed that scanning time was directly related to the distance between the objects, thus supplementing Cooper and Shepard's evidence for the second-order isomorphism of controlled imagery.

The work described by Cooper and Shepard and by Kosslyn *et al.* deals with control of images within a single plane. Other work by Shepard (Shepard and Metzler, 1971) has produced evidence of image rotation in depth by means of comparative judgments of diagrammatic representation of 3-dimensional objects. Of more recent studies in this area that by Pinker (1980) is especially interesting. He used the mental scanning technique of Kosslyn *et al.* but had his subjects learn to image an open box in which 5 objects were suspended. In one experiment he found the time taken to mentally scan from one object to another was directly related to the distance *in space*, rather than to the angular distance, between them. This finding, Pinker notes, suggests that a 3-dimensional imaginal representation of the box (he coins the term *sand-box* model) exists rather than a visual

2-dimensional *snapshot* of it. But when asked to imagine they were viewing the box through a rifle sight and scanning from one target to another subjects produced scanning times directly related to the *angular* distance. This was also found when the box was imagined from a novel 'viewing' angle. Taking his results together Pinker concluded that the box and objects were not represented in memory either as a sand-box model or as a visual snapshot. Instead, imagery seems to have $2\frac{1}{2}$ spatial dimensions! Sufficient information was retained on inspection of the box to support the imaginal construction of perceptual-like effects in 2 dimensions and to adjust these effects by means of information about the third dimension.

Are images epiphenomenal?

Shepard and Kosslyn clearly believe that imagery is actually instrumental in the completion of certain tasks. In contrast Pylyshyn (1973) has argued that neither their results nor subjects' reports that they do indeed make use of imagery force such a conclusion. Pylyshyn does not deny the subjective reality of imagery but he points out that just because the experience of imagery accompanies the comple-tion of a task it does not necessarily follow that imagery is *causal* in determining performance. In other words, imagery may merely be a *by-product* of activity taking place with purely symbolic, non-visual, representations of external objects, i.e. imagery is an *epiphenomenon*.

Kosslyn (e.g. Kosslyn, 1980; Kosslyn *et al.*, 1981) agrees that information about visual experience may be stored in a non-visual code. According to his view, expressed in his *cathode ray tube protomodel*, such non-visual codes are analogous to those in a computer holding information in the form of electrical charges the patterns of which bear no direct relation-ship to the visual displays which may be constructed from them on a cathode ray tube. More importantly though, imagery is considered analogous to the visual display and the model emphasizes that this display is 'read' by the 'mind's eye' and then utilized by an executive or decision-maker. This is in stark contrast to Pylyshyn's view which emphasizes the possibility that the visual display is doing no more than merely reflecting the internal, symbolic workings of the computer.

The controversy between the epiphenomenalists and those who believe imagery has some function has continued over the years and Pylyshyn's later views are conveniently expressed alongside those of Kosslyn in Block (1981). In his contribution to this volume Pylyshyn sees the central theoretical question in the controversy as being whether certain imagery phenomena require explanations in terms of *analogue* processes and mechanisms or in terms of *cognitive penetrability*. In other words, are the results of mental scanning and mental rotation studies the inevitable consequences of the intrinsic nature of the imagery medium, or do they depend consciously or unconsciously on the subject's tacit knowledge of geometry and dynamics and what they believe the experiment's expectations to be? Pylyshyn describes some results obtained with the mental scanning paradigm and which support cognitive penetrability. One group of subjects in the study were instructed to imagine a dot moving between two locations and to indicate when it reached the target. Another group were simply instructed to mentally focus on one location, then on another and to indicate when they had done so. Importantly, this group were given no indication of how the relocation of attention should be achieved. The first group produced response times directly related to the inter-location distances. The second group, though, produced no such relationship thus showing that relocating attention within an image does not *demand* uniform movement through the imagery medium. Instead, subjects can produce such movement if the instructions imply that they should. Mitchell and Richman (1980) have reached a similar conclusion.

Kosslyn (Kosslyn *et al.*, 1981) rejects the claim that task demands and tacit knowledge account for his own and similar results. In doing so he refers to a study in which subjects were asked to image pairs of dots moving towards the outer limit of the imaginal 'field' and to indicate when they were not distinct from each other. A control group was shown the instructions given to the imagery group and asked to speculate about how they had responded. While the controls correctly believed that the fusion point would be further towards the periphery with increasing inter-dot distances, they did not estimate the detailed relation actually found between the two. Thus tacit knowledge and task demands cannot account for the data. The same is true for the greater visual acuity for vertical than for oblique imagined stripes mentioned in the previous section: very few people are aware of the phenomenon with real stripes!

The charges that tacit knowledge and task demands, rather than the nature of imagery itself, account for the results of mental scanning and rotation studies are possible to the extent that subjects may have direct control over the phenomena under investigation. Kosslyn has attacked such charges by bringing forward situations where subjects' tacit knowledge does not predict the empirical outcome. A different approach to the study of imagery which does not seem so open to such criticisms has been pursued by Baddeley (see Baddeley, 1983; Baddeley and Lieberman, 1980). This approach identifies visual imagery as one component of a *working memory* system (which is discussed in Chapter 4) and relies particularly on interference techniques. One of Baddeley's findings demonstrates a spatial component of imagery by showing that tasks which may be assumed to rely on spatial aspects of imagery suffer more from spatial interference (tracking an auditory signal while blindfolded) than from visual interference (tracking a visual signal). It is not difficult to see how the detailed experimental manipulation of interference within these modes might lead to a convincing analysis of 'visual' imagery.

Summary

It seems necessary to distinguish between a number of ways in which visual stimuli may be represented in memory. Evidence points strongly to the presence of a precategorical iconic memory but there is a need to elaborate the model proposed by Sperling to take account of recent findings. The icon must be distinguished from the visual codes identified by Posner with his letter-matching paradigm because it is more durable and not susceptible to masking.

Visual stimuli may invite thematic interpretation and verbal labelling, produce emotional responses, and have a number of other effects. It is to be expected, then, that recall and recognition of such stimuli depend on information other than the purely visual as was discussed especially in relation to pictures and faces. While there is evidence that representations of visual features may persist over various periods of time such representations are, on the whole, not very detailed.

The production and control of imagery, as suggested by subjective reports, provide an appealing account of phenomena ranging from letter-matching to problem-solving. Nevertheless, there is continuing debate about whether paradigms such as those involving mental rotation and scanning reveal much about the nature of imagery. Does imagery have a function in performing certain cognitive tasks or is it merely an epiphenomenon?

3 Auditory memory

The reader no doubt will have had the rather embarrassing experience of paying attention to something else while being asked a question. Sometimes in this situation the recipient of the question replies 'pardon?' and then gives the appropriate answer before the question has been repeated. He is able to retrieve the question from memory even though he made no effort to enter it there while his attention was directed elsewhere. Subjectively it often seems as though an echo of the speaker's voice is held in memory and because of this Neisser (1967) christened the store underlying the phenomenon *echoic memory*. Neisser pointed out that such a memory system appears vital for speech perception because identification of the initial segment of a word must often await knowledge of the final segment. Also, interpretation of a spoken sentence such as 'You will come?' as a question rather than a command depends on appreciation of a rising inflection. This in turn requires representation of initial sounds in memory for comparison with later ones.

The idea that stimuli must be represented in a temporary store whilst transfer of information to the next processing stage is completed was referred to extensively in the last chapter. A number of visual memory stores were discussed there, and it is tempting to consider Neisser's echoic memory as the auditory equivalent of iconic memory.

The first part of this chapter discusses several ways in which the persistence of echoic traces has been investigated. The second and third parts of the chapter deal with two phenomena, the *suffix effect* and the *modality effect*, both of which have been widely interpreted in terms of the persistence of traces in auditory memory but which continue to pose theoretical puzzles. The fourth part of the chapter deals briefly with some long-term auditory memory phenomena.

Before moving on to the first part of the chapter it will perhaps be useful to the reader to distinguish between the terms *auditory* and *acoustic* which are used extensively in this chapter. The term *auditory* is taken to mean *pertaining to the sense of hearing*. Thus *auditory memory* carries with it only the implication that this memory is concerned with the auditory mode of stimulus input: it is neutral with respect to the way information is coded within it, with its processes, etc. The term *acoustic*, on the other hand, refers to sound-like properties. Thus, it is possible to conceive of acoustic traces being stored in memory following visual input, and for visually coded traces to be stored in memory following auditory input, as we learned in the last chapter. *Echoic memory*, then, generally refers to an acoustic-based auditory memory.

Measuring echoic persistence

A variety of techniques have been employed to study echoic memory. Four representative techniques are discussed below.

Recognition of periodicity

Guttman and Julesz (1963) employed an ingenious procedure to estimate the persistence of echoic memory traces. They constructed a set of stimulus 'messages' by extracting short sequences from a recording of random noise. The extracts varied from 50 milliseconds upwards and the subjects heard one section repeated from end to end for a lengthy period. In this way a 50-millisecond extract recycled 20 times a second, while a 250-millisecond extract recycled 4 times a second. The subjects' task was to report what they could hear, especially if they were aware of any periodicity (e.g. regular beats) in the sound. The logic behind this study rests on the assumption that for periodicity to be recognized, memory for any component of the extract must persist long enough for it to be integrated into a perceptual unit. Thus, the reports of subjects that clear periodicity occurred with the 250-millisecond extract (it sounded like a motor boat engine) indicates that auditory traces persist for a quarter of a second. The task of interpretation is complicated by the subjects' reports that some periodicity was experienced with extracts as long as 1 second although this was less distinctive than with the 250-millisecond extract. Thus, it may be that auditory traces persist for as long as one second. But, it is possible that if sounds can be perceived as units as short as 250-milliseconds, the periodicity reported with longer repetition cycles represent the perceptual grouping of shorter units. Possibly, therefore, the 250-millisecond trace represents what may be appropriately referred to as *preperceptual auditory memory* (Massaro, 1972), but the perception of longer cycles may reflect some other form of short-term auditory memory.

Auditory masking

Massaro (1970, 1972), amongst others, has used an auditory analogue of Sperling's visual masking procedure, discussed in the previous chapter, to study echoic memory. In one of his studies subjects were presented, on each trial, with one of two possible tones (high or low) and required to identify it. These tones were of only 20 milliseconds duration and because the identification process takes longer than this the tones must have been represented in memory for the process to be completed. A masking tone was presented at various intervals between 0 and 500 milliseconds following the offset of the target. The subjects' ability to correctly identify the tone rose steadily as the interval between target and mask increased up to 250 milliseconds but showed no increase at longer delays. This result is precisely what would be expected if the target was represented in an acoustic code while the identification was carried out: the acoustically coded representation of the auditory mask would then be capable of interfering with the target trace. The finding that the mask had no further effect on performance when it was delayed by 250 milliseconds or more suggests that traces of the target had decayed by that time so no further interference was possible.

The estimate of a quarter of a second obtained by Massaro for the delay at which the mask produces no further interference is similar to the estimate of echoic trace persistence which may be derived from the results of Guttman and Julesz. Nevertheless it is possible that Massaro's method underestimates the persistence. Notably, it is possible that all the useful information had been extracted from the traces within 250 milliseconds and that given more complex stimuli and a more difficult task the mask would have been effective at longer delays. Conversely, it is possible that echoic traces had decayed by the time the mask arrived and it is the identification process rather than echoic storage which is disrupted. This possibility is supported by results showing that auditory masks are effective up to only 100 millisecond delays when detection rather than identification of tones is required (e.g. Deatherage and Evans, 1969). Efron's findings (e.g. Efron, 1970) also indicate a somewhat similar limit to the duration of auditory sensory memory. He required subjects to adjust the onset of a light so that it appeared to correspond with the offset of a tone and found the longest offset-onset interval (i.e. the duration of *apparent* persistence) to be about 100 milliseconds.

The three-eared man experiment

Darwin, Turvey and Crowder (1972) investigated auditory memory in a situation analogous to that of the inattentive listener mentioned at the beginning of this chapter. Their investigation extended an earlier one by Moray, Bates and Barnett (1965) and used an auditory equivalent of Sperling's visual partial-report procedure. Of course, with the auditory mode it is impossible to present a simultaneous array of items exactly analogous to those used by Sperling. However, it is possible to get something approaching it if stereophonic headphones (or two loudspeakers) are used. If one list of items is presented through only the left headphone, a second list through only the right, and a third list through both simultaneously the subject has the distinct experience of hearing the messages from three locations, to the right, to the left, and centrally. In addition, the apparent locations make it easy to attend to one of these sources, or channels, and ignore the others. It was this phenomenon which Darwin *et al*. utilized to study immediate auditory memory.

Subjects were presented with a list of 3 items (digits and letters) on each channel. Three items, one from each list, were presented simultaneously and 3 triplets were presented within 1 second. This arrangement is depicted in Figure 3.1.

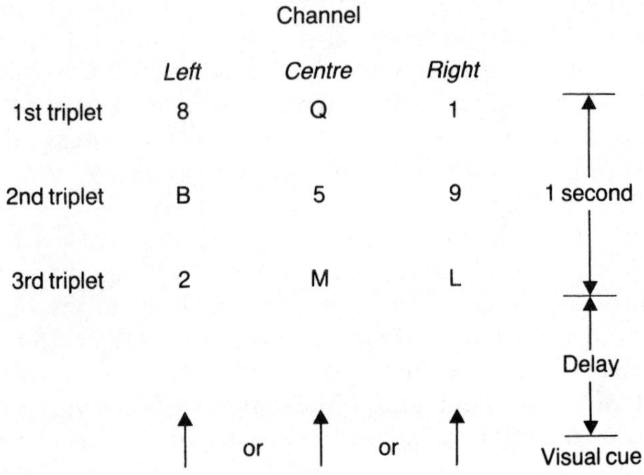

Channel

	Left	Centre	Right	
1st triplet	8	Q	1	
2nd triplet	B	5	9	1 second
3rd triplet	2	M	L	
	↑ or	↑ or	↑	Delay
				Visual cue

Figure 3.1:   *The 'three-eared man' procedure*

In the *whole report* condition subjects were required to recall as many of the 9 items as possible immediately the third triplet had been presented. In *partial report* a visual signal, indicating which *channel* should be recalled, was presented 0, 1, 2, or 4 seconds after the third triplet. Figure 3.2 shows the mean number of items available in memory, the calculation being based on the same logic as that employed by Sperling.

Figure 3.2 shares several general features with Figure 2.1 in which Sperling's results for iconic memory are shown and interpretation of both sets of results can follow the same reasoning. Thus, the fall in partial report superiority with increasing cue delay indicates two important points. First,

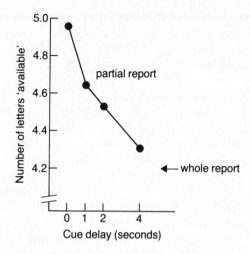

Figure 3.2: *Estimated number of letters available as a function of cue delay (adapted from Darwin et al., 1974)*

echoic information on each channel has a 'life' of about 4 seconds. Second, the superiority of partial report over whole report was not due solely to reduced output interference. Furthermore, since the recall cues were based on the apparent physical location of the channels their effectiveness is consistent with the idea that the partial report superiority stems from a store located prior to the verbal categorization process. But such evidence is not conclusive on this point because it does not rule out the possibility that *both* categorical and physical information are represented in the store. Darwin *et al.* investigated this issue by following Sperling's argument that if semantic categories are represented in the store then cueing recall of letters only or digits only should give rise to a partial report superiority. Their second experiment was similar to the first except that the cues indicated whether subjects should attempt to recall all the digits or all the letters from the 9 items presented on the three channels. Contrary to expectations based on a precategorical locus of immediate auditory memory, a small advantage to partial report over whole report was found. Thus it seems that the 'three-eared man' procedure employed by Darwin *et al.* does not give an entirely unambiguous insight into echoic memory if this is taken to include only sources of information prior to the verbal categorization process.

Memory for 'unattended' messages

The partial-report technique employed by Darwin *et al.* to study echoic memory, and by Sperling to study iconic memory, are similar in that they present many items to the subject in a brief time interval. This makes it very difficult for the subject to categorize any more than a small proportion of the items before the partial-report cue is presented and so helps to ensure that recall depends almost entirely on the sampling of uncategorized acoustic or visual traces. Another method of trying to sample uncategorized traces is to divert the categorization process to one source of stimulation, or input channel, while simultaneously presenting stimuli on another, unattended, channel. If the subject's attention is 'switched' from one channel to the other it should be possible to sample uncategorized stimulus information from the originally unattended channel. This approach is well illustrated by the study of Eriksen and Johnson (1964). Subjects were asked to read a novel thus directing attention to the visual input mode. During the 2-hour session a faint tone was sounded at irregular intervals. At times ranging from 0 to 10 seconds following the tone the reading light was switched off and subjects were required to state whether the tone had occurred or not during the last 15 seconds or so. In order to check on the guessing rate there were some occasions when no tone was present in the interval before the light was turned off. The *correct* detection rate fell from just under 50 per cent when the 'report' signal followed the tone immediately, to about 25 per cent with a 10-second delay. This pattern of results suggests that the tone is indeed represented in memory and that the trace decays over the 10-seconds period. However, the reading activity was uncontrolled so the subjects might not have attended to the book the whole time. Possibly, therefore, they were paying attention to the auditory channel some of the time and if the tone sounded while they were doing so they could record the fact in post-categorical memory. The fall in performance with delay in recall would then represent forgetting in post-categorical memory rather than properties of a precategorical, acoustic trace. This objection was met to some extent by the inclusion of another condition in which subjects were instructed to pay attention to the book but to report the occurrence of the tone without waiting to be signalled. In this condition, the detection rate was much lower than in the cued condition thus showing that subjects in the cued condition were not spontaneously switching attention from the book sufficiently often to account for their detection rates.

Eriksen and Johnson's estimate of 10 seconds for the duration of echoic memory traces is longer than that obtained by Darwin *et al.* based on the partial report of verbal stimuli. Possibly, then, Eriksen and Johnson were tapping a different type of auditory memory from these other researchers. Or more likely, perhaps, their procedure was not tightly controlled despite the indication of their control group results. This conclusion is supported by the fact that Glucksberg and Cowan (1970) reported an estimated acoustic trace duration of 4 or 5 seconds using recall of digits. Glucksberg and Cowan had subjects shadow (i.e. repeat) a sequence of prose presented to one ear while a different prose passage was presented to the other, non-attended ear. The non-attended message contained digits presented at irregular intervals and subjects were interrupted to report any digits that may have been presented. The results showed a systematic drop in the number of digits reported correctly as the delay between occurrence and report increased with minimum performance being reached after about 5 seconds. This dichotic presentation procedure is a big improvement on that of Eriksen and Johnson because it enables the experimenter to ensure that the subject is correctly shadowing the attended channel. While it does not *guarantee* that subjects cannot rapidly switch attention from one channel to another and still complete the shadowing task, it does go some way towards controlling attention.

The inclusion of a prose passage on the non-attended channel is an interesting feature of Glucksberg and Cowan's procedure. They incorporated this feature because if only digits are presented on the non-attended channel at irregular intervals the sudden appearance of a stimulus might cause the subject to switch attention. This problem was minimized by embedding the digits in the continuous prose passage.

How persistent is echoic memory?

Glucksberg and Cowan agree with Darwin *et al.* in producing estimates of 4-5 seconds for the persistence of traces in echoic memory. It seems, then, that their procedures tap a different auditory memory from that revealed by studies such as those of Guttman and Julesz and of Massaro. Possibly, therefore, there is justification for distinguishing between different levels of auditory memory as Massaro (1972) has done. Massaro attributed the results obtained with the recognition-of-periodicity and recognition-masking paradigms to *preperceptual auditory memory*. This is considered equivalent to iconic memory, being sensory, short-lived and subject to backward masking. The results obtained with the three-eared man and sampling of unattended messages procedures are attributed to *short-term auditory memory*. This holds information that has been 'perceived' and may be considered analogous to the short-term visual memory identified by Posner in the letter-matching task and which is not subject to backward masking. Massaro maintained that both types of auditory memory have a role to play in speech perception. Put crudely, he suggested that preperceptual auditory memory operates at a fairly primitive level of perception, possibly at the level of the syllable. Short-term auditory memory, in contrast, is involved in the perception of phrases or sentences, and it is this memory which gives rise to the 'double-take' phenomenon mentioned at the beginning of this chapter.

Not everyone agrees with Massaro's model of auditory memory, or the evidence which favours an echoic interpretation of it. Some object to it on the grounds that several studies have shown that auditory masks are effective up to only 100 milliseconds when detection of a tone is required rather than the 250 milliseconds estimated by Massaro with tone identification. Efron's findings with the simultaneity judgment task also suggest a somewhat similar limit to the duration of auditory sensory memory. In contrast, other theorists disagree with Massaro's model in the belief that preperceptual or somesuch traces can persist long enough to account for phenomena which he attributes to short-term auditory memory. In the next part we look in detail at studies of one such phenomenon, the *auditory suffix effect*, and the evidence which favours an echoic interpretation of it.

The auditory suffix effect

A large body of research on auditory memory has been concerned with the *suffix effect*. The effect is most strikingly obtained in the serial recall of auditory sequences containing 8 or 9 items, usually digits, presented at about 2 items per second. In the *control* condition only the to-be-remembered items are presented, but in the *suffix* condition a redundant auditory item is added to the list. The identity of this suffix is kept constant throughout the experiment and it need never be recalled. Nevertheless, its presence has a dramatic effect on recall. Figure 3.3 depicts the typical suffix effect. The reader should note that performance is plotted in terms of number of *errors* as is common for serial recall. This pattern of results, in which the suffix effect is restricted largely to the last few serial positions, has been reported by a number of experimenters (e.g. Crowder, 1967; Crowder and Morton, 1969), and so is a robust phenomenon. It is possible that any small increase in errors which occurs across *all* serial positions as a result of presenting a suffix (see Figure 3.3) can be explained in terms of the small increase in delay before recall takes place, or some such general effect. The same is not true for the large decrement in performance on the last few items: some special explanation is required for this.

A number of theorists have suggested that the high level of recall on the last few items in the control condition is due to the persistence of acoustic traces and that the suffix has its effect by interfering with these traces. What is possibly the most influential account of the suffix effect follows this line of reasoning. It was put forward by Crowder and Morton, and

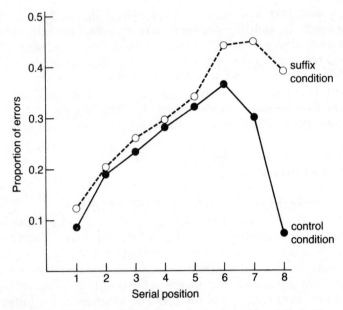

Figure 3.3:   *Typical suffix effect obtained with serial recall*

is based on what they call *precategorical acoustic storage* (PAS). The similarities between PAS and Massaro's preperceptual auditory memory, which was discussed earlier, will become apparent in what follows.

PAS theory

According to Crowder and Morton (1969) the suffix effect may be explained by assuming the presence of a memory store capable of holding one or possibly two items in the form of relatively 'raw' acoustic traces, and susceptible to interference by subsequent auditory stimuli. Because this store is assumed to be specific to auditorily presented items it is placed prior to the point at which stimuli are categorized into verbal units, it being assumed that the categorization process is common to stimuli presented in the visual and in the auditory mode. Hence the name *precategorical acoustic store (PAS)*.

Figure 3.4. gives a simple representation of the relation-

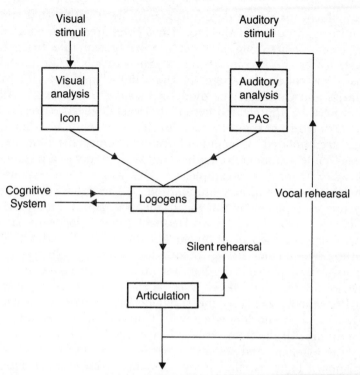

Figure 3.4: *Crowder and Morton's model of immediate memory (adapted from Crowder and Morton, 1969)*

ship between PAS and several other theoretical components of the memory system. It is assumed that visual and auditory stimuli reaching the sense organs undergo various analyses and transformations as a result of which their physical features become represented by internal codes. It is these codes which PAS and iconic memory are presumed to hold and which provide the basis for the categorization into verbal units carried out by the *logogen system*. Morton (e.g. 1969) developed his logogen model to deal with various perceptual phenomena such as the identification of words under impoverished stimulus conditions. The logogens accumulate information from the visual and acoustic codes. In the early model on which Figure 3.4 is based, it was assumed that the same logogens accumulate information from both visual and auditory stimuli. But the model has been greatly elaborated in recent years, one new feature being separate logogen systems for the two input modes. Such details of the model need not concern us here: in the volume in this series by Harris and Coltheart the model is discussed extensively. All that need be appreciated here is that each logogen represents a word, letter, or digit, and makes this item available when it has accumulated sufficient information. Once the item has been made available it may be dealt with in any of a number of ways. It may, for example, be given as a spoken response in which case auditory stimulation will feed back into the system as depicted by the vocal rehearsal loop in Figure 3.4. Silent articulation also gives feedback into the logogens thus enabling continued silent rehearsal to be accomplished. Other alternatives include storage in long-term memory, which is not specifically depicted in the diagram but which may conveniently be considered part of what is labelled the *cognitive system*.

PAS theory explains the serial position curves shown in Figure 3.3 in the following way. Consider first the control condition. All the items recalled must have been categorized by the logogens and so were retrieved from post-categorical memory. Thus, the fall in performance from early to later serial positions may be accounted for partly by the assumption that the subject's capacity to rehearse the items, and otherwise establish them in a relatively durable post-categorical store, must be shared amongst progressively more items as presentation of the list proceeds. Additionally, because recall must take place in serial order, later items presumably suffer from interference due to the act of recalling earlier items. The dramatically high performance on the last item in the control condition is explained by the benefit bestowed on it as a result of its representation in PAS: the acoustic trace supplements information in post-categorical memory. The benefit is limited largely to the last item because successive items interfere with any acoustic traces already in PAS. When the suffix is added to the list the last to-be-remembered item no longer enjoys its special end-of-list status, its representation in PAS suffers interference and performance is accordingly reduced.

How is PAS utilized?

In the serial recall paradigm recall must proceed from the first to the last serial position in order. If information in PAS is to supplement recall of the last items by being used *directly at the time of recall* it must persist long enough for the first items to be recalled. We noted earlier that Darwin *et al.* (1972) and Glucksberg and Cowan (1970) produced estimates of about 4 or 5 seconds for echoic persistence using other recall procedures. It seems unlikely that it would take subjects as long as 4 seconds to recall 6 digits, hence it is possible that information in PAS could indeed survive long enough to be used *directly* at recall. However, the information which can survive such periods might be adequate to perform one task but not another. Thus, the *useful* life of acoustic information in the serial recall paradigm may be less than 4 seconds and this, indeed, is one interpretation which may be put on the results obtained by Crowder (1969).

Crowder delayed the suffix by 0.5, 2, 5 or 10 seconds and found that it produced the suffix effect only at the shortest delay. This is what would be expected if traces persisted in PAS for less than 2 seconds because after a 2-second delay no useful information would remain for the suffix to interfere with. In that case, because it surely takes more than 2 seconds to get around to recalling the final list item, no useful information about it would be present in PAS at the time of recall even if no suffix were presented. Any advantage to the final item as a result of its representation in PAS would, therefore, arise from the *indirect* use of acoustic traces rather than from direct use at the time of recall. Following the earlier comments concerning Massaro's tone identification experiment, it should be clear that an alternative interpretation of Crowder's data is that traces in PAS may last longer than 2 seconds but all useful information has been extracted in that interval. This interpretation, also, implies that PAS is used indirectly to facilitate recall.

There have been several suggestions as to how indirect utilization of PAS is achieved. For example, Morton (1970) proposed that unless a suffix interferes with it information about the last item is transferred automatically from PAS into post-categorical memory while the first items are being recalled. According to Crowder (1972), the subject uses PAS within 2 seconds to rehearse the last item or two and check their identities. However, for the present purpose of giving a general outline of PAS theory it is not necessary to go further into the distinction between these two versions.

Critical features of the suffix

If the suffix interferes with precategorical acoustic traces as PAS theory insists, then its effect should be modality-specific. Evidence that this is so comes from studies which find that no suffix effect occurs when an auditory suffix follows a visual list (Crowder and Morton, 1969), nor when a visual suffix follows an auditory list (Morton and Holloway, 1970). There is, of course, a potential problem with these cross-modal situations in that subjects may not attend to the suffix (with a visual suffix the subjects may close their eyes!). Morton and Holloway neatly avoided this problem by requiring subjects to write down whether each suffix was a tick or a cross.

Further evidence that the suffix effect is acoustically based was provided in an extensive study by Morton, Crowder and Prussin (1971). They found that the size of the suffix effect was related to the physical similarity between list and suffix such that, for example, the effect was reduced when there was a difference in the sex of the speakers, and when the same voice was used but list and suffix differed in loudness. In addition, a number of studies have shown that the suffix must be *acoustically* speech-like if it is to influence recall. Morton *et al.* (1971) found that a burst of white noise had little effect on recall even though it covered the range of sound frequencies spanned by the human voice. Also, Morton and Chambers (1976) showed that a synthetically produced *zero* suffix has little effect on recall. In contrast to these findings, a human grunt does produce a suffix effect, and Crowder and Raeburn (1970) obtained the effect with a suffix constructed by reversing a section of tape containing a recorded word thus making it unintelligible. Taken together, these findings show that it is the physical rather than the semantic aspects of the suffix that are important.

Results reported by Morton *et al.* (1971) also support this

view. In one of their experiments Morton *et al.* constructed
lists of either 6 animal names or 6 kitchen utensils and found
that a suffix had a similar effect on recall whether it came
from the same or different category as the list items. This
finding supports the precategorical locus of the suffix effect
by showing that it was not influenced by the *semantic*
relationships between list and suffix and is entirely in accord
with PAS theory. But other findings show that semantic
relationships *can* influence the magnitude of the suffix effect.
For example, Salter and Colley (1977) have shown that the
suffix effect may be *reduced* if the suffix is a synonym of the
final list item (see also Salter, 1975). Although these results
may appear to conflict with PAS theory by suggesting that
the suffix may indeed depend on semantic relations between
list items and the suffix, it is possible to achieve a
reconciliation. This may be done by following Salter and
Colley's suggestion that their subjects used the meaning of
the suffix to assist storage of the final item in post-categorical
memory thus offsetting any acoustic interference the suffix
may have produced in PAS. Thus, Salter and Colley's
findings need not contradict PAS theory. Rather, they seem
to complement it by supporting the assumption made by
both Morton and Crowder that in serial recall *all* those items
which are recalled come from post-categorical storage
whether a suffix is present or not.

Other aspects of the auditory suffix effect
Earlier in this section when describing the suffix effect it was
noted that the suffix may have an influence at serial positions
throughout the list rather than merely on the final position.
This phenomenon, illustrated in Figure 3.1, was dismissed
rather cursorily because the relative size of the 'terminal'
suffix effect suggests it has a different origin from the effect
over preterminal items. But, on this evidence alone, it may
be argued that the acoustic store holds at least some
information about each of as many as 7 or 8 items and the
suffix interferes with all such information. On the other hand
Salter and Colley's findings, discussed above, suggest that
the terminal suffix effect may be influenced by factors
generally regarded as operating only in post-categorical

memory. Considerations such as these have encouraged attempts to clarify the relation between terminal and preterminal suffix effects. In one such study Balota and Engle (1981) varied the rate at which digit lists were presented (6, 3, or 1.5 digits per second) and the amount of practice subjects had with suffix and no-suffix conditions. Briefly, their rationale was based on the idea that at slow presentation rates subjects should be better able to employ those strategies necessary to encode and retain items in post-categorical storage, and with practice to avoid any disruptive influence of the suffix on those strategies. In contrast, any aspects of the suffix's effects which are *structural*, i.e. not amenable to changes of strategy, should remain uninfluenced by these experimental manipulations. The results showed that the disruptive effects of the suffix over preterminal positions was indeed reduced by practice and by increased presentation rate, but the effect on the terminal item was largely uninfluenced by these variables. Thus, Balota and Engle were able to conclude that the terminal suffix effect originates in some structural component of memory such as PAS, while the preterminal effect arises because the suffix also disrupts rehearsal and other strategies necessary to retain items in post-categorical memory.

The findings reported by Baddeley and Hull (1979) also support the distinction between terminal and preterminal suffix effects. In a series of experiments they found that the length of the suffix (e.g. Rhyl vs Abergavenny) influenced recall of terminal and preterminal items in different ways: longer suffixes produced greater decrements at preterminal positions but *smaller* decrements at the terminal position. Again, it seems easy to explain the effects of suffix length at preterminal positions in terms of increased retention interval and disruption of the attention allocated to the items in post-categorical memory. However, the effect at the terminal position is not so obviously explained. Although perhaps unjustified, it is tempting to draw an analogy between Baddeley and Hull's finding and other findings that three auditory suffixes, presented one after the other in rhythm with the list, produce a smaller suffix effect than does a single suffix (Crowder, 1978; Morton, 1976). Crowder (1978) has used this phenomenon to argue that forgetting in PAS takes place through *inhibition* rather than *overwriting* or *displacement* of information. Essentially, he points out that if items are removed from PAS then three suffixes should produce as large an effect as a single suffix, if not a larger one. But, if successive items merely *inhibit* previous items in PAS the successive suffixes should inhibit the effects of previous suffixes thereby reducing the suffix effect. Crowder's theory is very provocative and detailed, and it could conceivably provide a clue as to why multi-syllable suffixes produced a smaller suffix effect than did single-syllable ones in Baddeley and Hull's study.

The weight of evidence concerning the auditory suffix effect discussed in this section supports the idea of a precategorical, short-lived, acoustic store of small capacity. But there is other evidence that calls into question any interpretation of the suffix effect based on such a store and hence the usefulness of the suffix paradigm for investigating echoic memory. Some of this evidence is discussed later in this chapter. First, though we look at the *modality effect* which has also been widely attributed to echoic memory.

The modality effect

Figure 3.5 (a) shows some typical serial position curves for immediate serial recall. Performance is shown following auditory or visual (i.e. graphic) presentation of items and it should be noted that for the purpose of comparison scores are expressed in terms of the proportion of items *correctly* recalled. It can be seen that performance of the last few items is typically superior when presentation is auditory rather than visual but earlier items are little affected by the mode of presentation. This pattern of results is known as the *modality effect* and is found in a number of paradigms although with detailed differences. Typical free recall results are shown in Figure 3.5 (b) to illustrate some of these differences.

One widely accepted explanation of the modality effect is that it arises in echoic memory, as does the auditory suffix effect. Two main bases of this belief, the effects of varying

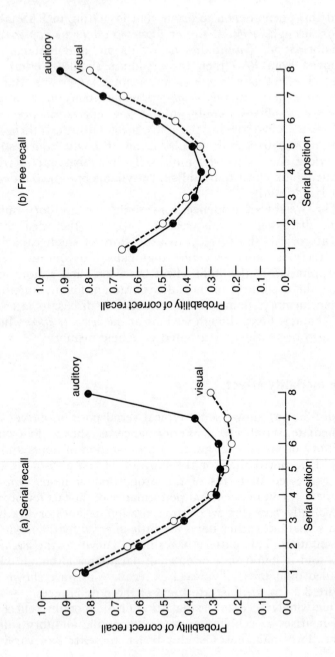

Figure 3.5:   *Typical modality effect in (a) serial recall, and (b) free recall*

phonological similarity among list items and of introducing delayed distraction, are now discussed.

Effect of phonological similarity
Strong support for the acoustic basis of the modality effect comes from studies which show that the effect is reduced when list items are phonologically similar to each other, i.e. share the same speech sounds. Darwin and Baddeley (1974) established this phenomenon with immediate serial recall of syllables (e.g. BAH, DAH, GAH) and Watkins, Watkins and Crowder (1974) did so with words (e.g. BAKE, ACHE, CAKE) for both free and serial recall. In one of their experiments, Darwin and Baddeley constructed short sequences from sets of syllables which differed in acoustic confusability. For example, BEE, BIH, BOO is a more distinct set than BAH, GAH, DAH, in that they can be distinguished more readily when presented auditorily in noise. Serial recall performance was assessed in conditions where the items were presented visually and either read silently or vocalized by the subject. (This latter procedure yields results almost identical to those obtained when subjects listen to the experimenter speaking the items.) The results showed that the modality effect was present with the acoustically distinct set but not with the similar set. This is precisely what would be expected if the modality effect were based on information stored in an acoustic 'format'. In that case the traces representing acoustically similar items would be difficult to distinguish from one another and recalling them in the required order would be difficult. In their second experiment Darwin and Baddeley studied the *auditory suffix effect* and found that this effect, like the modality effect in the first experiment, was obtained with acoustically distinct items but not with similar ones. These results are important for a number of reasons. They do, of course, strongly indicate an acoustic basis of both the modality effect and auditory suffix effect. Also, as Crowder (e.g. 1978) has argued, the dependence of the modality and suffix effects on the phonological nature of the list items excludes several theories not based on the notion of acoustic storage, including Kahneman's (1973) influential *attention-grouping theory*. It is

worth looking at this theory in a little detail.

In essence, Kahneman's theory maintains that items lying on the boundaries of perceived stimulus groups, such as lists, attract special types and amounts of attention. It is this which is assumed to give rise to the high levels of recall for items near the beginning and end of a list. The suffix effect is explained by the idea that, to the extent that it cannot be distinguished from the list, the suffix removes the special end-of-group status for the last item. In this way the theory is able to account for variations in the suffix effect which are associated with changes in the physical relationships between suffix and list items. To account for the modality effect the theory would have to maintain that an auditory list is more distinguishable than a visual list from the background environment. This position seems quite reasonable because, on the whole, the modality effect has been studied in quiet but well-illuminated laboratories. Thus, the end of an auditory list may well have a more definite perceived 'boundary' than the end of a visual list in such circumstances with the consequences that items at the end of auditory lists attract special attention. Nevertheless, several objections can be made to this account of the modality effect. First, an auditory advantage would be expected at the beginning of the list but this is not usually found. Second, Hitch (1975) found that recall of the later items of visual lists was actually diminished when the quiet, light environment was darkened – a manipulation which should have increased the perceived boundaries of these lists. And third is Crowder's point, mentioned above, that the modality effect should not be influenced by the phonological similarity of list items because this should not affect the perceived grouping of the lists.

Effects of delayed distraction

The effects of phonological similarity strongly suggest that the modality effect and suffix effect have a common origin in an acoustically based store peculiar to the auditory mode. PAS theory, derived principally from evidence on the auditory suffix effect, maintains that precategorical acoustic traces are fully utilized within about 2 seconds. If the modality effect is to be explained in terms of PAS it must arise from the indirect use of these traces. In contrast there are a number of theorists who, while advocating the idea that some sort of acoustic or echoic store is responsible for the modality effect, quarrel with certain aspects of PAS theory. Amongst these theorists are Broadbent (e.g. Broadbent, Vines and Broadbent, 1978) and the Watkinses (e.g. Watkins and Watkins, 1980) who believe that the constraints placed by PAS theory on the size and useful life of echoic memory are not justified. Rather, they believe that acoustic traces can persist for at least 18 seconds, and so can be utilized directly at the time of recall provided no auditory events occur in the retention interval.

The theories of Broadbent *et al.* and of Watkins and Watkins are broadly similar. Interestingly, though, Broadbent *et al.* label the acoustic traces as *sensory* thus indicating a relatively primitive level of analysis. In contrast Watkins and Watkins largely avoid commitment concerning the level to which these traces have been processed and accordingly refer to them less specifically as *echoic*. But in earlier studies they found that the modality effect extends over the same number of serial positions no matter whether single-syllable or 4-syllable words make up the list (e.g. Watkins, 1972). Thus, their conceptualization of echoic memory may be seen as not merely analogous to a tape-recorder being limited by the number of sound waves which can be represented on a given length of tape. Rather, by the time information is stored in echoic memory it has been analysed to the extent that units of sound which represent words have been identified. And it is in terms of these units that the capacity of echoic memory is limited. Nevertheless these echoic traces, like the sensory traces of Broadbent *et al.*, seem more similar to Massaro's preperceptual traces than his short-term auditory memory traces in so far as they are susceptible to backward masking by auditory events occurring in the retention interval.

It is easy to identify at least one set of conditions which will test between theories advocating that the modality effect arises from the indirect, and those advocating the direct, utilization of acoustic traces. Clearly, both types of theory predict that the modality effect will be reduced by auditory but not by visual events when they occur immediately following the end of the list. But, different predictions emerge when these distracting events are delayed by more than, for example, the 2-second interval which PAS considers to be the useful life of acoustic traces. This point is conveniently pursued by looking at one of the experiments reported by Watkins and Watkins (1980). In this experiment they presented auditory or visual lists of 9 letters for delayed serial recall. In one condition recall was preceded by an unfilled interval of 18 seconds. In the second condition 4 digits were presented visually after an unfilled interval of 15 seconds with serial recall of the letters taking place immediately these digits have been written down. The third condition was identical to the second except that the digits were presented auditorily. A clear modality effect was obtained with the unfilled delay. But this, on its own, does not establish that acoustic traces persisted up to the time of recall. PAS theory can account for this finding by the indirect utilization of echoic traces merely by making the plausible assumption that any advantage in post-categorical memory bestowed on final auditory items by PAS is maintained over the unfilled 15-second interval. However, Watkins and Watkins argued that, since the digits in the two distractor conditions had to be copied, it was necessary to categorize them; hence, whether presented visually or auditorily they should have interfered equally with post-categorical memory for the letters. The results showed that auditory distractors reduced the modality effect more than visual distractors thus supporting the view that *direct* utilization of acoustic traces is responsible for the modality effect, even after delays of 18 seconds. Gathercole, Gregg and Gardiner (1983) showed these results to have some generality by obtaining a similar pattern of interference in the free recall of word lists.

In rejecting the limit of 2 seconds on the persistence of traces in PAS Watkins and Watkins did not ignore Crowder's (1969) finding that there was no suffix effect when the suffix was delayed by 2 seconds or more. They point out that Crowder used a presentation rate of 2 items a second in combination with all suffix delays. It is possible, therefore, that presenting the suffix out of rhythm differentiated it from the list items in much the same way as do differences in voice or volume (Morton *et al.*, 1971). Thus, the absence of the suffix effect with a delay of 2 or more seconds could have been due to differentiation between suffix and list items and not to an *absence* of information in PAS. Watkins and Watkins found that when suffix and list items were presented rhythmically there *was* a suffix effect with a delay as long as 4 seconds. Accordingly they concluded that the theoretical constraints on PAS which dictated the indirect utilization hypothesis are unnecessary. However, Crowder (1978) insists that the suffix effect is not directly dependent on the degree of rhythm between list and suffix presentation. But Crowder's experiments involve suffix delays of up to 2 seconds only and it is conceivable that at longer delays some different mechanism which is influenced by rhythm is involved in the suffix effect. Whatever the outcome of this particular controversy the theory of long-lived echoic traces may be seen as an impressive attempt to provide a single, comprehensive account of the modality and suffix effects.

Problems for echoic theories
Compelling though the notion of long-lasting echoic traces might be as an explanation of the modality effect, several findings cast doubt on it including those reported by Gardiner and Gregg (1979). They varied the standard free recall procedure by making subjects count aloud before and after every word in the list, including the last one. The expectation was that the modality effect would be eliminated by the massive amounts of auditory interference originating from the counting but, surprisingly, they found the modality effect was present. It may seem possible to explain this finding when the words are spoken by the experimenter and the distractors by the subject on the grounds that list and distractor items may be differentiated in memory on the basis of acoustic features of the two voices. This explanation would be akin to that adopted by Morton *et al.* (1971) to explain the dependence of the *suffix effect* on the physical similarities between list and suffix. However, any such explanation is strained by the finding that the modality effect was obtained when the list and distractor items were spoken

by the same person. But the strongest evidence against an interpretation in terms of echoic trace persistence is the finding by Gregg and Gardiner (1984) that the modality effect obtained with 'through-list' auditory distraction is not influenced by phonological similarity amongst list items. If the modality effect can occur under conditions which are least favourable to the persistence of echoic traces (high phonological similarity in conjunction with massive amounts of auditory distraction), it is not clear when the effect in other circumstances should be attributed to echoic traces, if at all!

Somewhat similar doubts have arisen about echoic interpretations of the suffix effect be they based on the idea of indirect utilization of short-lived traces or direct use of long-lived traces. Amongst the findings which have contributed to these doubts is that reported by Ayres, Jonides, Reitman, Egan and Howard (1979). In that study all subjects received auditory word lists. For one experimental group each list was followed equally often by one of the speech sounds *da*, *pin*, *wing* and *wa*, while for another group each suffix was one of the musical sounds *a muted trumpet*, *a plucked violin string*, *a bowed violin string*, or *wa*. The critical feature of the experiment was the inclusion of the ambiguous *wa* suffix in both conditions. Ayres *et al.* reasoned that this suffix would be interpreted as a speech sound by one group of subjects but as a musical sound by the other group. If the suffix effect arises in a precategorical acoustic store it should not depend on how *wa* is categorized. The results showed clearly that the suffix effect was smaller when *wa* was interpreted as a musical sound rather than a speech sound and so were contrary to a precategorical locus of the effect.

Another striking result was reported by Spoehr and Corin (1978). They obtained the suffix effect when an auditory list was followed by a suffix which was silently articulated by the experimenter so that the subject had to lip-read it. The complementary result of a suffix effect when an auditory suffix follows a lip-read list was obtained by Campbell and Dodd (1980), and Gathercole, Gardiner and Gregg (1981) obtained a similar effect of a lip-read suffix on a lip-read list. These results stand in contrast to the findings, mentioned earlier, that no suffix effect occurs when an auditory suffix follows a visual list in *graphic* form, nor when a graphic suffix follows an auditory list. It seems, then, that the lip-read mode is more similar to the auditory mode than to the graphic mode with respect to the suffix effect, and hence that the suffix effect does not depend on auditory stimulation. And furthermore, according to the results of Gardiner, Gathercole and Gregg (1983), the same seems true of the modality effect. They showed that a lip-spoken sequence of distractor items reduced the auditory advantage over graphic lists much the same as does auditory but not graphic distraction.

The presence of *cross-modal* interference (e.g. lip-spoken lists with auditory distraction) indicate that the suffix and modality effects can arise at a point in the processing sequence which is common to lip-read and auditory modes but not shared with stimuli presented graphically. This in turn suggests that *speech* perception mechanisms rather than merely *auditory* perception mechanisms may be involved in the effects. However, the situation is further complicated because Shand and Klima (1981) obtained a suffix effect when list and suffix items were presented in American Sign Language to profoundly deaf subjects! It is not clear at this point how these various findings may be accounted for (see Gardiner, 1983, for comprehensive discussion), but it is clear that they challenge those interpretations of the auditory suffix effect and modality effect which rely on echoic memory. This is true whether echoic memory is viewed as a small sensory store of limited useful life, or as containing long-lasting acoustic traces which may be utilized directly at the time of recall.

Long-term auditory memory

It is clear that the long-term storage of auditory information is necessary to explain, for example, musical skills, and the abilities to understand speech and identify environmental sounds. It is also clear that the form of such storage must be highly abstract since it is not susceptible to the interference effects which seem to characterize echoic memory.

A neat demonstration that auditory information can be

retained in long-term memory was made by Craik and Kirsner (1974) using the continuous recognition procedure. This procedure involves the presentation of a long sequence of items each of which is repeated after a predetermined interval. The subject responds to each item by indicating whether or not it had occurred earlier in the sequence. Craik and Kirsner presented half the words in a male voice initially while the other half were presented in a female voice. The second presentation was either in the same or different voice. Recognition performance was better with the same voice than with the different voice after intervals as long as 90 seconds. Clearly, the same voice advantage cannot be attributed to direct utilization of persisting 'sensory' or 'echoic' traces because these would have been eliminated by the presentation of other items in the same voices during the retention intervals. Also, it is difficult to see how the results could be explained in terms of a *modality-free*, post-categorical memory store. Presumably, then, the subjects retained representations of auditory aspects of the presentation episodes in some non-sensory memory store and used these in conjunction with verbal memory to complete the recognition task.

Memory for voices
Other evidence of long-term memory for auditory stimuli is provided by the general ability to identify a familiar voice, and by findings that it is often possible for listeners to recognize which of several unfamiliar voices a message was spoken in after long periods of time. In their study of the long-term identification of voices Meudell, Northern, Snowden and Neary (1980) presented subjects with recordings of famous voices made over a 50-year period by the British Broadcasting Corporation. The subjects, aged between 48 and 67 years, were asked to identify each voice and were able to recall the name of the speaker on about 30 per cent of trials with recordings made as far back as the 1930s. Even for those voices where names were not recalled recognition scores were well above chance.

The recognition of *unfamiliar* voices was investigated in an early study by McGehee (1937; see, too, Clifford and Bull,

1978, Chapter 5). In this study, McGehee included one set of conditions in which each subject listened to a 56-word prose passage read by a single speaker. After various retention intervals subjects heard the passage read by five different readers, one after the other, and were asked to indicate the original voice. Performance was maintained at about 82 per cent over retention intervals of up to seven days, but fell to 35 per cent after three months and to 13 per cent (actually below the chance level of 20 per cent) after five months. Since the readers were unknown to the subjects and had no extraordinary accents it seems that recognition must have been based on something other than simple verbal labels. While it is tempting to conclude that performance must, therefore, have reflected merely the retention of physical features of the voices some further evidence of McGehee warns against this. McGehee found that, overall, men were better than women at recognizing the voice in which the passage had been read. But, there was an interaction between the sex of the listener and the sex of the subject such that men were better at recognizing female rather than male voices, while women could recognize male voices best. Clearly, this interaction cannot be explained by the voices of one sex possessing physical features which generally lend themselves more readily to retention than those of voices of the other sex. More plausibly, it seems that emotional and semantic factors are involved in voice recognition, as they are in facial recognition.

Memory for music

Relatively little experimental work has been carried out on memory for music. However, amongst the interesting results are those obtained by assessing the recognition of familiar melodies which have been distorted in various ways. The logic behind this procedure is that the effects of distorting a particular component of a melody should indicate its prominence in the melody's representation in long-term memory. The study by White (1960) exemplifies this type of research. White distorted familiar melodies such as 'Yankee Doodle' and 'On Top of Old Smokey' by changing the pitch intervals between successive notes in a number of ways.

Some of these distortions, e.g. decreasing or increasing the interval by a constant number of semitones, preserved the *melodic contour* (the simple pattern of ups and downs). Generally, such distortions reduced recognition from the 94 per cent obtained with undistorted melodies to about 80 per cent. Even when all the intervals were set at one semitone, thus largely eliminating information about pitch but preserving contour, performance was still at the 60 per cent level. But when contour was not preserved as, for example, when the pitch intervals between successive notes were changed randomly, performance fell to about 45 per cent. White showed, then, that changes in both contour and pitch intervals influence recognition of melodies, and so it may be concluded that both are represented in long-term memory (see, too, Dowling and Fujitani, 1971, Experiment 2).

Dowling and Fujitani (1971, Experiment 1) have shown that melodic contour is also important in short-term memory for unfamiliar sequences of tones. On each trial they presented a random 5-note sequence followed almost immediately by a comparison sequence. Subjects reported the comparison as being the same melody as the standard provided the contour was unchanged, even though it had been transposed to another key and the pitch intervals between successive notes changed. According to Dowling (1978), *scale*, in addition to contour, is an important component of short-term memory for melodies. A musical scale is an established set of discrete steps in pitch, typically with 5 or 7 steps in the octave, and constituting a framework of familiar pitches which guides the perception and production of melodies. Dowling illustrates the role of scale in short-term memory using a procedure similar to that of Dowling and Fujitani (1971, Experiment 1) but in this later study, unlike in the earlier one, using standard melodies which were tonal, i.e. the notes were on a scale familiar to the subject. The results showed that *atonal* comparison sequences were less likely than *tonal* ones to be recognized as the standard melody when transposed to another key and the pitch intervals modified but the contours preserved. Thus, scale and contour seem to be interdependent components of memory in that contour is a more effective cue to recognition with tonal than with atonal melodies.

Summary

The general idea that stimuli must be represented in a temporary store while they are 'worked on' by the cognitive system gives rise to the notion of an acoustically based store fairly early in the processing sequence for auditory stimuli. Estimates of echoic persistence are variable. Procedures involving masking of tonal detection and simultaneity judgments have produced estimates of about 100 milliseconds. Recognition of periodicity and recognition-masking paradigms have yielded estimates of about 250 milliseconds while durations of 4 or 5 seconds have been derived from the 'three-eared man' procedure and the sampling of unattended messages. It is possible that some of this variability can be accounted for by differences in task demands but there seems no compelling reason to conclude that all these estimates refer to a single, sensory, auditory memory store.

The general notion of echoic persistence provides credible accounts of both the suffix and modality effects. Precategorical acoustic storage theory insists that acoustic traces with a useful life of no more than about 2 seconds contribute indirectly to performance on the last one or possibly two list items. But, there is at least some evidence that favours the idea that echoic memory persists over quite long periods and so may be utilized directly at the time of recall. However, any explanation of the modality and suffix effects in terms of echoic memory face a number of challenges. Notable are those challenges rising from findings that lip-spoken, and even signed stimuli behave very much like auditory items when employd in the to-be-remembered lists or as distractors.

Finally, memory for voices and melodies illustrate situations in which the long-term representations of auditory stimulation in non-sensory form must be involved.

4   Short-term verbal memory

The work on iconic and echoic memories discussed in the last two chapters draws heavily on the concept of temporary buffer stores which hold information while it is operated on, e.g. categorized into verbal units. Numerous models of *post-categorical* memory have also incorporated the buffer concept by maintaining that, when categorized, items are held in a temporary store while they are coded for more permanent storage. This dichotomous view of post-categorical memory was prevalent during the 1960s and, in one form or another, still exerts an influence. In this chapter the development of certain ideas about short-term verbal memory is examined in some detail. While these particular ideas have demonstrable shortcomings they provide a useful framework for looking at some short-term memory phenomena which are dealt with in the second section of the chapter. Finally, some recent theoretical developments in this area are discussed.

Primary memory

One of the most influential of the two-component models is that proposed by Waugh and Norman (1965) in which they coined the terms *primary memory* and *secondary memory* to refer to the temporary and more permanent components of verbal memory respectively. It was William James (1890) who first used these terms although the dichotomy in memory components to which he referred was somewhat different from that envisaged by Waugh and Norman. James, basing his conclusions on introspection, distinguished between events which are still represented in consciousness and so form part of the psychological present (primary memory) and those which have left consciousness but which may be brought back into it at some later time. It is clear from James's description of primary memory that he considered it to contain images derived from sensory aspects of recent events and not just verbal items. In contrast, Waugh and Norman restricted their attention to verbal items but in what follows we shall see how James's view has, to some extent, been incorporated into recent models of short-term verbal retention.

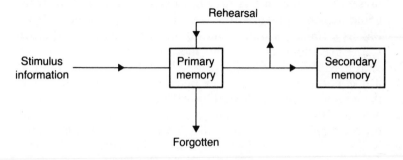

Figure 4.1: *Waugh and Norman's model of short-term memory (adapted from Waugh and Norman, 1965)*

The model developed by Waugh and Norman, which is represented in Figure 4.1, consists of two stores, primary memory (PM) and secondary memory (SM). Stimulus information is entered into the small capacity PM from where it may be copied into SM which is assumed to have virtually unlimited storage capacity. The model was developed in the context of experiments involving verbal items, that is digits, letters and words. Hence, while Waugh and Norman made no *strong* assumptions about the nature of coding in PM they did suggest that stimulus information has been fully categorized into verbal units before entering it. Subsequent work has supported this view by showing that the capacity of PM remains at about 3 words irrespective of the number of syllables they contain (e.g. Craik, 1968a). If PM were precategorical then it would be reasonable to expect that some unit of coding rather more primitive than whole words, such as syllables, would form the basis of coding and hence of capacity.

The model assumes that items held in PM may be displaced by subsequent items entering it unless they are deliberately maintained there by rehearsal. Also, while items are in PM they stand a chance of being copied into SM. Hence, by maintaining particular items in PM by rehearsal the subject is able to control the likelihood that they will be copied into SM. Furthermore, the model insists that the presence of items in SM may be achieved only via PM, there being no other possible route. Thus, SM depends entirely on PM as a source of input. In another sense, however, the two stores are independent. The model assumes that when an item is copied into SM the original 'item' may remain in PM if it is not displaced by other items while, at the same time, the copy may exist in SM. Thus, the probability that an item is in one store at a given moment is quite independent of the probability that it is in the other store: it may be in PM only, in SM only, in both PM and SM, or in neither.

Forgetting in PM: the probe-digit experiment

Waugh and Norman developed their model largely as a result of their interest in the causes of forgetting over short periods. Their account of forgetting is particularly interesting, therefore. They postulated that items are displaced from PM by other items rather than passively decaying, and devised an empirical test of these two possibilities. If trace decay alone is responsible for forgetting, they argued, then varying the number of other items presented between a particular item and the memory test should have no effect on performance provided the retention interval remains constant. On the other hand, if displacement is responsible the number of intervening items should be critical. In order to test this aspect of their model Waugh and Norman (1965) employed what they termed the *probe-digit* procedure. They presented sequences of 16 digits, following the last one by a further digit, the *probe*, this being identified by an accompanying tone. The subjects' task was to recall the digit which had followed the probe in the sequence. For example, the following sequence and probe (8) may have been presented:

$$901436248139052 5 8$$

As in all lists, the probe item occurs only once in the sequence and in this case the correct response is 1. It is easy to see how the number of items between presentation and test can be varied using this procedure. Also, recalling an item is assumed to act as an input to PM, and so as an additional interfering item. Thus, it is an advantage of the procedure that a single, specified position can be probed in each list, so avoiding such *output interference*.

In order to determine the relative effects of delay and number of intervening items on performance Waugh and Norman simply varied the rate at which the sequences were presented (1 item per second or 4 items per second) in addition to the serial position probed. Furthermore, since their intention was to study forgetting in only PM they instructed their subjects not to rehearse the digits but to attend to each one as it was presented. In this way it was hoped to minimize the copying of items into SM (since, according to the model this depends on rehearsal).

The results showed that the rate of presentation had only a small effect on performance compared to the number of intervening items thus indicating that displacement is the major source of forgetting in PM. The relation between performance and number of intervening items, averaged over the two presentation rates, is shown in Figure 4.2.

It can be seen that the most rapid drop in performance takes place with 1 to 5 intervening items, but there is a continued fall with up to 13 items. This may appear to show that displacement from PM is still taking place after as many as 13 intervening items. But, as Waugh and Norman point out, it may be that subjects were not able to carry out instructions to avoid rehearsal completely. Hence, the forgetting curve may have been influenced by the presence of information in SM thus making the curve less steep than

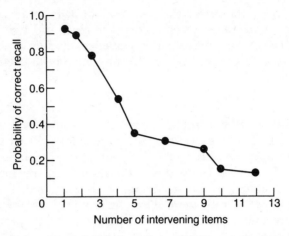

Figure 4.2: *Performance on the probe-digit task (adapted from Waugh and Norman, 1965)*

would otherwise have been the case. Possibly, then, the initial steep drop may be correctly taken to indicate a PM capacity of about 4 or 5 items, this being roughly in line with estimates obtained with other techniques and discussed later in this chapter.

Dissociation between recency and prerecency positions
The results of the probe-digit experiment certainly suggest that displacement from a limited-capacity store is taking place but, on their own, they do not force the conclusion that *separate* stores exist. Possibly the strongest and most extensive evidence favouring the existence of independent PM and SM components of short-term retention comes from studies using the free recall paradigm.

Immediate free recall of word lists produces what should by now be the familiar serial position curve with a marked recency effect (see Figure 4.3.). The Waugh-Norman model accounts for this curve by maintaining that items from later serial positions have a high probability of being in PM when recall begins and hence are very likely to be successfully recalled. Earlier items, however, must largely be retrieved from SM, the chance being that subsequent items have displaced them from PM. The postulate that recency and prerecency portions of the serial position curve are largely dependent on different memory stores is supported by findings that certain variables affect them in different ways. For example, the rate at which words are presented affects performance on prerecency items but not on recency items. By contrast, a period of distraction activity, such as backward counting, imposed between the end of the list and recall, drastically reduces recency but not prerecency performance (Glanzer and Cunitz, 1966). These two effects are illustrated in Figure 4.3. Taken alone, either of these dissociations provides only weak support for the postulate that recency and prerecency effects have separate origins because it is possible to explain either of them by effects taking place in a single store. When taken together, however, the *double* dissociaton is difficult to account for by a single origin. The Waugh-Norman model, of course, accounts for the effect of post-list distraction by displacement of recency items from PM, and the effect of presentation rate is attributed to increased opportunity for rehearsal and hence for copying into SM.

Craik (1970) reported an interesting finding which is consistent with the Waugh-Norman model. He gave subjects a series of trials on each of which a different word list was presented and immediately free recalled. When this series of immediate free recall tests was completed subjects were unexpectedly asked to free recall the words from all the lists they had been tested on. Performance on both initial and final tests, averaged over all lists, is illustrated in Figure 4.4 where it can be seen that final free recall gave rise to what Craik termed *negative recency* even though initial recall produced the usual *positive* recency effect. It is easy to argue that this negative recency is precisely what the Waugh-Norman model predicts in these circumstances because it assumes that items are rehearsed during list presentation so as to copy them into SM. When recall is signalled at the end of the list the contents of PM are output immediately thus giving rise to the recency effect, but rehearsal then ceases because no further test is expected. Since the later items in the list spend least time in PM they will be least likely to

have been copied into SM and so will be recalled least well in the final recall test. This interpretation of negative recency is supported by the results obtained by Rundus (1971) with a technique in which subjects were asked to 'think aloud' while rehearsing the words during presentation. In this way it was possible to record the number of times each list item was rehearsed before recall was signalled. The results showed a pattern of rehearsal similar to the final recall curve obtained by Craik.

A problem for the Waugh-Norman model

If the two-store interpretation of negative recency is accepted then certain findings make it necessary to reconsider at least one feature of the Waugh-Norman model. As we have seen, this model accounts for negative recency in terms of the amount of rehearsal each item receives. But, the assumption that copying by rote rehearsal is the only way to establish SM traces seems wrong intuitively. Furthermore, as we shall see in the next chapter, there is strong, objective evidence that subjects engage in activities involving imagery, organiz- ation and other complex strategies in order to set up long-

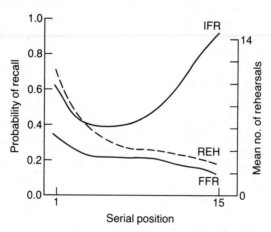

Figure 4.4: *Serial position curves for immediate free recall (IFR) and final free recall (FFR) (adapted from Craik, 1970). The curve labelled REH shows the number of rehearsals of items in each serial position (adapted from Rundus, 1971)*

term traces for lists of unrelated words. Thus, it is possible that negative recency arises from differences in the *quality* of rehearsal rather than the *quantity*. This point was made by Watkins and Watkins (1974) who argued that the use of constant list length by Craik (1970) and Rundus (1971) enabled the end of the list to be anticipated. Thus, it is possible that subjects changed their strategy from one intended to effectively set up traces of early items in SM to merely maintaining the later items in PM ready for immediate output. Watkins and Watkins examined this possibility by employing conditions in which the list length was either known or unknown before presentation started. The results showed that the usual recency effect was obtained with immediate free recall in both the 'known' and 'unknown' conditions. But negative recency did not appear in final free recall when subjects could not anticipate the end of the list. Since the later items have the same *opportunity* for rote rehearsal irrespective of condition, the differences in final free recall indicate differences in the way these items are dealt with. It seems that when the list length is unknown, a deliberate attempt is made to establish all items in SM, but when the list length is known subjects switch to the strategy of merely maintaining later items in PM by rote rehearsal. These results suggest not only that copying into SM can be rapid, given the appropriate strategy, but that rote rehearsal is not an effective means of copying. This latter conclusion is supported by the findings of Craik and Watkins (1973) that the probability of recall from SM is not related to the number of rote rehearsals when this is explicitly controlled by the experimenter. Although there are now a number of studies which show that SM performance is improved by longer periods of rote rehearsal, and especially so with recognition tests rather than recall, it remains that the crucial determinant of transfer to SM is the *type* and not the *quantity* of rehearsal (see Craik, 1983, for discussion of this point). We shall return to this issue in Chapter 5 where the relation between the nature of processing strategies at presentation and long-term remembering are discussed in some detail.

Capacity of PM

How many items can PM hold? There are several basic methods for calculating the capacity of PM, each one making different assumptions and yielding slightly different estimates. The most commonly used methods are described and critically discussed by Watkins (1974), hence the three mentioned here are dealt with only briefly in the context of free recall.

The assumption that PM and SM are independent stores leads to the following equation which was adopted by Waugh and Norman (1965). It gives the probability, R_i, of recalling an item in serial position i as:

$$R_i = PM_i + SM_i - PM_i \times SM_i \qquad (1)$$

where PM_i and SM_i are the probabilities that the item is present in PM and SM respectively. The equation states that the probability of recalling an item is the probability that it is in PM or in SM with a correction being made for the assumption that if it is in both stores it can only be retrieved from one of them. Rearranging the formula gives:

$$PM_i = \frac{R_i - SM_i}{1 - SM_i} \qquad (2)$$

Since R_i is the observed probability of recall the only difficulty in obtaining PM_i is estimating SM_i. A convenient means of doing so is to take the mean probability of recalling items from the central serial positions and assume that this value applies for recency items as well. The capacity of PM is then found by summing the values of PM_i over the recency serial positions. This method usually yields estimates of PM capacity of just less than 3 items.

One criticism of the Waugh-Norman method is its assumption that the value of SM_i is constant for all recency positions. This assumption conflicts with the interpretation placed by the Waugh-Norman model on the negative recency effect which requires that the likelihood of an item being in SM decreases over the final positions. Hence the Waugh-

Norman equation underestimates PM capacity.

Raymond (1969) suggested that rather than taking the estimate of SM_i from the prerecency asymptote of immediate recall, it should be based on delayed recall. Imposing a distractor task, such as backward counting, between the list and recall leaves performance wholly dependent on SM. Thus, a separate estimate of SM_i can be obtained for each serial position giving:

$$PM_i = \frac{I_i - D_i}{1 - D_i} \qquad (3)$$

where I_i and D_i are the probabilities of recalling the item in the ith position with immediate and delayed recall respectively.

This method suffers from having to assume that imposing the delay does not influence the probability of recall from SM. This assumption is generally unfounded since performance over the prerecency positions usually falls with increasing delay thus leading to inflated estimates of PM_i (D_i is smaller than it should be).

Tulving and Colatla (1970) proposed that an item be attributed to PM if no more than a certain number of presentation and recall events involving other items have intervened between its own presentation and recall. Choice of the critical number of intervening events is somewhat arbitrary but when it is set at 7 the PM capacity is found to be about 3.6 items.

Which is the best method to use for estimating PM capacity? Watkins (1974) cleverly argued that the purpose of the procedure is to separate two independent components of recall. That being so the best method must be the one which yields the greatest dissociation between estimates of PM and SM.

By way of illustration consider the effect of presentation rate on free recall (see Figure 4.3). The best method of calculating the PM component should leave PM capacity least affected and the SM component most affected by manipulation of rate. It emerged that the Tulving and Colatla method proved best.

The capacity measure remains fairly constant whether the items are digits, letters or words and it is unaffected when word length is varied from 1 to 4 syllables (Craik, 1968a). Such findings suggest that PM is post-categorical as Waugh and Norman speculated. Indeed, the finding by Glanzer and Razel (1974) that capacity is about 2 when whole proverbs constitute the 'items' suggests that PM is able to hold 'ideas' as well as words, digits and letters. Possibly, however, the redundancy of proverbs enables the retention of a single 'key' word to cue correct recall of the whole proverb.

Atkinson and Shiffrin's model

The Waugh-Norman model is essentially a *structural* model in that the routes of information flow are fixed, and memory stores have certain rigid characteristics such as capacity, coding and the course of forgetting. However, the model is not entirely structural in that rehearsal, and hence the copying of items into SM, is under conscious control. Unfortunately Waugh and Norman did not make clear if PM is merely a storage space or if the process controlling rehearsal is included in it also. This omission no doubt arose because the point is not crucial to the interpretation of those short-term retention phenomena the model was intended to explain. However, if the structures and processes underlying short-term retention are to be understood fully the relation between storage space and control processes must be considered. Atkinson and Shiffrin (1968, 1971) dealt with this issue explicitly.

The main features of Atkinson and Shiffrin's model are shown in Figure 4.5 which is adapted from their 1971 paper. The model maintains that stimulus information is first held briefly in sensory registers such as the echoic and iconic stores discussed in Chapters 2 and 3. This information is then passed on to the short-term store (STS) which holds categorized verbal codes in what is referred to as the *auditory-verbal-linguistic* (AVL) component of short-term storage. From STS the information may be passed on by rehearsal, or some other coding process, such as imagery, to the long-term store (LTS) which, largely for theoretical convenience, is assumed to retain everything entered into it more or less permanently.

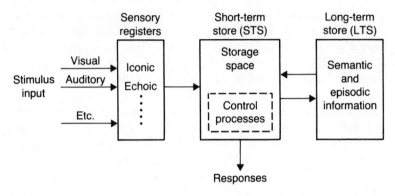

Figure 4.5:   *Atkinson and Shiffrin's model of short-term memory (adapted from Atkinson and Shiffrin, 1971)*

In *broad* terms the Atkinson and Shiffrin model is not unlike that proposed by Waugh and Norman with its STS and LTS corresponding to PM and SM. However, the models differ in a number of important ways. For example, STS is more than a temporary storage space for items on their way to LTS. It contains both storage space and the control processes which direct the flow of information within the memory system as a whole. These control processes allow a good deal of flexibility within the structure indicated in Figure 4.5, and include decision-making about what should be entered into STS from the sensory registers, which items should be coded for storage in LTS, how this should be done and how best to retrieve required information from LTS. Items may be copied, or in Atkinson and Shiffrin's terms, coded into LTS by circulation in the *rehearsal buffer* which corresponds closely to Waugh and Norman's PM, but which constitutes only part of STS. Other ways of coding items for retention in LTS include the use of imagery and other strategies which will be discussed in Chapter 5.

Importantly, it is assumed that the capacity of STS has to be shared amongst these processes so that high demands by one lead to a reduction in the capacity available to others. For example, it is possible to maintain a maximum of 5 or 6 items in STS by rehearsal because demands made by mere rehearsal are small. However, copying these items into LTS by this means is rather slow and the subject might decide to use another, faster, process such as imagery. This process is considered so demanding that only the item being coded in that way can be maintained in STS: there is insufficient capacity to do that and rehearse other items at the same time. By allowing imagery to be utilized in STS, Atkinson and Shiffrin acknowledge the possibility of non-verbal components existing alongside the AVL component. Presumably such components would account for findings such as those obtained by Posner *et al.* (1969) with the letter-matching task and which seem to depend on short-term visual codes (see Chapter 2). Thus, STS is seen as a *working buffer* in which information is controlled and utilized, and as such, it is crucial for input to and output from LTS.

There are several aspects of Atkinson and Shiffrin's model which deserve comment at this point. The model shares a problem with the Waugh-Norman model by insisting that storage in LTS can be achieved by rote rehearsal. As we have seen, this may not be a valid assumption (Craik and Watkins, 1973), but this problem is alleviated by the provision of alternative means of coding for long-term retention. Another point worth mentioning concerns the 'recognition' process whereby stimulus information is categorized into verbal units. The mechanism proposed by Atkinson and Shiffrin arises from their assumption that both episodic and semantic information is stored in LTS. Information from the sensory registers is fed into STS and used to search LTS for the appropriate name and meaning which, in turn, are entered into STS. This may seem a rather roundabout means of categorizing items especially as the coded information is then put back into LTS for long-term retention. But, in broad terms, the arrangement is not much different from placing the logogens prior to STS as is done in Crowder and Morton's model (Figure 3.4). However, as we shall see in Chapter 6, there are important theoretical consequences arising from the assumption that episodic and semantic memories are contained in the same store.

Two-component interpretation of short-term retention

The most important feature of the Waugh and Norman model is the independence of PM and SM. This feature, which is incorporated into Atkinson and Shiffrin's model and shared with a number of other models (see Murdock, 1971), makes it possible for short-term retention to be based on two sources of information each with different characteristics. This in turn, facilitates the understanding of a number of phenomena which are difficult to account for on the basis of a single memory process. The dissociation between recency and prerecency serial positions in free recall is one of these phenomena, as already noted. In what follows, the ways in which the two-component view has helped in understanding other short-term retention phenomena are discussed. The short-term component will be referred to as STS rather than PM, and the long-term component as LTS rather than SM, unless there are good reasons for doing otherwise.

Short-term forgetting

Brown (1958), closely followed by Peterson and Peterson (1959), studied the retention of small numbers of verbal items over intervals up to about 30 seconds. Basically, their procedures consisted of presenting a small set of to-be-remembered items, say 3 consonants, and filling the retention interval with some rehearsal-preventing task such as backward counting. Typical results for this Brown-Peterson paradigm, in which each subject performs a number of trials at each retention interval, are shown in Figure 4.6.

The results obtained by Brown and the Petersons were surprising at the time they were reported because they conflict with *interference theory* which was the currently prominent explanation of forgetting. In essence, the theory conceived of verbal learning as the formation of associations between items with forgetting being the result of competition between new and old associations. The Brown-Peterson results are difficult to explain because, according to this theory, there is no reason why the digits in the distractor task should interfere so effectively with the to-be-remembered

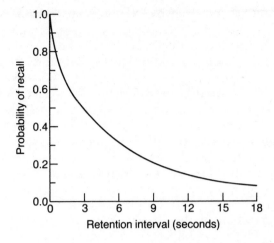

Figure 4.6: *Typical results obtained with the Brown-Peterson technique*

items which were in a different verbal class. Consequently, the rapid forgetting was interpreted as arising from decay of memory traces taking place over time and quite independently of the nature of the distractor material. It follows from this conclusion that if interference provides an adequate account of forgetting in long-term retention then separate memory systems underlie long-term and short-term retention, one system being susceptible to decay, the other to interference.

Arguments against the division of verbal memory into two separate systems soon appeared, amongst them being that of Keppel and Underwood (1962). They showed that if only the first trial of the Brown-Peterson paradigm is considered performance is nearly perfect irrespective of retention interval. On the second and third trials, however, the forgetting curve became progressively similar to that shown in Figure 4.6 which arises when performance is averaged over a large number of trials. Thus, Keppel and Underwood were able to claim that the forgetting observed by Brown and the Petersons was due to interference arising from prior lists (proactive interference) and not from decay. This argument was one of several used by Melton (1963) in his influential paper in which he advocated a unitary verbal memory system: if interference occurs in both short- and long-term retention then separate *systems* corresponding to the *paradigms* are not required. It was at this point that Waugh and Norman introduced their distinction between primary and secondary memory. As we have already noted, their model assumes that secondary memory may be involved in both long- and short-term retention situations. Thus, it is possible to subscribe to a two-store view of verbal memory *and* accept that interference can occur at both long- and short-retention intervals simply by maintaining that interference is a secondary memory, or LTS phenomenon.

Interpretation of the Brown-Peterson forgetting function in terms of STS and LTS seems straightforward, superficially at least. Since the distractor task prevents rehearsal, performance must depend on those items copied into LTS during presentation. This interpretation is not necessarily entirely correct, however, because there is evidence that subjects can, and do, surreptitiously rehearse while performing the distractor task, and that this affects the shape of the forgetting function. Such evidence comes from the study by Posner and Rossman (1965). They varied the difficulty of the distractor task by having subjects either read out digit pairs at 1 pair per second (easy task) or add the digits and classify the number as odd or even (difficult task). More forgetting occurred when the task was difficult than when it was easy, this being consistent with the idea that the additional rehearsal with the easy task facilitated the copying of items into SM. Clearly, this effect of task difficulty is quite contrary to any account of short-term forgetting based solely on time-dependent decay. More direct evidence that rehearsal during the period of distraction affects the forgetting function comes from Reitman (1974). She had subjects perform a tone detection task either as distraction in the Brown-Peterson paradigm, or when no memory load was imposed on them. Some subjects showed a marked drop in tone detection when the memory load was imposed relative to the control condition, others did not. This suggests that some of them were diverting attention away from the distractor task and engaging in rehearsal. Importantly, the presumed rehearsers showed less rapid forgetting than did the presumed non-rehearsers.

If subjects can rehearse during the period of distraction why should performance not reflect merely the likelihood that items are maintained in STS, rather than the contents of LTS? There are several reasons for favouring the LTS interpretation. First, Dillon and Reid (1969) found that forgetting was less if the first half of the distractor period contained an easy task and the second half a difficult task, than if the order was difficult-easy. Thus, it is possible that an initial easy task permits items to be copied into LTS before rehearsal is prevented. With an initial difficult task rehearsal is prevented immediately and copying into LTS is thwarted. If performance on the memory task reflected only the contents of STS then performance would be poor no matter which period the difficult distraction occurred in. A second reason for believing that performance is based on LTS is the finding that it depends on the number of repetitions given to the items before the distractor task begins (Hellyer, 1962). And finally, the LTS interpretation fits with the dependence of proactive interference on semantic factors, the subject of the next section.

Release from PI
It is now well established that performance in the Brown-Peterson paradigm falls progressively over successive trials if similar to-be-remembered items are used on all trials. But if, after several trials, the items are changed from one verbal class to another (e.g. from consonant trigrams to digits, or from letters to words) performance increases dramatically. Figure 4.7 depicts typical results of such a manipulation. Both the control and experimental groups are treated identically up to trial 4 when the experimental subjects are switched to a new class of item. The resulting increase in performance has been termed *release from PI* on the assumption that any fall in performance over early trials is attributable to a build-up of proactive interference, as Keppel and Underwood suggested. This phenomenon has been extensively investigated by Wickens (see, e.g., Wickens,

1972). 'Release' has been shown to occur with changes from one verbal class to another, such as from consonant trigrams to digit triplets, or from one semantic category to another (e.g. from items of furniture to types of food). Smaller release occurs when the change is from one *connative* class of word to another, such as from 'good' words (e.g. *mother, wise, able*) to 'bad' words (e.g. *kill, fire, hate*), or vice versa. In contrast, shifts in grammatical class, such as from verbs to nouns, produce little release if any.

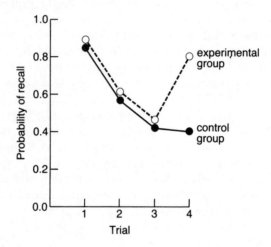

Figure 4.7: *Idealized pattern of results obtained with the release from proactive interference paradigm*

Wickens (1972) adopted the view that if a shift in material along a certain stimulus attribute leads to release from PI then that attribute must be contained in the memory representation on which performance is based. Consequently, he pointed out, the release from PI phenomenon offers a means of exploring just how items are coded in memory. However, it is possible that release from PI can be accounted for in a somewhat uninteresting way.

It is conceivable that the fall in performance over trials is due to boredom or fatigue and that the change in stimulus class arouses the subjects' interest. In this way, there is nothing theoretically striking about release from PI since it could reflect merely better learning as a result of greater attention. However, such an explanation is difficult to maintain in the light of findings by Watkins and Watkins (1975). They argued that if the release from PI arises from better storage of items in LTS then these items should be better recalled than items from the prior lists on a final recall test in which items from *all* lists are required. Thus, their logic is similar to that used by Craik (1970) with respect to negative recency (see page 97). In essence, Watkins and Watkins found that items from 'release' trials were recalled no better than items from prior trials thus showing that better storage in LTS is not responsible for release. It seems, then, that initial performance suffers because items which are in memory are not retrieved. This view is strongly indicated by the results of a study by Gardiner, Craik and Birtwistle (1972).

Gardiner *et al.* tested subjects on four trials of the Brown-Peterson paradigm and employed a shift in semantic category on the fourth trial which was so subtle that it was unnoticed by subjects unless pointed out to them. This involved either a shift from garden flowers to wild flowers, or from indoor games to outdoor games. The control subjects were given four trials and nothing was said about the category change. These subjects showed no release from PI showing that the change was indeed unnoticed. There were two experimental groups. One of these was told of the category change *before* the fourth list was *presented*. The other group, in contrast, was not told about the change until just before they were about to *recall* the fourth set of items. Importantly, *both* the experimental groups showed the release effect. These results show clearly that the progressive fall over trials in the Brown-Peterson paradigm arises because of effects on the retrieval of items rather than on storage. If the way in which items are *stored* is affected then release should not have occurred for the informed-at-retrieval group because they were treated identically to the control subjects at the time of presentation.

Studies of release from PI serve to emphasize two points which are relevant here. First, they demonstrate the involvement of semantic factors in short-term retention and so support the presence of an LTS component in such situations. Second, they show the importance of *retrieval* in such situations.

Memory span
Basically, the span of immediate memory is defined as the longest sequence of items the subject can recall in their correct order. It has traditionally been employed in standard tests of cognitive ability and its inclusion is justified by its positive correlation with IQ scores.

It has long been known that memory span is fairly constant across different materials. For example, the average is about 7 unrelated items whether these are digits, letters or words. This was acknowledged by Miller (1956) in his classic treatment of the topic, in which he argued that the apparent invariance of span reflects the principle that the unit of short-term retention is what he called the *chunk*. Chunks may be formed by coding several stimulus items into a single conceptual unit. Thus, a sequence of 4 letters may represent 4 chunks (e.g. NPTI) or 1 chunk (e.g. PINT) depending on whether they can be coded as a word or not. According to Miller, then, memory spans average about 7 *chunks*. He quotes binary to octal recoding as another example of chunking. If the task involves remembering a long sequence of *ones* and *zeroes*, as can happen when setting switches on a computer, it is possible to reduce the sequence to be retained by using the following technique: represent 000 by 0; 001 by 1; 010 by 2; 011 by 3; 100 by 4; 101 by 5; 110 by 6; 111 by 7. It is now possible to convert the to-be-remembered sequence, e.g. 001011110111101011 to 136753, thus reducing the number of *chunks* to be retained from 18 to 6. At recall the 6 chunks are simply converted back to the binary digits.

There is, of course, a danger of circularity in the definition of a chunk. Unless there is some unambiguous means of establishing the coding employed by the subject it is possible to 'establish' that 7 chunks are recalled merely by dividing the recall protocol into 7 portions. However, when there is good reason for choosing a particular definition, such as unrelated words rather than individual letters, Miller's 'magical number seven, plus or minus two' seems to adequately describe the average memory span (see also, Simon, 1974, for further discussion).

What are the processes underlying memory span performance? Are both STS and LTS involved? The involvement of the STS rehearsal loop is indicated by findings that span for words is negatively related to the number of syllables in them: the longer the words the smaller the span (Baddeley, Thomson and Buchanan, 1975). While this finding is *consistent with* the dependence of span on difficulty of rehearsal it does not constitute direct evidence. Baddeley *et al.* obtained more direct evidence by showing that the effect of word length is eliminated when rehearsal is suppressed by a simultaneous articulation task. They then showed that it is not word length *per se* that is important for span but the time taken to articulate the words, as would be expected if subvocal rehearsing were involved.

According to the two-component models of short-term retention, span is too large to reflect only the output from STS, so LTS must contribute to it, also. There is some evidence for this view. Craik (1970) obtained measures of the STS and LTS components of free recall from individual subjects together with their memory spans. He found that the correlation between span and the LTS component was higher than between span and the STS component and took this to indicate that span was more dependent on LTS than on STS. Likewise Watkins (1977) argued that both STS and LTS contributed to span, but on the basis of the effect of word frequency of usage. He divided the word sequences used in the experiment into two portions each containing either common, high frequency (H) words or uncommon, low frequency (L) words. In this way memory span was determined for four types of sequence, HH (high frequency words in both portions), LL, LH and HL. The corresponding spans were 5.82, 4.24, 4.65 and 5.19. It can be seen that span is most affected by differences in frequency occurring in the first half of the sequences (HL vs LL, and LH vs HH). Watkins interpreted these results by drawing on Raymond's (1969) conclusion that word frequency affects the LTS but not the STS component of recall. In this way he was able to conclude that the early list items were recalled from LTS whilst the later items were maintained in, and recalled from, STS. Thus memory span for words, at least, seems to depend on both STS and LTS.

Phonological errors in short-term retention

The results of Baddeley *et al.* (1975) on memory span demonstrated the involvement of speech-based processes in short-term retention, this being in line with the Waugh-Norman and Atkinson-Shiffrin models which maintain that items are held in STS by rehearsal. But it should be realized that this work followed on from a large body of research concerned with the type of codes employed in short-term memory and which dealt specifically with the patterns of errors made by subjects. Conrad (1964) noticed that when subjects recalled sequences of letters their errors usually involved the substitution of similar-sounding letters, rather than those of similar visual shape, even though the stimuli were presented *visually*. For example, if the sequence KHBTRC was presented for serial recall and the fourth letter, T, was incorrectly recalled, it was more likely to be replaced by the phonologically similar P than the phonologically dissimilar F. Thus it seems that the short sequences of letters were stored in some phonological, i.e. speech-based, code as could be expected if they were maintained in STS by rehearsal. In order to firmly establish the nature of the confusions he observed Conrad determined the pattern of errors subjects made when they attempted to identify auditory letters presented in a background of white noise. As would be expected, the pattern of errors involved letters which sounded alike, that is, the confusions were *acoustic* in nature. For example, a subject might have been told that the letters to be identified, one by one, would come from the set BCPTVFMNSX. On those occasions when V was misidentified, B was most frequently given as the response, C was the next most frequent error, and X least frequent of all. When Conrad compared the pattern of errors made in the listening task with that from the memory test there was a significant degree of similarity between them. Hence, he was able to conclude that verbal stimuli presented visually are stored, over short intervals at least, in an acoustic code.

Conrad's investigation involved tests of short-term retention but he was not concerned with distinguishing between the STS and LTS components of performance. Strictly, therefore, it is not clear from his results whether acoustic confusions are appropriately viewed as originating in STS rather than LTS. If the coding employed by STS is to be determined then some way of separating out the two components must be found, and Kintsch and Buschke (1969) decided that Waugh and Norman's probe technique offered a way of doing so. In one experiment they presented lists of 16 words, each list being followed by a probe word. The subjects were required to supply the word following the probe. In one condition all the words in each list were unrelated, while in the other condition 8 pairs of synonyms were distributed through the list so that the members of each pair did not occur in adjacent serial positions. The results showed that the presence of synonyms increased the difficulty of the task over the early but not the later positions. Application of the Waugh and Norman formula confirmed that the LTS component was affected but not the STS component. In their second experiment Kintsch and Buschke employed lists containing pairs of homonyms (e.g. knight-night) and once again performance was depressed by the presence of similar items. This time, however, it was the STS component which suffered and not the LTS component. Taken together the results of the two experiments indicate that STS employs mainly acoustic coding while LTS employs mainly semantic coding.

Acoustic or articulatory coding?
The term *acoustic confusions* was used by Conrad to describe the errors occurring in his tests of immediate recall, because of the close similarity between them and the errors made in hearing tests. However, if visual stimuli are recoded into the speech-based codes used in rehearsal it might be expected that errors should reflect the similarities in the way items are *produced* rather than the way they sound. In other words, the errors should be *articulatory* rather than *acoustic*. Taking up this point, Hintzman (1967) noted that the patterns of errors

in auditory perception are not the same as the patterns of articulatory similarity amongst letters. Hence, he argued, it should be possible to decide between the two types of coding by looking for articulatory confusions in memory.

Hintzman employed the 6 stop consonants shown in Table 4.1 for his research. The stop consonants /b/, /d/, and /g/ (as in bav, daf, and gaf) are all *voiced* in that the vocal chords vibrate when they are spoken. The consonants /p/, /t/, and /k/ (as in pav, taf, and kaf) are *unvoiced*, that is, the vocal chords do not vibrate when they are spoken. The 6 consonants also differ with respect to whether air pressure is released at the front, middle, or back of the mouth. Hintzman noted that earlier work had shown that voiced and unvoiced consonants are rarely confused in tests of auditory identification even when they share the same place of articulation (e.g. /p/ is rarely confused with /b/). Also, /b/ is no more likely to be confused with /d/ rather than /g/ although /d/ is more similar in terms of place of articulation. Thus, place of articulation has little or no influence on auditory perception and so, if STS codes are articulatory rather than acoustic, errors involving place of articulation should appear in immediate recall. Hintzman's results for serial recall of nonsense syllables incorporating the stop consonants (e.g. pav, taf, gaf) showed that /p/ was more likely to be replaced by /t/ than by /k/, and /d/ was more frequently substituted for /b/ than was /g/. Hence, it may be concluded that articulatory coding was being employed.

Some doubts about the STS-LTS distinction

Some of the available evidence showing both phonological and semantic coding in short-term *retention* has now been

Table 4.1

| | Place of articulation | | |
	Front	Middle	Back
Unvoiced	/p/	/t/	/k/
Voiced	/b/	/d/	/g/

discussed in this chapter. Phonological coding was demonstrated by Conrad and by Hintzman, while semantic coding is indicated by PI and release from PI together with 'chunking'. Baddeley (e.g. 1972) has argued, and we have already noted, that the existence of both types of coding in short-term retention may be accounted for by attributing phonological coding to STS and semantic coding to LTS. But this straightforward account is challenged by evidence of phonological coding in long-term retention. This is illustrated by the study of Gruneberg and Sykes (1969) in which subjects were presented with a list of to-be-remembered words and about 20 minutes later given a recognition test. More false recognitions occurred with distractors which were acoustically similar to target items than to those which were not. Clearly, these confusions cannot be attributed to STS and it must be concluded that LTS can utilize acoustic codes. Hence the distinction between STS and LTS is not synonymous with that between phonological and semantic coding.

It is worth emphasizing that there is no conflict between a conclusion that the confusions made by the subjects in Gruneberg and Sykes's experiment were *acoustic* and Hintzman's conclusion that errors in short-term serial recall are *articulatory*. There is no reason why acoustic features of items should not be preserved in long-term recall while articulatory coding can only be preserved so long as articulatory rehearsal is possible. Possibly, though, it it best to use the more neutral term *phonological* where it is not necessary to distinguish between the two types of code.

Shulman (1971) proposed that just as phonological codes may exist in LTS so semantic codes may be utilized by STS, and the distinction between STS and LTS is superfluous. Shulman argued that semantic codes take longer to set up than do phonological codes and evidence of semantic coding is not usually found in tests of immediate memory because they can be completed using the more convenient phonological codes. Shulman (1970) tested his ideas by using an immediate memory task for which semantic coding was essential. Subjects received lists of 10 words followed by a probe and, depending on the condition, they were required to indicate whether or not the list contained a word which was identical to, or a synonym of, the probe. When the proportion of correct responses was plotted against serial position there was a strong recency effect for both conditions. Hence Shulman was able to argue that if the recency effect is attributed to STS, as two-component models insist, then this must utilize semantic coding and the STS-LTS distinction is not necessary.

Baddeley (1972), amongst others, has challenged Shulman's conclusion. He pointed out that it is not necessary for the semantic information utilized to complete Shulman's task to be present in STS. It is possible, for example, that when the probe is presented it is immediately translated into the phonological representation of a synonym and this is used to probe STS. In this way the decision could be made entirely on the basis of phonological codes. Levy and Craik (1975) also concluded that where semantic coding is evidenced in short-term retention it seems best to attribute it to LTS. Nevertheless Shulman's arguments should alert us to the possible complexity of STS. Indeed, as we shall now see, the concept has been elaborated to the point where it is not difficult to see that semantic information could be held somewhere within the system.

Further developments: working memory

It has been emphasized throughout much of this chapter that Atkinson and Shiffrin conceived of STS as a limited-capacity system which functions both as a temporary store and an executive system which controls processes such as rehearsal. While this conceptualizaton of STS is more flexible and detailed than Waugh and Norman's primary memory it, too, is concerned principally with the temporary storage of verbal items while they are coded in LTS. Subsequent views on STS have accepted that it is more complex even than Atkinson and Shiffrin proposed (see, e.g., Shiffrin, 1976), but perhaps the most important developments of the concept have arisen from the idea that it has a role to play not only in remembering lists of verbal items but in cognitive tasks generally. Views along these lines have long been held by a number of people including Broadbent (1971) and Lindsay and Norman (1972), but there was not much evidence to back up this notion until Baddeley and Hitch (1974) initiated what has become a long and productive research effort into the nature and function of what they call *working memory*.

Basic findings and ideas
Part of the research by Baddeley and Hitch draws on the idea that if STS acts as a general purpose working memory then a cognitive task performed simultaneously with a short-term memory task must compete for the same limited working capacity. In one set of experiments (Baddeley and Hitch, 1974) they required subjects to perform a verbal reasoning task while remembering from 1 to 6 digits. The reasoning task involved presenting a statement concerning two following letters, e.g. *A is preceded by B – BA*, with subjects indicating whether the statement was true or not. False sentences, such as *A is preceded by B – AB*, and more complex ones such as *A is not preceded by B – BA*, were also included. Times to respond *true* or *false* and accuracy were recorded. On each trial the set of digits was presented first, then the reasoning task was performed, and finally the digits were recalled. Thus, the demands put on working memory were varied by the number of digits in the memory set. The results showed that even when subjects were instructed to give priority to remembering the digits correctly neither speed nor accuracy of verbal reasoning was impaired by a memory load of 1 or 2 items. With 6 digits, however, there was a marked decrement in reasoning performance.

Baddeley and Hitch accounted for their results by maintaining that working memory has a limited capacity which is shared between the executive processor which plays a part in most 'non-routine' cognitive activity and the articulatory loop which acts as a temporary store for verbal items. The articulatory loop is considered to be essentially a 'slave' system controlled by the executive and which was devoted to holding the digits involved in the memory task. Importantly, if the number of items being rehearsed is small, or the subject is required to repeat a redundant sequence such as *1, 2, 3*, then rehearsal makes little demand on the executive. But, when the number of items in the memory set exceeds the size of the rehearsal loop some of the executive's capacity must be used to make rehearsal more efficient or to draw on long-term storage. By showing that a memory load of 6 digits gives rise to a decrement in the verbal reasoning task Baddeley and Hitch were able to conclude that the same, albeit complex, system – working memory – is involved in both tasks.

The need to include the articulatory loop in any comprehensive model of short-term memory has been shown by phenomena discussed in the previous section, namely, the presence of articulatory confusions in short-term recall of visually presented items, and the effects of word length on memory span. While a role of the articulatory loop in short-term retention has been established, it is pertinent to ask if it, like the central executive, has a function in other cognitive activities. Several studies have been reported dealing with its role in mental arithmetic (e.g. Hitch, 1978) and many more with its role in reading. This latter role is now discussed briefly. (For a more detailed treatment of reading the reader is referred to the volume by Harris and Coltheart (1986) in this series.)

The idea that inner speech is involved in reading has a long history. One method which has been used to establish whether or not this is so is to make electrical recordings around the larynx and so detect muscular activity while the subject is reading. Hardyck and Petrinovitch (1970) used this procedure and concluded that articulatory activity is not necessary for reading and comprehension of simple prose but it is used when the passages are difficult.

Another, well-established technique for studying the role of inner speech is that of articulatory suppression. Here the subject is required to articulate some irrelevant item or set of items such as 'hiya' or '1, 2, 3, 4' repeatedly while reading. Several sets of experimental results show that articulatory suppression reduces what the subject remembers about the exact wording of the sentences but not their meaning (e.g. Levy, 1978, 1981). Of course, where the information uptake in reading is assessed by what can be remembered there is the possibility that articulation suppresses not the reading process but the transfer of information to memory. Accordingly, Baddeley, Eldridge and Lewis (1981) investigated the effect of suppression more directly. They required subjects to read passages of prose and to detect sentences which contained an anomalous word or a reversal of two words creating an anomalous sentence. Articulatory suppression did not affect the time taken to read the passages but it did affect the detection of anomalies.

It seems, then, that the articulatory loop fulfils only a subordinate and peripheral role in normal reading. It is not directly involved in the comprehension of written material but may be called upon as a supplementary store when the passage is difficult enough to over-tax the central executive or when the surface details of the materials are important as in the detection of order errors and when verbatim recall is anticipated. It is encouraging for proponents of the working memory model that it is possible to fit into this general pattern of conclusions the role of the articulatory loop in learning to read (Baddeley, 1979) and in dyslexia (Jorm, 1983).

Other components of working memory

The other components of working memory which have so far been firmly identified are the *visuo-spatial scratch pad* and the *phonological store*. The visuo-spatial scratch pad supports the use of imagery and, like the articulatory loop, is considered to be a slave of the central processor. Because imagery was extensively discussed in Chapter 2 this component will be mentioned here merely to note that while it has not received as much attention as the articulatory loop some progress has been made in exploring its characteristics within the working memory framework (e.g. Baddeley and Lieberman, 1980).

The reasons for including a phonological store in the model, in addition to the articulatory loop, are rooted in the adverse effects of high phonological similarity and increasing word length on recall. It is now well established that both these effects are removed by articulatory suppression when the items are presented visually but not when they are presented auditorily. The explanation of this situation favoured by Baddeley is that auditory items are fed straight into a speech-based store with which they are highly compatible. With visual presentation, though, access to this store is gained only via the articulatory loop. Additional support for this view comes from a series of experiments reported by Salamé and Baddeley (1982) in which irrelevant speech was presented while the subject saw the lists of to-be-remembered digits. The presence of the irrelevant speech disrupted memory for the visual digits but the difference between this condition and the control (no irrelevant speech) condition disappeared when articulatory suppression was introduced. Thus far the evidence points to the articulatory loop as the locus of the interfering effects of the speech. But the further finding that long words produced no greater disrupting effect than short words, as they should if they entered the articulatory loop, was taken by Salamé and Baddeley as arguing against the loop as the locus of the effect. Instead, some other store is implicated. Finally, the phonological nature of this store was indicated by the sensitivity of the interference produced by unattended speech to phonological similarity between the to-be-remembered digits and the speech no matter whether the speech was composed of words or non-words.

The recency effect reconsidered

It was noted earlier that the two-component view of short-term verbal memory derives some of its strongest support from the dissociation between recency and prerecency portions of the serial position curve in free recall. The effects of distraction interpolated between the list and recall (Glanzer and Cunitz, 1966) and the negative recency phenomenon (Craik, 1970) exemplify this dissociation and so support the idea that the recency effect arises from the direct retrieval of items from STS. However, several sets of findings cast doubt on this aspect of two-component models, and the working memory model acknowledges these findings by accepting an alternative explanation of recency.

Some of the findings which argue strongly against the STS account of recency were reported by Bjork and Whitten

(1974) and by Tzeng (1973). These studies employed a rather bizarre technique which was intended to equate the amount of rehearsal given to each list item. Each to-be-remembered word (or pair of words), including the last word in the list, was preceded and followed by a period of distractor activity such as rapidly counting backward by threes. Typically, these periods were about 12 seconds, but the final period (immediately prior to recall) was as long as 30 seconds. Under these circumstances, especially in view of the usual effects of a period of post-list distraction, the two-component models predict that no recency effect will be found. It is surprising, therefore, that both studies showed that the recency effect, which is abolished when distractor activity occurs after the last item, is reinstated by the addition of distraction between items.

Is there any way in which two-component models can accommodate the appearance of recency with through-list distraction? One possible way would be to insist that the distraction task does not entirely prevent rehearsal and subjects are thus able to maintain the last few items in the short-term store. This explanation seems implausible because recency appears under conditions which are similar to those used by Bjork and Whitten except that learning is incidental, i.e. subjects are required to attend to the list items but do not expect a memory test (Baddeley and Hitch, 1974). Under these circumstances subjects have no reason to maintain items in STS. Other evidence against an account of recency in terms of surreptitious rehearsal has been obtained by Glenberg, Bradley, Stevenson, Kraus, Tkachuk, Gretz, Fish and Turpin (1980). They showed that varying the difficulty of the arithmetic task which comprised the through-list distraction influenced recall over the prerecency region but did not affect recency. This strongly suggests that while the prerecency performance may be influenced by the ability to rehearse or use other strategies, recency arises from some other origin which by all accounts cannot be STS.

If recency in immediate free recall is not attributed to STS then the explanation of Craik's *negative recency* phenomenon in those terms must be reassessed. Several plausible explanations, which do not rely on the two-component view of short-term retention, are available. For example, it is known that when an item is presented twice in a list recall increases as the interval between presentations increases (see, e.g., Melton, 1970). If it is assumed that recalling an item acts as a second presentation then items in later serial positions, which tend to be recalled early, will have their effective presentations closer together than items presented early and recalled late. Accordingly, negative recency could reflect the influence of these two events on memory traces in a single store.

The recency effect is not restricted to recall in a laboratory context. It appears, also, when subjects are asked to recall the names of American presidents (see Crowder, 1976, page 459), and when rugby players are asked to recall teams they played against in the current season (Baddeley and Hitch, 1977). Thus, recency seems to be a general phenomenon and so would seem to require a general explanation which, of course, output from STS cannot provide. At this point it is worth noting that proponents of two-component models may object that recency in immediate free recall is due to output from STS, whereas recency in other situations is due to some other origin. Certainly, it must be accepted that recency can be influenced by instructed attempts to maintain the last few list items in STS by rehearsal (see Shallice, 1975). However, this is not a usual strategy as evidenced by findings that the recency effect in recall is not affected when rehearsal is suppressed by some other vocal activity (Richardson and Baddeley, 1975), and shows no evidence of phonological coding (Glanzer, Koppenaal and Nelson, 1972).

Faced with their unexpected finding of recency Bjork and Whitten (1974) argued that their results are consistent with a theory of recency in which retrieval of items from memory depends on the discriminability of temporally ordered traces. Basically, they suggest, the ability to discriminate the trace of one item from that of another depends on the temporal interval between successive list items (t_1) and the time that elapses from presentation to recall (t_2). Retrieval depends on the ratio of t_1 to t_2 such that as t_1 is made smaller or t_2 made larger so retrieval becomes more difficult and recency is reduced. It is possible to draw an analogy with a spatial arrangement. Distinguishing between equally spaced lamp posts when looking along a straight road depends on both the distance between them and how far away the observer is from them: it is easy to distinguish between those nearby, but not those far away. By analogy, Bjork and Whitten's account of recency maintains that subjects 'scan' back through the recent past and attempt to discriminate one trace from another. In immediate free recall, of course, t_1 is usually comparable to the value of t_2 for recent items and recency is obtained. With a 2-second presentation rate and 30-second post-list delay (a typical delayed recall arrangement), t_1 is small relative to values of t_2 and little recency, if any, is obtained. When distraction is added between items, however, t_1 is increased relative to t_2 and recency again appears.

It is not difficult to appreciate that temporal discriminability between traces at the time of recall can account for recency when rugby games are recalled because these games are part of the players' past experience. But it is more difficult to see how such a principle deals with recency in the recall of American presidents since this information is not based entirely on subjects' direct personal experiences and so need not be temporally ordered.

Returning to Baddeley and Hitch's conceptualization of working memory, they accept that the articulatory rehearsal loop is not responsible for recency in free recall. But, they insist that it is responsible for phonological confusions in short-term retention and plays an important part in tasks such as memory span.

Summary

This discussion of short-term verbal retention has traced one line of theoretical development. This started with the Waugh-Norman model which has its origin in the controversy over the unity or otherwise of the verbal memory system. Atkinson and Shiffrin developed the two-component approach by making explicit the allocation of STS capacity to storage space and the central executive and by emphasizing the distinction between structure and process in their model. These two-store models, and others like them, have distinct advantages over unitary models in understanding a number of short-term memory phenomena. However, it is likely that they in turn do not do justice to the complexity of the system underlying short-term memory performance. Baddeley and Hitch set about elaborating the original two-store models into the working memory model. They challenged the view that phonological coding is an essential route into LTS and have attempted to identify components of working memory and determine their characteristics and the relationships among them. Also, they have extended the involvement of the short-term memory system to cognitive activities generally. The primary memory of Waugh and Norman has survived as the articulatory loop in these developments but recent views, represented by the working memory model, seem to have incorporated James's original notion of primary memory as holding the contents of consciousness, whatever form they may take. Nevertheless, it seems clear that if the working memory model is to go further than merely recognizing the presence of several rather than merely two components of short-term retention, there must be more attention directed towards the nature of the central executive. At present, almost nothing has been proposed about what properties this component might have.

5 Encoding in long-term storage

The term *encoding* is used here to refer to the establishing of episodic information in memory. We saw in Chapter 4 that merely maintaining items in the articulatory rehearsal loop does not lead to effective encoding in long-term storage, hence the question arises, 'What strategies do people employ when trying to learn verbal items in the laboratory?' This chapter begins by looking in some detail at two common types of encoding strategy. The first type makes use of imagery and involves the cognitive *elaboration* of the nominal stimulus. The second type of strategy utilizes semantic relations between list items to integrate them into organized memory units. This may be seen as a form of *reduction* coding in that the organization reduces the amount of information that need be retained.

The second part of the chapter concentrates on incidental learning. It explores some of the factors that determine what may be learned in the absence of any intention to learn and discusses some theoretical developments originating from the study of such learning situations.

The third part considers some effects of processes involved in comprehending sentences and passages of text on what is encoded in memory.

Intentional learning

Imaginal elaboration
Subjects often report the intentional use of imagery when

attempting to learn lists of words even when no specific instructions to use it are given. Thus, it seems, subjects realize the benefits of using imagery for learning and remembering, and this is even more strongly suggested by findings that under certain circumstances instructions to use imagery at presentation can lead to quite dramatic levels of performance. An example of such circumstances is provided by the use of the *method of loci*, the mnemonic device developed by the Greek Simonides around 500 BC, and used extensively ever since (see Yates, 1966). This method involves forming an image of a familiar room or other space, and imaging the to-be-remembered items each in a specific location. At the time of recall, the locations in the image are inspected and the items incorporated in them are identified. Some idea of the effectiveness of this mnemonic device is given by the results of Ross and Lawrence (1968). They instructed subjects to use familiar places on a walk around their university campus as loci to learn a list of 40 words presented once only at a rate of 3 seconds per word. Immediate recall was very impressive (a mean of 38.2 words), as was recall after 24 hours (a mean of 38.4 words). Furthermore, it was possible for the subjects to form a new set of images for another list in a single trial and achieve high levels of performance on immediate and delayed recall of the new list.

The *pegword* method, also, relies on imagery but employs familiar objects instead of loci as mnemonic 'pegs'. First, in this method, pegwords are associated with numbers by means of a rhyme such as *one-bun, two-shoe, three-tree*, and so on. The objects represented by the pegwords are then combined with images of the to-be-remembered items. Thus, given a list beginning with *plate, flower, snake*, the images could be a bun on a plate, a flower growing out of a shoe filled with soil, and a snake coiling around a tree. At recall the numbers are used to generate the pegwords and each of them used to produce its image which will be combined with that of the required item. The pegword technique and method of loci produce very similar levels of remembering (see, e.g., Bower and Reitman, 1972), but the pegword technique has the advantage that an item in a particular serial position can be quickly recalled without having to count around the loci in sequence.

Mnemonic devices such as those involving pegwords and loci can be employed with verbal items only to the extent that they give rise to images. There is, of course, no direct way of assessing the images evoked by particular words, and any comparisons of word imageabilities (the readiness with which images are evoked) are necessarily based on subjective reports. However, words that have high imageability are better remembered than those with low imageability in typical free recall, paired-associates learning, and recognition, and furthermore, these differences are increased when instructions to employ imagery are introduced. Paivio (1971) has offered an explanation of these findings that relies on the idea that imaginal codes are more readily established in memory for high rather than low imageability words and that these codes facilitate remembering. According to Paivio's *dual coding theory* there are two basic cognitive systems for encoding, organizing, storing and retrieving information, one verbal, the other imaginal. The theory, which has remained essentially unchanged over the years (see Paivio, 1979), maintains that superior memory for high imageability words arises because they are readily encoded in both the imaginal system *and* the verbal system whereas low imageability words are likely to be encoded only in the verbal system. Thus, highly imageable words are better remembered because they are represented in memory by two types of representation rather than one. Clearly, Paivio accepts both the functional importance of imagery and the reality of imaginal representations in memory, and, unlike theorists such as Pylyshyn whose views were discussed in Chapter 2, he believes that verbal processing and imaginal processing give rise to representations in separate storage systems.

It should be obvious that while superior memory performance for high over low imageability words is consistent with dual coding theory, there are other possible explanations. One possibility is that some word characteristic strongly correlated with imageability may underlie the superiority and that an account not based on imagery is called for.

Despite findings that imageability is related to memory performance when other word characteristics such as meaningfulness, frequency of everyday usage and lexical complexity are experimentally or statistically controlled (e.g. Paivio, 1971; Kintsch, 1972), the possibility that some other characteristic is responsible can never be ruled out entirely. Nevertheless, the relationship between word imageability and performance can be seen as one of several strands of evidence that converge on the dual coding theory. Other evidence used by Paivio to support his theory is based on differences in the readiness with which verbal and imaginal codes are generated and the independent effects of verbal and imaginal processing on performance. Some of this evidence is now discussed.

Paivio noted that the verbal system may have evolved initially to deal with spoken language and so should be best equipped to deal with information sequentially. The imaginal system, on the other hand, deals mainly with material in which numbers of features are presented simultaneously and so must be processed in parallel. Although such views are controversial Paivio incorporated them into the dual coding theory and one important consequence of doing so is the prediction that imaginal encoding should be an advantage only in certain circumstances. It should be of little or no help in performing tasks in which serial ordering of items is crucial, but should be of assistance when order is not important. A test of these predictions was carried out by Paivio and Csapo (1969) who employed pictures of nameable objects, concrete words, and abstract words in tasks dependent on serial order (memory span and serial learning), and tasks where serial order is not important (free recall and recognition). Pictures were included in the experiment because they should give the fastest access to imaginal codes but slowest access to verbal codes and so should provide important evidence bearing on the theory. The results of this study are complex but some of the principal findings support the dual coding theory. Generally, on sequential tasks pictures were inferior to words at fast rates of presentation but not at slow rates, presumably because of the comparative difficulty in gaining access to verbal codes from pictorial stimuli. On the non-sequential tasks the superiority of concrete words over abstract words increased with slower presentation as would be expected if imaginal codes were increasingly accessible, and more so for the concrete words.

Another line of evidence converging on the independence of imaginal and verbal coding in memory was provided by a further study of Paivio and Csapo (1973). They investigated the effect of repeating items in the presentation list. Generally, as would be expected, this has been found to increase retention but the effect is usually small when repetitions are successive and greater when they are widely spaced (see Melton, 1970). Paivio and Csapo included picture-picture word-word, picture-word and word-picture repetitions, the last two conditions involving the name of an object and the corresponding picture of that object. Picture-picture and word-word repetitions increased recall relative to single presentation but not as much as if the two presentations were independent in their effects. In contrast, word-picture and picture-word repetitions were additive in their effects on recall, this being in line with the assumption of dual coding theory that verbal and imaginal codes are distinct from one another.

While the results of Paivio and Csapo's experiments do provide support for the dual coding theory the evidence that imaginal encoding accounts for them is somewhat indirect. Because of this a number of investigators have felt it necessary to provide stronger tests of the theory. One approach which has been adopted to meet this challenge is to interfere with imaginal processing. The rationale here is perhaps most easily understood in terms of the working memory model. Assuming that the visuo-spatial scratch pad is employed in the imaginal encoding of words this process should be disrupted by a task which makes demands on that system and which is performed concurrently with list presentation. The study by Baddeley, Grant, Wight and Thomson (1975) exemplifies this approach. They first of all showed that a concurrent pursuit tracking task interfered with the ability to perform several tasks involving imagery, such as constructing and recalling an imaginal matrix into which digits were placed as directed by auditory instructions. They then had subjects learn lists of concrete (e.g. *table-square*) or abstract (e.g. *idea-original*) noun-adjective pairs with or without the concurrent pursuit tracking task and found that the usual advantage to concrete over abstract pairs was not diminished by tracking. At first sight this result seems very embarrassing for the dual coding theory because it shows that the advantage for concrete words is not dependent on imaginal activity. But this is only so if it is assumed that imaginal encoding is solely dependent on the construction of conscious images in a system such as the visuo-spatial scratch pad. Baddeley *et al.* recognized this point and J.T.E. Richardson (1980) pursued it by emphasizing the distinction between what he terms the *constructive* and *elaborative* uses of imagery. He considers the construction of conscious images to be useful for various tasks of the sort discussed in Chapter 2, and may, when constructed via techniques such as the method of loci, be associated with high levels of remembering. But the images themselves are not stored in long-term memory nor do they give rise to long-term codes. Instead, facilitation of remembering by word concreteness and imageability is seen to arise from the production of elaborative codes which may be evoked and registered in long-term memory without the creation of images in working memory. Thus, elaborative coding, and hence the advantage in learning of concrete over abstract words, is not prone to the influence of visuo-spatial tracking tasks as Baddeley *et al.* found.

Richardson favours the view, shared with Pylyshyn (see Chapter 2), that imaginal elaborative codes are not stored separately from verbal codes in long-term memory, as dual coding theory insists, but rather are stored in a common format. Although he argues that it is really not possible to distinguish empirically between the dual- and single-format theories he notes that certain considerations seem to favour the latter theory. These include findings that instructions to use verbal encoding strategies, such as seeking out relations between to-be-remembered items and organizing them into higher-order units, can often lead to levels of performance as impressive as those obtained under imaginal instructions. It is to such verbal encoding strategies that we now turn.

Organizing

We noted in Chapter 4 that memory span seems limited to 7 ± 2 *chunks*, as Miller (1956) called them. According to Miller, chunking is an effective aid to remembering because each chunk enables several items to be efficiently stored and retrieved so circumventing the limited capacity of short-term memory. The idea that somewhat similar limitations exist in long-term memory for word lists developed during the 1960s and was taken to its extreme by G. Mandler (e.g. 1967). Mandler had subjects sort a set of randomly selected words into as many sub-sets as they thought appropriate on the basis of any conceptual relations they could discover among them. He then asked for free recall and found that the number of words recalled increased with the number of sets used for sorting, but only up to about 7 sets. Other research (e.g. Mandler and Pearlstone, 1966) found that the number of items recalled from each sub-set had a similar upper limit of about 7. Mandler concluded that there are strict upper limits on long-term storage and that these can only be circumvented by chunking or *organizing* the nominal list items into functional units.

It was not long before objections were raised against Mandler's strong principle of limited capacity and these were expressed notably by Postman (1972). One objection arises from findings that more than 7 chunks can be recalled if, as with lists containing taxonomically related words, each chunk can be named (e.g. *flowers*, *metals*) and the name used as a cue at recall (Tulving and Pearlstone, 1966). Such findings show that, with respect to the recall of chunks at least, the limit on recall is in *retrieving* not *storing* information. Another, different, kind of objection concerns the irrefutability of the limited capacity notion: no matter how many list items are recalled it is possible to argue that the *chunks* have been organized into *superchunks*, even though their identity remains obscure. Also, it is simply not possible to obtain proof that more than 7 items cannot be recalled in the absence of chunking activity in any circumstances whatever! A weaker and hence more tenable position maintains merely that organizing the to-be-remembered material into higher-order functional units may enhance retention but is not essential for the long-term recall of more than a small number of items. This position gained wide support and is well summarized by Bower when he states, 'a preferred strategy of the adult human in learning a large body of material is to "divide and conquer", that is to subdivide the material into smaller groups by some means, and then learn these parts as integrated packets of information. . .' (Bower, 1970, page 41). A good deal of evidence upon which this view is based consists of differences in the order in which items are presented and that in which they are output in free recall. The assumption is that recognizable groupings of items at output which were not present at input reflect organizational processes in the subject.

Early evidence of organization in free recall comes from the study by Jenkins and Russell (1952). Their subjects were presented with a list containing 24 pairs of highly associated words (e.g. *table-chair*, *black-white*), the order throughout the list being haphazard such that members of each pair did not occur in successive positions. Despite this haphazard order of presentation it was found that the associated pairs tended to be clustered together in recall. Taxonomic categories may also provide the basis for clustering in recall as Bousfield (1953) showed. He presented a list of 60 words comprising 15 instances of each of the 4 taxonomic categories *animals*, *professions*, *vegetables* and *names*. Although the order of word presentation was completely randomized the free recall protocols showed that items from a common category clustered together at a greater level than could be expected by chance.

How can we be sure that associative and categorical clustering reflects encoding processes and not *merely* processes occurring at retrieval? After all, clustering does take place at recall! Is it possible, for example, that clustering is entirely the result of only one key item from each categorical or associative group being recalled, the remaining items being merely generated on the basis of long-established semantic structures and verbal habits? This extreme possibility can be rejected on the grounds that at least two accomplishments at encoding are necessary if the clustering data are to be accounted for. First, the subject must detect the categorical or associative relationships in the list. Evidence that this is so comes from studies showing the recall and clustering are increased by presenting the items blocked by category rather than randomly (Cofer, Bruce and Reicher, 1966), or by revealing the full categorical structure of the list beforehand (Bower, Clark, Lesgold and Winzenz, 1969). The results of an experiment by Hudson (1969) also implicate, and strongly so, processes at encoding. He used lists containing words from categories such as 'round' (e.g. *globe, balloon, button*) and 'white' (e.g. *snow, ivory, linen*) and required free recall. The results showed that compared to an uninstructed control group, informing subjects about the identity of the categories increased clustering when it was done *before* but not *after* list presentation. Finally, evidence of organizational activity during list presentation comes from some studies in which subjects were encouraged to perform their rehearsal of list items overtly (e.g. Rundus, 1971). These showed a strong tendency for related words to be rehearsed together even though the presentation order was haphazard.

The second accomplishment at encoding which is necessary to account for the recall of related items is that the items presented in the list and which belong to a particular associative or categorical relationship must be differentiated from other words sharing that relationship but which were not presented in the list. It cannot be that items are simply generated from semantic memory purely on the basis of category membership and linguistic habits or there would be large numbers of intrusions into the recall protocols, contrary to general findings. Theoretical accounts of just how the occurrence of particular items in specific episodes is encoded in memory and how such information is used to 'edit' the output are dealt with in the next chapter so the matter will not be considered further here.

In the studies discussed above the associative and categorical relationships used as criteria for clustering were determined by the experimenter and the presence of clusters is not difficult to detect. In contrast, if the to-be-remembered lists are constructed with essentially 'unrelated' words, drawn randomly from a large pool of words, there is no *a priori* basis for identifying the organization employed by the subjects. How then may organizational processes be revealed with such material? One method of doing so was introduced by Tulving (1962) who argued that items encoded together into higher-order units will tend to cluster together in recall and that this *subjective organization*, as he called it, will become apparent over successive free recall trials with the same set of words; even though the words are presented in a different order on each trial, consistencies in the output sequence should appear. Basically, he used information theory to devise an index of subjective organization, the SO score, based on constant pair-wise groupings in successive outputs. This index has a value of *zero* if the output sequence on trial n has no pairs in common with trial $n–1$, increasing to a value of *one* if the sequences are identical. Another index of subjective organizaton, the ITR (inter-trial repetition) measure, is similar to SO being based on pair-wise consistencies, but ignores the order in which the items within a pair are output.

Generally, experimental results have confirmed that measures of subjective organization correlate positively with the number of items recalled as would be expected if recall is dependent on the development of organization (Tulving, 1962; see too, Sternberg and Tulving, 1977). However, SO and ITR scores often remain quite low even though recall performance is perfect, and sometimes the correlation between these measures and recall is not statistically reliable. Such findings seem to show that subjective organization plays only a small part in determining recall performance but this is not a necessary conclusion. It is possible to argue, as has Postman (1972), that the fault lies not in organization theory but in the indices of organization. This point has been taken up by Pellegrino and Ingram (1979) who emphasized that SO and ITR scores do not adequately reflect either the complexity of subjective organization or the flexibility with which it is expressed in the output. This can be seen in the simple example shown in Table 5.1. Here the to-be-remembered words, which are presented in a different random order on each trial, are shown in the left-most

column and successive recall attempts by a single, hypothetical subject are shown in the remaining columns.

It can be seen in Table 5.1 that five consistent groupings emerge; *goal* and *hole* form a pair based presumably on a phonological relationship; *coat* and *wool* (clothing); *ant*, *bird*, *daffodil* (living things); *lake*, *cave*, *valley* (geographical features); and *court*, *line*, *partner* (tennis). Neither the order of items within groups nor the ordering of groups are consistent and the pairwise sequences on which the SO score is based are very few; on trial 2 there are 0 such sequences, 1 on trial 3, 1 on trial 4, and 1 on trial 5. Yet it is possible to identify the groupings 'by eyeball' and to depict them by means of the network shown on the right of the table.

It is clear from the example that SO scores do not adequately reflect what seems to be the effective organization in the output (and inspection of the table shows that ITR does not do much better). Given this state of affairs it is not surprising that a number of techniques have been developed to more adequately reveal the nature of subjective organization. Friendly (1979) describes and assesses some of them. The simplest type of development is merely to ask subjects to indicate which items were 'recalled together' or 'were present in memory together' either by drawing lines between the groupings on the response sheets or by clustering them in some other way. More sophisticated procedures, requiring complex computer analysis, include Friendly's Proximity Analysis and Monk's Hierarchical Grouping Analysis. The first of these procedures involves assessing the distance between items in the output and constructing a network similar to that shown in Table 5.1 with the distance of each node from the left-hand side representing the average proximity amongst items nested under it. Monk's technique is even more sophisticated and identifies proximity groupings with constant, serial, or variable orderings of items within them.

Despite the effort expended on developing analytic techniques, interest in output organization, which was a major area of memory research for some twenty years following Bousfield's early work, has recently waned. As Puff (1979) notes, there are several reasons for this, one of them being the widespread acceptance that subjects do indeed engage in organizational activities at input. But perhaps the foremost reason for this decline in interest is the influence of the *levels of processing* approach to memory research which is dealt with in detail in the next section. This approach has focused attention on the way in which individual items are processed, to the neglect of inter-item relationships – a neglect which some investigators believe should not be allowed to continue (e.g. Battig and Bellezza, 1979).

Incidental learning

'Do you recall the circumstances in which you first heard that John F. Kennedy had been shot?' Brown and Kulik (1977) asked Americans questions such as this concerning events of national or purely personal importance and found that a high proportion of respondents confidently recalled the circumstances in which they had received the news, and seemed to do so with a perceptual-like clarity. Brown and Kulik referred to such memories as 'flashbulb memories' because of the indiscriminate way in which details seemed to be preserved. They noted that the important factors in the creation of such memories are the level of surprise, the intensity of the emotional reaction, and the consequences of the event for the individual's way of life. Apparently, then, flashbulb memories indicate the registration of detailed information, irrelevant to the main event, in long-term memory in the absence of any intention to do so. That is, they seem to show the presence of *automatic* rather *effortful* processes, to use the terms employed by Hasher and Zacks (1979) and discussed in Chapter 1.

Neisser (1982) points out that Brown and Kulik's study suffers from a failure to verify the subjects' descriptions of their circumstances. Nevertheless, there is ample evidence from carefully controlled studies for the long-term retention of situational details which are irrelevant to the task at hand. The study by Baddeley, Lewis and Nimmo-Smith (1978) illustrates this point. This study showed that when subjects were questioned about the previous occasion on which they had visited the laboratory at Cambridge they could remember details such as the sex of the experimenter, length of the session, and whether testing had been carried out individually or in groups, after intervals of 60 days or more even though there was no reason for them to believe they would be asked about such details later. This part of the chapter deals with some of the factors which determine such incidental learning and with theoretical accounts of it.

Experimental studies of incidental learning

Various procedures have been used to investigate incidental learning (see Postman, 1964 for a review). Essentially these procedures direct subjects' attention to the stimulus material by some means or other without informing them that a later memory test will be given. This approach is aptly illustrated by the study of Tresselt and Mayzner (1960) in which subjects were required to cross out the vowels in the stimulus words, copy the words, or judge the degree to which each word was an instance of the concept 'economic'. When recall was unexpectedly required, performance following the semantic judgment task was four times higher than following the letter cancellation task and twice as high as with copying. A later experiment by Schulman (1971) showed that recognition memory, also, is influenced by the nature of the orienting task. He required subjects to search a list of words for targets which were defined either in terms of their *structure* (e.g. containing the letter *a*) or semantically (e.g. denoting living things). Performance on the unexpected recognition test was best following the semantic task.

The results of the above-mentioned studies are typical in showing that semantic orienting tasks lead to better incidental learning than structural tasks, but how do these levels of performance compare with intentional learning? The study of Hyde and Jenkins (1969), in which both intentional and incidental learning groups were employed, is informative on this point. The intentional group was given the usual free recall instructions before list presentation, which was auditory. The incidental group was divided into three sub-groups, each of which was given a specific orienting task. In one task subjects had to indicate whether or not each auditorily presented word contained the letter *e*. The second task involved estimating the number of letters in the words, and the third task was to rate each word's meaning for pleasantness. Subjects performing the semantic task achieved a mean recall score of 16.3 items, this being almost identical to the score for the intentional group (16.1 items). Estimating the number of letters and checking *e* produced relatively low mean scores of 9.4 and 9.9 items respectively, as would be expected on the basis of the Schulman, and Tresselt and Mayzner results. Jenkins and his associates (see Jenkins, 1974a) have subsequently shown that other orienting tasks which produce levels of recall similar to those obtained under intentional instructions include writing relevant adjectives for target nouns, estimating frequency of use of words in everyday communication, and rating words on the dimension of activity-passivity. Other tasks giving rise to low levels of recall include counting the number of syllables, deciding whether words rhyme with one another, and deciding whether each word was presented in a male or female voice.

The findings of Jenkins and his associates support Postman's (1964) conclusion that it is the way stimulus items are dealt with by the cognitive system and not intention to learn *per se* which is crucial to memory performance. We have already seen that when intentional learning instructions are given, subjects engage in organizational and other encoding strategies which involve semantic processing of to-be-remembered words. Thus, it appears that performance is equivalent for intentional and incidental conditions if semantic processing is involved in both. It would be wrong, however, to conclude from this that the same sort of processing is employed. It seems unlikely, for example, that subjects will seek out and utilize semantic relationships *between* words under incidental conditions. If this is so, how is incidental learning to be explained? The ideas put forward by Craik and Lockhart (1972) help answer this question.

Craik and Lockhart's approach
Models of memory, such as that of Atkinson and Shiffrin which emphasize the role of intentional control processes in governing transfer to long-term storage from short-term

storage, have difficulty in accounting for the high levels of performance obtained under incidental learning conditions. An alternative approach to memory, described by Craik and Lockhart (1972), not only provides a basis for understanding incidental learning but gives a more flexible framework generally than do models based more directly on the information processing analogy. However, this *levels of processing* approach, as Craik and Lockhart chose to call it, was developed partly from the Atkinson and Shiffrin model and so shares some features with it. It also has points in common with suggestions made by Baddeley and Patterson (1971) and Cermak (1972). Generally, the emphasis is on the recording in episodic memory of the cognitive processes carried out on stimuli, rather than on direct representation of the stimuli themselves. As such the levels of processing approach has much in common with the Russian view of learning through experience rather than intention (Smirnov and Zinchenko, 1969).

In the initial description of their views Craik and Lockhart (1972) followed Treisman (1964) and others by arguing that *perception* involves a hierarchy of processing *levels* or *stages*. According to this view, early stages of analysis are concerned with physical stimulus features such as brightness and pitch, while later stages are concerned with the semantic features. Following the assumption that perceptual processing is hierarchical the early stages have been referred to as *shallow* levels of processing, while the later, semantic stages being carried out further into the cognitive system have been referred to as *deep* levels. Craik and Lockhart adopted this terminology and accepted that the depth to which an item is processed depends on such factors as its meaningfulness (words may be processed to a deeper level than digits), and the requirements of the task being performed. For some tasks, such as counting the number of letters in words, only a shallow level of processing is required, whereas judging the pleasantness of words involves a deep level.

The link between perceptual processes and memory is provided by Craik and Lockhart in their suggestion that a record of the perceptual analyses is made in memory. As Craik and Jacoby (1979) explain, this link may be understood by analogy with the proceedings of a law court. The verdict of the court summarizes the proceedings and prescribes appropriate action. Similarly, the action taken after perceptual analysis of a stimulus may be seen as a summary of the analytical processes. However, just as the proceedings which lead to a verdict in court are recorded for later consultation, so the processes involved in perception leave a record in memory. It is further suggested that the persistence of these memory traces depends critically on the depth of processing carried out; deeper levels are associated with longer-lasting traces. Thus, it does not matter whether deeper processing is achieved as a result of intentional learning or some other activity, the record laid down in memory will be relatively durable.

Craik and Lockhart argue that it is possible to place too much reliance on concepts borrowed from information processing science when constructing models of human memory. They point to a number of problems arising from strict adherence to models involving a series of stores, each supposedly with specific properties such as storage capacity and code, and forgetting rate. These problems are exemplified by the difficulty in determining whether performance limitations are due to constraints on *storage* capacity or on *processing* capacity (e.g. the adequacy of control processes). Also, it has proved difficult to determine the coding employed by a specified store (for example, whether STS can hold semantic information or not – see Chapter 4). In addition, the point is eventually reached with such models where so many separate stores are required to deal with different aspects of memory that the system becomes unwieldy. The levels of processing approach represents an attempt to move away from the constraints of formal information processing models to a more flexible account of memory in which the emphasis is on the recording of the cognitive operations carried out on the stimuli rather than the controlled, hierarchical transfer of information from one store to another. Nevertheless, the approach retains a number of important features of the original Atkinson and Shiffrin model, including the concept of short-term store or primary memory. Craik and Lockhart assume a primary memory system which functions much as does Baddeley and Hitch's working memory. It is responsible for rehearsing 'chunks' of information at any particular level of analysis, e.g. phoneme, word, idea. This *Type I* processing, as it is called, is considered to have a purely maintenance function; it does not lead to an increment in trace durability. *Type II* processing, in contrast, involves directing attention to deeper level of processing and so enhances retention.

The levels of processing approach to memory has several attractive features. It emphasizes memory as an integral part of cognitive activity as a whole. It avoids the temptation to think too rigidly in terms of formal information processing models, and incorporates a flexible approach to 'primary memory' as does Baddeley and Hitch's working memory model. Also, of course, it provides an account of incidental learning. Nevertheless, there have been criticisms of the approach some of which are discussed shortly. One general criticism, made by Baddeley (1978) amongst others, concerns the fact that *levels of processing* as described by Craik and Lockhart (1972) is no more than an *approach* to memory. It is not a formal theory. While it gains by escaping some of the problems associated with a rigid adherence to information processing principles it loses in specificity. Thus, there is a danger that the approach can accommodate almost any finding, but is capable of predicting very few.

Assessment of depth
A number of critics of the 'levels' approach (e.g. Baddeley, 1978; Eysenck, 1978; Nelson, Walling and McEvoy, 1979) have noted that unless an independent measure of *depth* can be obtained there is a danger of circularity in the arguments. It is all too easy to infer the level of processing involved in a particular orienting task from the amount remembered, and then explain the amount remembered by the depth of processing. If the levels of processing approach is to be theoretically useful, i.e. something more than a mere rule of thumb about which tasks are likely to give rise to high retention, then some independent measure of depth must be obtained.

Craik and Lockhart (1972) proposed that the levels of

processing form a hierarchy with deep levels requiring more time to complete than shallow ones. Thus, the time taken to perform an orienting task should provide an index of depth. In one of their experiments Craik and Tulving (1975) did indeed find that reaction times were shortest for a structural task (e.g. 'Is the word in capital letters?'), longer for a phonemic task (e.g. 'Does the word rhyme with weight?'), and longest for semantic questions (e.g. 'Is the word a type of fish?' or 'Does the word fit the sentence *He met a — in the street*?'). This result seems to support the levels idea. But, it is possible to produce structural orienting tasks which take longer to complete than those involving semantic questions, as Craik and Tulving showed in another of their experiments. In this experiment superficial processing was induced by having subjects decide whether target words conformed to a particular pattern of vowels (V) and consonants (C). They were shown a series of words, each accompanied by a matching or mismatching pattern of vowels and consonants (e.g. TABLE-CVCCV or UNCLE-CVCVC). In the semantic orienting task they classified a sentence frame as appropriate or inappropriate for the target word (e.g. 'The man threw the ball to the —. – *baby*'). Although the letter-sequence task took longer to perform it was the semantic task which gave rise to the better retention. Thus, the time taken to complete the orienting task does not offer a direct index of processing depth.

Johnston and Heinz (1978) adopted the notion of *expended processing capacity* as an index of depth. Their subjects were presented with two messages, simultaneously and dichotically, and required to shadow one message, as it moved from one ear to the other, either on the basis of speaker's voice (male or female) or semantic category (animal names or male first names). Concurrently, subjects pushed a button as quickly as possible in response to a randomly occurring light. It was argued that the shadowing and reaction time tasks shared processing capacity, hence the reaction times provided an index of the demands made by the shadowing task. Reaction times were shorter when shadowing was by voice than when it was by category, thus showing that selection of stimuli for attention on the basis of superficial features consumes less capacity than when semantic features are involved. In an unexpected memory test recognition of words from the shadowing sequences was best following the category task.

The advantage of expended processing capacity over times to complete orienting tasks as an index of depth is shown in the study of Eysenck and Eysenck (1979). They found that the times to complete the superficial orienting task used in one experiment were longer than for the semantic task while for the tasks used in a second experiment the reverse was found., Despite this, estimates of expended processing capacity were greater for the semantic tasks in both experiments and these tasks produced the highest levels of recall. Expended capacity, then, seems to offer an independent index of depth. But the very concept of depth itself has been called into question, as we shall now see. Nevertheless, it is possible that the notion of expended processing capacity can help avoid the circularity which has been such a problem with the original levels of processing formulation.

Elaboration, compatibility and uniqueness
The original levels of processing view put forward by Craik and Lockhart maintains that processing *depth* lies on a continuum. This, in turn, implies that stimuli are processed by a fixed series of analysers ordered from structural to semantic. This idea is unsatisfactory because it seems unlikely that a full structural analysis is necessary before semantic analysis can begin: it is not necessary, for example, to establish whether a word is printed in upper-case letters, or whether the vowels and consonants conform to a particular pattern, to begin semantic analysis. Furthermore, if reading involved the fixed sequence of visual analysis followed by phonological analysis with this, in turn, being followed by semantic analysis, it would not be possible to know whether the printed word *sail* referred to ships or shops! Another problem with the original notion of *depth* arises from findings that different semantic tasks give rise to different levels of retention. Such findings require that some distinction be made between processes at a particular level. Some of these findings are discussed below, but the

important point to appreciate here is that they, together with the problems inherent in a fixed, serial order of processing levels, forced modification of the original approach.

Craik and Tulving (1975), and Lockhart, Craik and Jacoby (1976) acknowledged problems of the sort mentioned above by adopting the view that there are *domains* of encoding rather than a depth continuum. Several domains, corresponding to the structural, phonemic and semantic tasks that had been used in experimental studies, were assumed to exist. Thus, the types of processes necessary to complete different tasks were seen as being grouped together in domains rather than distributed along a depth continuum. The concept of depth has not entirely vanished in this reformulation in that at least *some* processing in the structural domain is necessary before semantic processing can begin, but the attempt to break away from the troublesome concept of depth is clear.

It can be argued that the introduction of *domains*, rather than *levels*, of processing does no more than acknowledge in a very crude way that perception and comprehension of verbal materials is not merely a fixed, serial process. Nevertheless, the idea is important for two other modifications to the original levels approach. These modifications involve the concepts of *compatibility* and *elaboration* and were introduced by Craik and Tulving (1975).

The modification involving compatibility was made largely in response to Craik and Tulving's (1975) finding that items given a positive response in the orienting task were recalled better than those given a negative response (see also Schulman, 1971). Thus, when the orienting question was 'Is the word a type of fish?' the target word *shark* would be recalled better than *heaven*. In terms of the original depth analogy both target words must be analysed to the same depth in response to the same question. It is difficult, therefore, to account for the difference in memorability in terms of depth. Instead Craik and Tulving attribute this phenomenon to the greater *compatibility* between the encoding context created by the question and the positive, compared to the negative, item. The idea here is that positive items combine with the question to form an integrated idea which, in turn, produces a coherent memory trace which is relatively easy to retrieve. Unfortunately it has proved difficult to establish an independent index of compatibility and without this the concept has a dubious theoretical utility.

The concept of *trace elaboration* was introducd to account for findings that retention is related to the elaborateness of the orienting task within a single processing domain. The study of Klein and Saltz (1976) provides a good example of such findings. They required subjects to rate the meanings of nouns on semantic dimensions such as *pleasant-unpleasant* and *fast-slow*. Incidental learning was better for words rated on two dimensions than for words rated only on one. For words rated on two dimensions recall was higher when the dimensions were unrelated to each other than when they were related. Retention, then, increased with the number and variety of processes carried out, this presumably determining the richness or elaborateness of the memory record (see also Auble and Franks, 1978).

The concepts of elaboration and compatibility must be considered jointly because increasing compatibility may lead to greater elaboration. Indeed, one possible reason for the superior recall of items giving rise to positive decisions over those giving rise to negative ones is that more elaborate processing must be carried out to reach a positive decision. The two concepts are brought together in one of Craik and Tulving's (1975) experiments. Subjects were presented with sentence frames of high, medium or low complexity and required to decide whether or not the target word accompanying each sentence could appropriately fit the frame. The following are examples of the sentence frames used: low complexity – 'He dropped the —'; medium complexity – 'The — frightened the children'; high complexity – 'The great bird swooped down and carried off the struggling —.' After making decisions about 60 words, 20 at each level of complexity, and half requiring positive responses, subjects were unexpectedly asked to free recall them. The results showed an increase in recall with sentence complexity for positive but not for negative words. It seems, then, if the target word is compatible with the sentence frame an integrated 'idea' can be achieved and this will be more elaborate with increasing complexity of the sentence frame.

Moscovitch and Craik (1976) and Jacoby (1974) have proposed that distinctiveness or *uniqueness* of a memory trace is also an important determinant of how well it is remembered. The idea here is that the record left by semantic processing is less likely to be confusible with the records of other semantic processings than is that left by structural processing with those of other structural processings. This notion of trace uniqueness is bound up with trace elaboration in that the more elaborate the trace the more distinct or unique it will be (see Craik and Jacoby, 1979 for further discussion).

Study-test interactions
Bransford (e.g. Morris, Bransford and Franks, 1977) and D.L. Nelson (e.g., Nelson, 1979; Nelson, Walling and McEvoy, 1979) have made proposals which differ from the levels of processing framework in some crucial respects. One important difference is the denial by Nelson and by Bransford that structural processing cannot leave an enduring memory record. Nelson refers to his *sensory-semantic* conceptualization, while Bransford refers to the notion of *transfer-appropriate processing*. Both conceptualizations insist that the free recall and recognition tests used to validate the levels of processing approach have been largely biased in favour of semantic processing. When tests are used which are *appropriate* for assessing visual or phonological memory codes high levels of performance can be demonstrated following structural orienting tasks. This has been shown in a number of studies. Morris *et al.* (1977), for example, gave subjects orienting questions concerned with meaning (e.g. '— has ears. – *dog*') or rhyme (e.g. '— rhymes with log. – *dog*'). Following this, in one part of the study, a group of subjects were presented with a set of words and asked to decide whether or not each of them rhymed with any of the target words presented in the context of the sentence frames. Recognition of rhymes was better after rhyming questions than after meaning questions for periods of up to 24 hours. Stein (1978) provides further evidence of the persistence of

'structural' traces. This study included a structural orienting task (e.g. 'Does this word have a capital D? – *raDio*'), and a semantic task (e.g. 'Does this item use electricity? – *raDio*'). A forced-choice recognition test was then given in which the target items had to be selected from a number of alternatives (e.g. radiO, raDio, rAdio, Radio). Here, semantic questions in the initial task led to lower recognition than structural questions.

The studies of Bransford *et al.* and of Stein illustrate the importance of the testing situation in addition to the encoding situation in determining memory performance: study and test situations may interact such that their combination is crucial (see Chapter 6). Retrieval mechanisms have not been neglected by adherents to the levels of processing approach (see Craik and Tulving, 1975, Experiment VII; Moscovitch and Craik, 1976), but those study-test interactions which reveal long-lasting structural traces must force further modification of the approach along the lines of the sensory-semantic or transfer-appropriate conceptualizations. Craik, Lockhart, Jacoby and others have always insisted that levels of processing is an *approach to*, or *framework for*, memory research and not a theory which may be tested in a formal way. The original formulation has been adapted to deal with new evidence, as we have seen, and there seems to be no reason why long-lasting traces resulting from structural processing should not be incorporated in it. But, as we have already noted, such flexibility carries with it the loss of predictive power. Amongst other things, the looseness of the formulation permits *depth* to be replaced by *elaboration*, *compatibility* and *uniqueness* which themselves appear to be rather vague.

Despite the authoritative criticisms made against 'levels' by Baddeley (1978) and Nelson *et al.* (1979), for example, Craik and Lockhart's original paper must be seen as an important contribution to the study of memory. It expresses a movement away from formal information processing models and provides a basis for dealing with incidental learning. By maintaining that records of cognitive processes are kept in memory the approach complements Tulving's episodic ecphory theory which is dealt with in the next chapter.

Comprehension and memory

When people read a story their attempts to comprehend the material involve the extraction of a theme, or themes, and the making of inferences. By way of illustration consider the following opening lines of a story:

> It had been a trying day. Thompson opened the door with his key, went into the lounge, sat in the armchair, and made himself comfortable.

At this point the reader may well go beyond what is actually printed and infer that Thompson had come home after a hard day at work. But read on.

> He took out the revolver and checked it. No sooner had he done so than he heard Martin returning home.

So, it was not Thompson's home! It now seems reasonable to infer that Thompson is about to shoot Martin in Martin's home. Also, the theme of an assassin preparing to shoot his victim seems to emerge.

What influence does the *construction* of themes and inferences have on what is remembered about stories and other passages of text? One possibility is that inferences become incorporated into memory as if they had been explicitly stated. Another possibility is that while the theme is well remembered surface details of the text are forgotten so that retelling the story involves a *reconstruction* based on the theme. In this part of the chapter we consider briefly the influence of construction and reconstruction on what is remembered. We begin with an example of the importance of themes to both comprehension and memory.

Constructive processes at encoding

Bransford and Johnson (1973) presented the following passage to their subjects.

> The procedure is actually quite simple. First you arrange items into different groups. Of course one pile may be

sufficient depending on how much there is to do. If you have to go somewhere else due to lack of facilities that is the next step; otherwise, you are pretty well set. It is important not to overdo things. That is, it is better to do too few things at once than too many. In the short run this may not seem important but complications can easily arise. A mistake can be expensive as well. At first, the whole procedure will seem complicated. Soon, however, it will become just another facet of life. It is difficult to foresee any end to the necessity for this task in the immediate future, but then, one can never tell. After the procedure is completed one arranges the materials into their appropriate places. Eventually, they will be used once more and the whole cycle will then have to be repeated. However, that is part of life. (Bransford and Johnson, 1973, page 722).

Subjects who were given no clue about the topic of the passage rated it as incomprehensible and were able to recall very few ideas contained in it. Other subjects who were supplied with the topic 'Washing Clothes' *before* presentation rated it as comprehensible and recalled more than twice as many ideas from the passage as did the 'no topic' group. A third group who received the topic *after* presentation of the passage, but before recall, did no better at recall than the 'no topic' group. These results demonstrate the importance of extracting a theme from material both for comprehension and for remembering. Also, they show that the provision of the theme at retrieval alone was not helpful, presumably because much verbatim information had been forgotten and it was not possible to reconstruct the ideas from what had been retained.

Other work by Bransford has demonstrated that making inferences during comprehension affects what is remembered. In one study (Bransford, Barclay and Franks, 1972) one group of subjects were presented with sentences such as 'Three turtles rested on a floating log and a fish swam beneath them.' (The inference here, of course, is that the fish swam not only under the turtles but under the log also. A recognition test was then given which included new sentences which were logically implied by the initial ones, such as 'Three turtles rested on a floating log and a fish swam under it.' Subjects in this condition were much more likely to falsely identify such *new* sentences as *old* than were subjects who had initially received sentences with no such necessary implication, e.g. 'Three turtles rested beside a floating log and a fish swam beneath them.'

In another study Johnson, Bransford and Solomon (1973) showed that subjects were likely to incorrectly recognize new passages containing implicit inferences, that is, inferences implied but not logically demanded by the initial sentences. For example, some subjects were presented with sentences including 'John was trying to fix the birdhouse. He was pounding the nail when his father came out to watch him and to help him do the work.' This passage implies, but does not demand that John was using a hammer, and these subjects were very likely to falsely recognize the sentence 'John was using a hammer to fix the birdhouse when his father came out to watch him and to help him do the work.' This was not so for other subjects who had initially received the sentence with 'looking for' substituted for 'pounding'. Bransford (e.g. 1979) concludes from his own and other results that subjects *construct* meanings and inferences to comprehend sentences and passages, and that these constructions are remembered rather than what was actually presented. However, it would be wrong to conclude from this that Bransford believes surface details of verbal material are lost from memory within a matter of seconds as some researchers have claimed (e.g. Sachs, 1967). We have already noted in an earlier section of his chapter that Bransford's notion of *transfer-appropriate processing* was specifically conceived to acknowledge that retention of superficial features can often be revealed if the appropriate test conditions are created. It is worth adding here, therefore, that memory for the formal wording of sentences has been shown to persist over long periods of time. One such demonstration was provided by Keenan, MacWhinney and Mayhew (1977) who tested recognition memory for statements made during a research group discussion. Statements having what the authors termed 'high interactional content' (high IC) were particularly well retained in verbatim form. Examples they give are 'Would everyone please shut up' (high IC), as distinct from 'Would you please stop talking' (low IC), and 'I think there are two fundamental tasks in this study' (low IC) as distinct from 'I think you've made a fundamental error here' (high IC).

Reconstruction at retrieval

Kintsch (1976) describes an experiment in which subjects read texts on topics with which they were generally familiar, such ˙as the biblical story of Joseph and his brothers. Immediately following this a recall test for the topics was given and this, in turn, was followed a day later by another recall test. On immediate recall the errors were mainly due to subjects omitting information. In contrast, after 24 hours what was recalled reflected what subjects had known about the topic before the experiment rather than the text as presented. In particular, there were many importations of material from the prior knowledge. These findings accord with what Bartlett (1932) observed with recall of the 'War of the Ghosts' (see Chapter 1): his subjects, too, appeared to remember the gist of what had been presented and to *reconstruct* details according to their beliefs about what must have been true.

The hypothesis that distortions in remembering arise from reconstruction at retrieval stands in contrast to Bransford's constructivist view referred to in the previous section. Bransford, of course, ruled out the possibility that subjects were merely reconstructing the 'Washing Clothes' passage at retrieval because supplying the topic label after presentation did not facilitate recall. But presumably the passage contained a number of ideas that would not be generated spontaneously as a description of the topic. Not surprisingly, therefore, Bransford has argued that his results are of limited generality and that construction and reconstruction each operate in a wide variety of circumstances. Certainly, the active nature of retrieval has become increasingly accepted over the last few years and this is apparent from the growing interest in what is known as *recollective experience* and which is discussed in Chapter 6.

The reconstructive hypothesis draws attention to the possibility that new information can influence memory for previous experiences by forming a new basis for remembering. A substantial amount of evidence shows that this does indeed happen. The study by Snyder and Uranowitz (1978) is particularly interesting because of the implications of its results for social psychology. These authors presented groups of students with a single narrative containing a detailed description of the life of a woman named Betty. Amongst the details given was the statement that Betty dated occasionally. After reading the narrative subjects in one group were told that Betty is now a lesbian, while the other group was told she is heterosexual. At a later date memory for the details of Betty's life was tested by a multiple-choice recognition test, and of special interest here is the item which gave as alternatives (a) Betty occasionally dated men, (b) she never went out with men, (c) she went steady, (d) no information was presented. The subjects' choices showed the influence of the post-narrative information: those who learned that Betty is now a lesbian were likely to remember that Betty never went out with men even though they had not been informed as such. Snyder and Uranowitz argue that the reconstructive process contributes to the persistence of social stereotypes because once an individual has been labelled it is difficult to remember anything about him or her without it being influenced by the stereotype.

The reconstructive hypothesis warns us that eyewitness testimony, also, may be distorted by exposure to misleading information after the event. Elizabeth Loftus has carried out extensive work on this possibility which her results confirm (see Loftus, 1979 for a review). In one of her earlier experiments (Loftus and Palmer, 1974) she showed students a film depicting a multiple car accident and then questioned them about what they had seen. One group of observers had among their questions 'About how fast were the cars going when they smashed into each other?' For another group the word 'hit' was substituted for 'smashed into'. A third group was not interrogated at this point. The results showed that the verb 'smashed' was associated with higher estimates of speed than was 'hit'. This suggests that the information implicit in the question had influenced what was recalled about the accident. One week later the three groups were asked 'Did you see any broken glass?' Of the group asked about the speed when the cars *smashed into* each other, 32 per cent said they did see broken glass. For the *hit* and 'not questioned' groups the percentages were 14 and 12 respectively.

There is now much evidence, in addition to that provided by Loftus and Palmer, that what a person remembers about an event can easily be altered by exposure to new information (see Loftus, 1979, 1983). In order to account for such findings by the process of reconstruction it is necessary to assume that the memory traces for the original event remain intact, and that the new information is also stored intact and is used to reinterpret the original traces. This 'coexistence' hypothesis requires that the original, unaltered memory can be recovered and Loftus (e.g. 1983) rejects it on the grounds that there is little evidence that this can be done. Thus, Loftus also rejects the reconstructive process, at least as an account of distortions to eyewitness testimony by post-event information. Instead, she proposes that the new information is incorporated within the original traces so that the original record of the event no longer exists. She refers to this alternative as the 'alteration hypothesis'.

Loftus's conclusions have been challenged by Bekerian and Bowers (1983) on the grounds that original memories *can* be recovered if the appropriate test conditions are established. They found that memory for a witnessed incident could be improved by matching the order of questions to the original ordering of events rather than arranging them haphazardly. Thus, it seems, the original memory can be recovered uncontaminated by post-event information if steps are taken to reinstate the 'context' of the incident. This possibility cannot be lightly dismissed because, as we shall see in Chapter 6, there is much evidence that re-establishing at test the context in which encoding took place can lead to enhanced recall and recognition performance. But, whatever the outcome of the controversy over the alteration and coexistence hypotheses, it is clear that the notion of reconstruction at retrieval has drawn attention to several important social and legal issues.

Summary

Encoding in long-term storage may be achieved through effortful strategies directed specifically at learning and remembering, or as a consequence of cognitive activity in the absence of any intention to learn. This chapter discussed both aspects of encoding.

Imaginal elaboration can be a very effective mnemonic strategy as the method of loci and pegword techniques demonstrate. Paivio accounts for the benefits of imagery strategies by his dual coding theory. This postulates separate verbal and imaginal systems and attributes the advantage of concrete over abstract words in free recall and recognition to the additivity of verbal and imaginal codes. The theory has come under attack for reasons that include the failure of certain non-verbal interference tasks to reduce the advantage enjoyed by concrete words.

Categorical and subjective organization in free recall protocols may be seen as evidence for the use of reduction coding to circumvent the limits of long-term memory. However, SO and ITR measures generally do not correlate at all highly with recall scores and this has led to more complex methods of analysing subjects' output sequences. Nevertheless, interest in organization has waned because the weaker forms of organization theory are widely accepted, and because of the influence exerted by the levels of processing approach.

The levels of processing approach views encoding as dependent on the nature of cognitive activity associated with item presentation rather than on intention to learn *per se*. In this way it provides not only an account of incidental learning but avoids some of the problems inherent in the more rigid models based on the information processing analogy. However, the approach has been criticized notably for the circularity in the notion of 'depth' of processing. Attempts to meet this objection and others by introducing concepts such as 'domains of processing', 'trace elaboration' and 'trace uniqueness' still leave some issues unresolved. This is especially true of findings that shallow levels of processing can indeed give rise to persisting memory traces. Despite these problems and the looseness of the formulation, 'levels of processing' continues to be very influential in memory research.

Both constructive and reconstructive processes influence what is remembered about sentences and passages of text. Errors in remembering suggest that inferences made during comprehension are incorporated into memory, and that themes are well retained and used to reconstruct the material influenced by prior knowledge.

The coexistence hypothesis maintains that distortions of memory arising from post-event information are due to influence on the reconstructive process by independent memory traces. The alteration hypothesis insists that new information is incorporated into existing memory traces so that the original traces cannot be recovered.

6 Retrieval

Memory tests may be classified according to the type of retrieval cue given to the subject. In recall tests the cue may be merely 'recall the words from the last list', or more specific cues such as those based on rhyme or categorical relationships (e.g. 'some of the words were animal names'). In recognition the test includes copies of the to-be-remembered stimuli as cues, the requirement being to decide whether such stimuli occurred in a particular presentation context. Different test procedures, then, appear to make different retrieval demands. Hence, the patterns of performance which arise under these various procedures may be informative about the processes involved in retrieval. This chapter emphasizes the importance of retrieval processes in remembering and looks in detail at some models of them.

Retrieval limitations

Availability and accessibility
Tulving (e.g. 1968, 1974) has distinguished between failures to remember which are due to the absence of the required information in memory, and those which occur because information which is present in memory storage cannot be retrieved. In Tulving's terms it is necessary to distinguish between the *availability* of information in memory, and its *accessibility*. The basis of Tulving's distinction is a body of research which demonstrates that items which cannot be recalled at one time may be recalled at a later time either

unaided or with the help of cues, even though no new opportunity for learning has occurred.

The unaided recovery of previously unrecallable items was demonstrated by Tulving (1967) in an experiment in which he gave subjects a single presentation of a word list and required three successive recall attempts. Although about half of the list words were recalled on each trial they were not all the same words. Thus, some words which were not recalled on one trial were recalled later, while others recalled on an early trial were not recalled in a subsequent one. The early failure to recall items which were later recalled cannot, of course, be attributed to storage loss because it would not then be possible to recover them at all. These items, therefore must have been available in memory but not accessible. An important aspect of Tulving's results is that although the actual words changed, the number of words recalled on each trial was nearly constant. This implies that, in some circumstances at least, there is a limit on the capacity of the retrieval process, i.e. only a certain number of items can be accessed on a particular trial.

The distinction between availability and accessibility is also strikingly illustrated by Tulving and Pearlstone's (1966) study which investigated the effects of providing cues at recall. In this study, subjects were presented with lists composed of words drawn from a number of taxonomic categories such as *furniture* and *fruit*. Items in each category were presented successively with each block of items being preceded by the category name. Essentially, the subjects were divided into two groups, one group being given the category names as cues at recall, the other group receiving no such assistance. The cued group recalled about twice as many words as did the non-cued group but this result was due to differences in the number of categories represented in the recall protocols and not the number of words recalled from each of those categories. Since both groups were treated identically up to the point of recall they should not have differed in the number of items available in memory. It seems, then, that the provision of cues must have affected accessibility and this view was confirmed by another recall test following the first, in which *both* groups were given the category cues. On that occasion the two groups differed very little in recall, this showing that the non-cued group did indeed have more information available than could be accessed on the first unaided recall test.

Encoding specificity hypothesis

Tulving and Osler (1968) took up the study of retrieval cueing from where Tulving and Pearlstone (1966) left off by investigating some of the circumstances in which cues are or are not effective. In the conditions which form the core of their experiment they presented 24 to-be-remembered (TBR) words, either alone (e.g. MUTTON) or paired with a weak associate (e.g. *fat*, MUTTON), telling the subjects that the accompanying words might be helpful in remembering the TBR words. Those subjects receiving the TBR words alone were tested either with free recall or cued with the weak associates. The other subjects, having the associates presented at the time of studying the TBR words, were tested with no cues, with the same cues (e.g. *fat*), or with different weak associates (e.g. *leg*). The results showed that recall was relatively good when the same cue, or no cue, was present *both* during encoding and at the retrieval, but performance was poor in those conditions where the encoding and test situations differed with respect to the cue. These results show that the effectiveness of a cue supplied at retrieval depends critically on the circumstances of encoding. Tulving and Osler concluded that 'specific retrieval cues facilitate recall if and only if the information about them and about their relation to the to-be-remembered word is stirred at the same time as the information about the membership of the to-be-remembered word in a given list' (Tulving and Osler, 1968, p. 593). This hypothesis, known as the *encoding specificity hypothesis*, expresses the idea that information about a cue must be 'attached' to the TBR word at encoding if it is to facilitate retrieval.

Of course, the cues such as *leg* and *fat* which are explicitly referred to in the Tulving and Osler study are only part of the cognitive and environmental contexts in which encoding and retrieval take place. If other aspects of the context are encoded with TBR words they, too, should act as retrieval cues and changing the context between encoding and test should remove them and so lead to a decrement in performance. This has been shown to happen when performance of subjects who have learned material in one room and are tested in another room is compared with performance of subjects who have experienced no such change of room (Greenspoon and Ranyard, 1957; see, too, Smith, Glenberg and Bjork, 1978). Also, Godden and Baddeley (1975) have demonstrated decrements in the memory performance of divers who, having learned material in one context (e.g. on land) are tested in another (e.g. underwater). Other changes in the context between learning and test which lead to decrements in remembering include changes in 'internal states' brought about by manipulation of drugs (e.g. Eich, 1977) or by induced emotional mood (e.g. Bower, 1981).

The encoding specificity hypothesis emphasizes the dependence of remembering on the relation between encoding and retrieval circumstances. Because of this it plays an important part in Tulving's views on recognition and recall which are dealt with later in this chapter. Further discussion of the hypothesis is left until then.

Intra-list cues

As we have noted, Tulving and Osler (1968) showed that the effects of supplying retrieval cues are not always beneficial. Another situation in which detrimental effects of cueing have been found is where some of the to-be-remembered items themselves are given as cues for the recall of the remainder. Where categorized lists are used it would be expected that supplying one item from a category would act as a cue for the category as a whole in much the same way as the category name and there is evidence that this is so (Hudson and Austin, 1970). But, there is often another, surprising, consequence of cueing with list items, as Slamecka (1968) found. In one of his experiments the provision of cues in the form of one or more words from each category represented in the list *impaired* recall of the remaining words relative to a group receiving no such cues. This result is surprising if, as seems reasonable, it is assumed that subjects utilize between-word associations when encoding. In that case, intra-list cues should facilitate recall by cueing other words encoded with them. And, of course, there are fewer items left to be recalled. Subsequent research has confirmed and extended Slamecka's finding. It is now known that the greater the number of cues provided from the list (intra-list cues) the lower is the probability of recalling the remaining items (e.g. Rundus, 1973), and this relationship also holds when the cues are extra-list items, i.e. are drawn from a category in the list but were not presented for learning (Watkins, 1975). This inhibitory effect occurs when the to-be-recalled list consists of randomly selected words and is even found in recall from semantic memory. This latter phenomenon was first reported by Brown (1968) who asked English subjects to recall the names of the English counties, giving one group half of them and requesting recall of the remainder. When recall of the remaining items was compared with recall of the same items by a second group who received no names it was found that the 'cues' had inhibited recall.

The inhibitory effect of intra-list cueing is not well understood. It has been suggested that the provision of cues merely produces non-specific interference or simply delays recall. But such artifactual accounts of the phenomena have been dismissed on a number of grounds which include the finding by Mueller and Watkins (1977). They presented subjects with categorized lists and cued recall either with category names alone, category names each accompanied by an intra-list cue from that category, or category names each accompanied by an intra-list cue from another category. Thus, any *general* effects of the intra-list cues should be equally evident for the two types of cue. But the same-category cues produced inhibition while the different-category cues did not.

Several prominent accounts of inhibition in intra-list cues rely, in one way or another, on the influential notion that the retrieval system has a limited capacity. We have already encountered this notion in connection with Tulving's (1967) finding that although different words were recalled on successive attempts to recall a list which was presented only once, the number of words retrieved on each trial remained remarkably stable. Other data which may be interpreted as showing retrieval limitations come from situations in which subjects are required to generate exemplars from a semantic category. Generally, subjects fail to produce all the exemplars they have knowledge of (Bousfield and Sedgewick, 1944). Indeed, it has been suggested that the proportion of items available in semantic memory which are retrieved in such a generation task may be as low as 20 per cent (Lazar and Buschke, 1972), but this figure depends on the way in which the number of available items is assessed.

According to Shiffrin (1970) *output interference* contributes to the limitations of retrieval capacity. Briefly, according to Shiffrin's model the to-be-remembered items, whether they be a set of items presented in a list or a category held in semantic memory, form a distinct 'pool' in memory. Retrieval takes place by sampling the items in the pool, the probability of drawing a particular item depending on the 'strength' with which it is connected to the retrieval cue (category name, label of subjective chunk, etc.). The strength of such connections is presumed to depend on degree of learning and strength of linguistic associations, amongst other things. If the item sampled from the pool has not been retrieved before, it is emitted as a response, otherwise it is withheld. Either way it is replaced in the pool. In this manner there comes a point where the probability of retrieving a hitherto unrecalled item becomes extremely small and the subject decides to discontinue the sampling. This brief account is an extremely simplistic summary of a complex model in which specific consideration is given to details such as the rules used to determine the order in which items are sampled and when sampling should be terminated. However, it is now possible to appreciate how, according to the model, accomplished retrieval actually inhibits the access to available but hitherto unretrieved items.

It is easy to see how Shiffrin's model can account for the inhibitory effects of intra-list cues. It is only necessary to assume that presentation of such cues places them in the pool of items in memory as if they had been retrieved and this, in turn, reduces the probability of retrieving the remaining items. The model accounts for the fall in recall of the remaining items with increasing number of cues by the corresponding decrease in the *proportion* of items in the pool which have not been 'retrieved'.

Watkins (e.g. 1979) has adopted an explanation of intra-list cueing effects based on what he terms the *cue-overload* theory. This involves the ideas that recall is always mediated by cues of one sort or another, and that there is a limit to the mediating capacity of each cue. Thus, as each cue is 'loaded up' with more items there is a fall in the probability of retrieving any particular item nested under it. Intra-list and extra-list cues are considered as additional items which become subsumed under the effective retrieval cues of category names, subjective chunk, or whatever. While there is some common ground between this theory and that of Shiffrin, Watkins does not attempt to specify particular retrieval mechanisms and places little emphasis on output interference. Instead, he sees cue-overload theory as organizing under a simple principle a wide range of experimental phenomena including the build-up of and release from proactive inhibition, and the relation between list length and the probability of recall, in addition to intra-list and extra-list cueing. This theory avoids some of the problems associated with Shiffrin's rather mechanistic sampling device and of other models based more or less directly on it, but seems to lose little in explanatory power (see Roediger and Neely, 1982 for discussion of these models).

So far in this chapter we have considered some of the situations in which the provision of cues is beneficial or detrimental to the retrieval of available information. We have not, however, included consideration of data from recognition tests. It is possible to argue that these tests involve the most specific retrieval cues of all, namely, copies of the to-be-remembered items, and so remove any problems of gaining access to information in memory. Because of this, the comparison of recall and recognition performances has provided the basis for much theoretical controversy. It is to this area of controversy that we now turn.

Recall and recognition

Consider a subject who is attempting to recall a list of words which he knows, either from cues held in memory or supplied by the experimenter, contained some animal names. A possible strategy of retrieval would be to generate animal names from semantic memory and use the resulting items as responses. However, the number of intrusions which occur in both free and cued recall is generally small, i.e. subjects respond with few words which were not presented in the list. This suggests that if our subject used category names to generate category exemplars from semantic memory they would not be given as responses willy nilly. There must be some editing device which withholds exemplars so generated which were not presented in the list.

The idea that recall consists of a generation process in which likely responses are retrieved from memory and passed on to a recognition process for editing is a feature of several models of recall, exemplified by those of Kintsch (1970), and Anderson and Bower (1972). Tulving (1976) is opposed to this view. He maintains that the division of memory processes into those of generating and editing is unwarranted. Instead, he maintains that the memory system only retrieves what it is instructed to retrieve and that, basically, recall and recognition processes differ only in the efficiency of the retrieval cues given to subjects. These three models are selected for discussion now to highlight some of the theoretical issues concerning retrieval.

Kintsch's two-stage model

Kintsch (1970) resurrected a model suggested by William James in 1890. According to this model recall consists of two *successive* stages. The first consists of a generation process which generates words from semantic memory. The second stage consists of a *recognition* process which edits words generated at the first stage by testing if they are recognizable as list members. Importantly, the model postulates that the recognition *process* in recall is identical to the process operating in a recognition *test*.

Kintsch (1974) has revised his ideas but it is his original

model which will concern us here. In it he maintains that the recognition process involves a decision based on the *familiarity* of a word's memory trace. The level of familiarity is assumed to depend on the frequency and duration with which the word has been experienced and how recently. Although Kintsch is not definite about the nature of *familiarity* the notion has an intuitive appeal about it. Figure 6.1 should help to explain the model further.

When a word is presented for study (e.g. *cow*) it has the familiarity of its representation in semantic memory incremented (shown by the bar on top). Thus, episodic information is assumed to be imposed on semantic information. When the word is presented in a recognition test (Figure 6.1(a)) direct *access* is gained to its representation in semantic memory and the familiarity information is automatically made available to the recognition process which

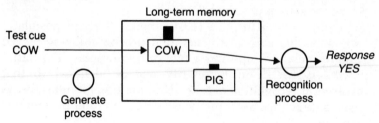

(a) Recognition test

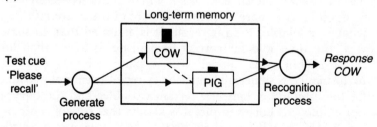

(b) Recall test

Figure 6.1: *A representation of recall and recognition processes*

assesses whether it is sufficient to indicate a target word rather than a distractor.

In free recall (Figure 6.1(b)) the item is not presented as a test cue so some other means of accessing its memory representation is necessary. Kintsch achieves this by the theoretical device of 'tagging' the semantic relationships between words in the list thus imposing a second type of episodic information on semantic memory. The notion of tagging is an important aspect of the model and by it Kintsch acknowledges the categorical associative and subjective organization which subjects employ when studying lists in anticipation of free recall. For example, if a number of *domestic animals* are in the list this relationship will be tagged. At recall, all words linked by this relationship are generated as candidates to be considered by the recognition process. Importantly, if *domestic animals* is tagged during encoding of the list then *all* domestic animals will be passed on to the recognition process. However, the number of candidates which are generated will be reduced if more specific tagging is undertaken, say, *farmyard animals*.

In summary, Kintsch's (1970) model of recall postulates two successive stages, a generation process utilizing tagged semantic relationships and a recognition process. This latter process is based on familiarity and is identical to that involved in recognition *tests* in which the test stimulus always ensures direct access to the item's representation in semantic memory.

Evidence for the two-stage model

The two-stage model was resurrected at a time when its main rival was the *threshold model*. This maintains merely that recognition is a more sensitive measure of trace strength (i.e. what is available) than is recall. It is assumed that, in some way, the threshold for correct recognition is lower than for recall. While this model will explain why recognition performance is generally superior to recall it cannot account for the interaction between certain variables and the type of test employed. For example, it is known that lists of common words are usually recalled better than uncommon words while recognition is usually superior for uncommon words.

The threshold model cannot deal with this interaction: if common words are better recalled they should also be better recognized. The two-stage model is able to account for these findings by assuming that the generation process is more effective for common words but the recognition *process* in both recall and recognition *tests* is superior for uncommon words (see Gregg, 1976).

There are a number of other interactions which are consistent with the two-stage model, including the one demonstrated by Bruce and Fagan (1970). They found that recall was superior for categorized lists of words relative to unrelated lists whereas recognition was not affected by the type of list. Presumably the list organization facilitated the generation process of recall but did not influence the recognition process. McCormack (1972) gives a full review of this and other such interactions which support the two-stage model.

Finally, the support for the two-stage model provided by Bahrick (1970) deserves mention. Basically he obtained free recall of word lists and then cued those words which were not recalled. The cues had been shown to elicit the list words with varying probabilities in free association tests carried out on another group of subjects. A third group was given a recognition test for the list words. Bahrick argued that the two-stage model predicts that the cues should generate target items as candidates for recall with probabilities indicated by the free association test, and these should then be submitted to the same process as in the recognition test. Thus, the probability of cued recall of a given word should be: probability (cue elicits word in association test) × probability (word is recognized). His findings were in line with this prediction.

Anderson and Bower's contextual model

Anderson and Bower's model of recall, like that of Kintsch, has independent and successive 'generate' and 'recognize' processes. The first process is based on marked semantic relationships, the marking being equivalent to Kintsch's tagging. The recognition process, however, is not based on the notion of 'familiarity' because this is easily shown to be incapable of accounting for many memory phenomena. For example, subjects can often correctly decide whether a test item has been presented once only and recently in a list, or twice much earlier in the list. Clearly, any crude notion of 'familiarity' would be hard-pressed to account for these findings. Therefore, its usefulness seems limited to tests in which subjects must decide if the last time they encountered the test word was more recently (during the experiment), or less recently (before the experiment began).

According to Anderson and Bower's model, information about *contextual elements* provides the basis for recognition decisions about the circumstances in which items were encountered. Essentially, representations of words in semantic memory are 'linked' to those elements which represent not only the physical aspects of a word's presentation but details of the environment, and the subject's emotional state, for example. In this way the model accounts not only for the ability to decide if the test word appeared in the experimental context, but how many times it appeared and, if several lists have been presented, which one the word appeared in. This account of Anderson and Bower's model does not do justice to its complexity. Even so, it has a more developed counterpart (Anderson and Bower, 1973). However, it is worth explaining that although Anderson and Bower have elaborated the notion of 'familiarity' (and Kintsch (1974) has done likewise), the model possesses the generic features of the two-stage model of recall, namely:

(1) In recognition automatic access is gained to the list item's representation in semantic memory.
(2) In recall, access is gained via marked semantic pathways.
(3) Recall consists of successive generation and recognition stages.

Tulving has attacked each of these features and we shall discuss the bases of his objections. First, however, it will be helpful if Tulving's alternative approach to recall and recognition is described.

Tulving's episodic ecphory theory

Tulving (e.g. 1976) rejects the view that recall consists of successive and independent generate and recognize stages. He also rejects the idea that the semantic memory system is tagged or marked, and so used in the generation of candidates for recall. Instead, he sees both recall and recognition as involving retrieval of information *only* from episodic memory, but differing in the type of information carried by the cues given at test. That is, recall and recognition are not fundamentally different. Tulving's theory will be considered in general terms before dealing with the relevant experimental evidence.

As we learned in Chapter 1 Tulving views the episodic memory system as quite separate from semantic memory. Whereas semantic memory contains information about word-meaning and linguistic rules, episodic memory contains a record of the way episodes are experienced. Thus, Tulving agrees with those who maintain that *familiarity* or any such simplistic notion is not adequate to represent what is stored in memory about the occurrence of a word in a list. But, unlike Kintsch, and Anderson and Bower, Tulving insists that this information is not 'attached' to existing word representations in semantic memory, but is contained in a separate system. This is not to say that subjects do not utilize the semantic properties of items to facilitate memory performance by engaging in the encoding activities mentioned in Chapter 5. However, in Tulving's view these activities based on semantic information influence performance because they form part of the episode itself and hence affect the record left in episodic memory (the reader may wish to refer back to the outline of Craik and Jacoby's courtroom analogy given in Chapter 5).

Clearly, if the semantic memory networks are not tagged or marked by episodic information they cannot be used to generate likely candidates for recall. How then is retrieval achieved in Tulving's model? It is assumed that the cues provided, such as 'recall', carry with them implications of something like 'the list of words presented in this room one minute ago'. The temporal and contextual information implicit in a cue is used to match it with part of the episodic trace. This matching constitutes the *ecphoric process* and a successful match results in *ecphory*. This term is borrowed from Semon (1909) who used it to refer to the 'activation of the latent engram'. The products of the ecphoric process are used to produce conscious memory of the original event and this, in turn, determines the overt response. Tulving does not make it clear exactly how the matching of the cue information and the episodic trace takes place but he has suggested that some form of pattern completion is involved. Alternatively, the cue may be seen to broadcast a signal which produces resonance in matching parts of the episodic trace (see, e.g., Lockhart *et al.*, 1976). One consequence of this theoretical approach is 'that the system never retrieves anything "incorrectly"' (Tulving, 1976, page 65). In other words, the episodic memory system only gains access to what it is directed towards and will retrieve it provided it is available. Thus, Tulving is able to dispense with the independent and successive stages of generation and recognition. The cues give direct access to episodic memory, so there is no need to generate candidates from semantic memory, and since the cues give access to only what they specify there is no need for editing by a recognition process.

The next few sections deal with evidence relevant to Tulving's model and which forms the basis of his attack on the generate-recognize models of recall.

Context effects in recognition
According to generate-recognize models the test item in recognition gives automatic access to the familiarity value, or to contextual information attached to its representation in semantic memory. The episodic trace model, in contrast, maintains that the test item is effective only to the extent that it re-establishes the encoding context and thereby gains access to the appropriate part of episodic memory. Hence, changing the context in which an item is encoded and tested should have no effect on recognition according to generate-recognize models but should do so according to episodic ecphory theory.

Evidence of context effects in recognition has been found by a number of investigators. Light and Carter-Sobell

(1970), for example, presented each to-be-remembered noun with an adjective which specified one of its several meanings, e.g. *strawberry* JAM, or *traffic* JAM. At recognition the TBR words were presented alone, with the same adjective, or with an adjective indicating another meaning. These conditions gave scores of about 43 per cent, 60 per cent, and 27 per cent respectively. Apparently then in recognition access to available information is not guaranteed as the generate-recognize models presume.

One way in which the generate-recognize models can possibly accommodate context effects is to insist that each meaning of a homographic word such as JAM has a separate representation in memory. The direct access assumption may then be maintained by assuming further that changes in context direct the recognition process to the inappropriate location. Anderson and Bower (1974) and Martin (1975), amongst others, have adopted this view. While this approach rescues the direct access assumption with respect to homographs it cannot account for the effects of changing the test context obtained with non-homographs by Tulving and Thomson (1971) nor indeed, with pictures of *faces* (Watkins, Ho and Tulving, 1976)! A similar problem is posed by further data from the study of Light and Carter-Sobell (1970) mentioned above. They showed that presenting JAM for study with *strawberry* and testing in conjunction with *apricot* gave lower performance than using *strawberry* on both occasions. To explain this, the generate-recognize models must accept that different *senses* of the same word have separate locations in semantic memory. At this point the models come close to admitting that retrieval cues, i.e. the test items, must reinstate the original encoding context if they are to be effective. This, of course, is more in line with episodic ecphory theory than the original two-stage model.

Failure to recognize recallable words

Another prediction of the generate-recognize models which has been subjected to experimental test is that recallable words should also be recognizable. In principle, if recall performance depends on the functioning of both generation and recognition processes, it cannot exceed recognition performance which relies on the second process only. Tulving and Thomson (1973) tested this prediction and obtained considerable amounts of *recognition failure*, that is, failure to recognize words which could later be recalled. Generally, their procedure was:

(1)   Presentation of TBR words, each with a weak associate (e.g. *ground* – COLD).
(2)   Subjects required to generate 4 free associations to a strong associate of each TBR word (e.g. *hot*). The intention of this was to mimic the assumed generation of TBR words by semantic cues in recall.
(3)   Subjects then indicated which of their associative responses were TBR words.
(4)   The original cues were supplied (e.g. *ground*) and cued recall of TBR words assessed.

In one experiment 66 per cent of the TBR words were generated at stage 2. Of these, 53.5 per cent were recognized at stage 3, this score being uncorrected for guessing. The cued recall score at stage 4, however, was 61 per cent and, crucially, a large proportion of these words had *not* been recognized earlier.

Tulving and Thomson claimed that their demonstration of recognition failure is quite inconsistent with the generate-recognize model, but is this so? Santa and Lamwers (1974, 1976) have challenged this conclusion on both logical and methodological grounds. They argue that recognition failure can be explained by two-stage models if it is at all possible that the task faced by the recognition *process* is more difficult in the recognition *phase* of the experiment than in the recall phase. It is possible, for example, that the distractors in the recognition test may have been more difficult to discriminate from TBR words than those generated internally in recall. It is also possible that the cued recall performance benefited from being preceded by the recognition test or the free association test.

These objections are partly, if not entirely, met by the fact that recognition failure has occurred in a large number of studies, including some which have omitted the free association phase and excluded difficult, semantically related distractors in the recognition test. In addition there is evidence that cued recall scores are unaffected by whether TBR words are included in the recognition test or not, although Vining and Nelson (1978) have shown this is not necessarily so. However, the difficulty of determining the comparability of the assumed recognition *stage* in recall and recognition *tests* makes it difficult to reject generate-recognize models merely on the grounds of recognition failure. But, Tulving has recently posed a new challenge to such models based on this very phenomenon and concerning the *recognition failure function*.

Flexser and Tulving (1978) considered the data from 33 experiments possessing the basic elements of the Tulving and Thomson paradigm and conducted by a number of experimenters. They plotted the amount of recognition failure against the recognition test scores and found a lawful relationship between them. This relationship is depicted by curve *a* in Figure 6.2, where, following Flexser and Tulving, the probability of recognizing recallable words (the complement of recognition failure) is represented on the ordinate.

Generate-recognize models maintain that recall is dependent on successful recognition, hence the probability of recognizing recallable words should be always unity (line *b*). If, however, recall does not depend on whether an item is recognized in a recognition *test*, the data will fall on the diagonal (line *c*). Nearly all the data points from the various studies fell close to line *a*!

The challenge Flexser and Tulving present to the two-stage notion is to account not only for the deviation of the data from line *b*, but for the *particular* shape of curve *a*. They developed a mathematical model based on episodic trace theory and this accounts for the data very well. It is not necessary to go into details here but in essence they maintain that recognition failure occurs because the cues employed in the cued recall phase of the Tulving and Thomson paradigm have been specifically encoded with the TBR words at presentation. Therefore they give better access to the episodic trace than the TBR words when presented alone in recognition. The degree of dependence of recognition failure

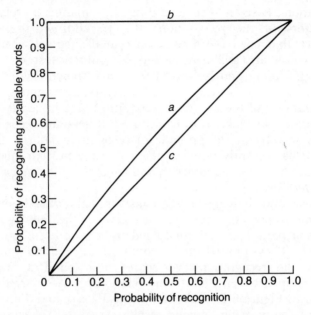

Figure 6.2:   *Recognition failure function: see text for explanation of lines a, b and c (adapted from Flexser and Tulving, 1978)*

on the level of recognition performance (reflected in the shape of curve *a*) is assumed to reflect the extent to which the retrieval context in recall and recognition gives access to the same information in episodic memory. Thus, recognition failure depends on the extent to which the context is changed between study and test for recognition relative to cued recall.

Strong associative cues
The encoding specificity hypothesis (introduced in an earlier section of this chapter) is an essential element of Tulving's episodic ecphory theory: it is only by incorporating cues into the episodic trace at encoding that they can provide access to a particular part of the trace in future. Thus, the hypothesis predicts that even cues which strongly elicit to-be-remembered (TBR) words in verbal association tests will not be effective if they were not encoded as part of the presentation episode. Indeed, in these circumstances such

cues should have detrimental effects on performance by directing retrieval to the wrong part of the episodic trace. In contrast, the generate-recognize models predict that strong associates of the TBR words will facilitate the generation of items from semantic memory even though they were not present during study. Thomson and Tulving (1970) tested these predictions in an extension of the Tulving and Osler (1968) study referred to earlier. Lists of TBR words were presented to one group of subjects without any accompanying associates (e.g. BLACK), to another group accompanied by weak associates (e.g. *train*, BLACK), and to a third group with strong associates (e.g. *white*, BLACK). At recall each group was divided into three sub-groups and required to *free* recall the TBR words, recall them cued with the weak associates, or recall them cued with the strong associates. The results are shown in Table 6.1.

Table 6.1

| Presentation condition | Number of items recalled | | |
	No cues	Cues at recall Weak associates	Strong associates
No associates	14.1	11.1	19.0
Weak associates	10.7˙	15.7	13.9
Strong associates	12.2	9.2	20.2

(from Thomson and Tulving, 1970)

The generate-recognize models predict that performance will be best under strong associative cueing, and worst when no cues are provided (even weak associates should give some benefit to the generation process). Clearly the results shown in Table 6.1 disconfirm this prediction. Instead, they are much more in keeping with the encoding specificity hypothesis because, with the exception of the no associate-strong associate condition, highest performance is obtained when the cues present at encoding and retrieval correspond. But how can the encoding specificity hypothesis, and hence the

episodic trace theory, explain the familiarity effect of strong
associates at test when they were not presented at encoding?
Although rather *post hoc*, this can be done by maintaining
that when no study cues are present encoding is uncon-
strained and strong associates are elicited by the TBR words
and so form part of the encoding context. Presumably, when
weak cues are present at study encoding is directed away
from these apparently extrinsic influences. Other experiments reported by Thomson and Tulving support this
interpretation. Nevertheless, Santa and Lamwers (1974,
1976), among others, have criticized this account of these
cueing effects. Their criticisms carry weight and are
considered in the next section along with other difficulties for
the encoding specificity hypothesis and hence for the episodic
ecphory theory.

Further views on retrieval

Tulving has provided an extremely forceful challenge to the
generate-recognize conceptualization of recall by demonstrating situations in which its basic tenets are contradicted. He
has shown that direct access to the item in memory is not
assured by a recognition probe, that items which are
recallable are not necessarily recognized, and that words
which generate targets with high probability in tests
concerned with semantic relationships do not always act as
effective retrieval cues in tests of episodic memory.

Powerful though Tulving's attack has been, his own
episodic ecophory theory has not escaped criticism. We have
already noted that any criticism of generate-recognize models
inherent in the principle of recognition failure of recallable
words is weakened by the possibility that the paradigms
employed to produce the phenomenon do not equate the
difficulty of the recognition *processes* in recall and recognition
tests. Furthermore, there is evidence that recognition failure
of recallable words is minimal when items are presented
singly as in the usual free recall paradigm (Watkins and
Todres, 1978). Hence it is conceivable that in this situation,
at least, the generate-recognize model may be appropriate

(as, indeed, Bahrick's study discussed earlier in conjunction with Kintsch's model suggests). The possibility that in some circumstances list items can be generated by *extrinsic* cues (not encoded at presentation of to-be-remembered items) is a very real one, therefore. While this does not necessarily damage Tulving's interpretation of the effects of differences in encoding and retrieval contexts, it does suggest that the episodic ecphory theory should be looked at in a wider perspective. This issue, which Tulving has always seen as a necessary consideration, forms the substance of this part of the chapter.

How many retrieval routes?
As we have noted above the generic generate-recognize model of recall, exemplified by the models of Kintsch and of Anderson and Bower, seem to have difficulty in dealing with most aspects of the Thomson and Tulving results. In contrast, the encoding specificity hypothesis, which forms a major plank of the episodic ecphory theory, gives a good account of the data. Nevertheless, the high level of performance in the no associate-strong associate condition cannot be dismissed lightly because the argument that the strong associates were elicited 'spontaneously' during encoding is *post hoc* and unverifiable. As such it represents a move away from a strong and testable hypothesis. It is interesting, therefore, that Tulving made a deliberate move towards a broader, but consequently weaker, position with the enunciation of the encoding specificity *principle*. This has been expressed in various terms but the form used by Wiseman and Tulving (1976) makes it clear:

> A to-be-remembered (TBR) item is encoded with respect to the context in which it is studied, producing a unique trace which incorporates information from both target and context. For the TBR item to be retrieved, the cue information must appropriately match the trace of the item-in-context. (page 349)

Essentially, the principle maintains that if an item *was* recalled in response to a cue then the cue information matched the trace. But if recall was not successful, then the cue information did not match the trace. This is a reasonable idea but it cannot be tested experimentally. In contrast, the encoding specificity *hypothesis* (stated on page 161) maintains that the circumstances of encoding influence the effectiveness of cues supplied at recall, in a specified manner. Since the encoding and retrieval circumstances can be manipulated and the consequent changes in recall observed, the *hypothesis* is capable of experimental test.

Returning now to Thomson and Tulving's results and the encoding specificity hypothesis, is it really true that subjects are unable to utilize retrieval cues that were not encoded at learning? Santa and Lamwers (1974) expressed the belief that subjects can do so and that Thomson and Tulving's results were the product of the peculiar experimental circumstances employed. They conducted their own study and found that subjects who were informed that the cues had been changed from weak to strong associates recalled nearly twice as many words as did subjects who were uninformed about the change. Thus, it is possible that Thomson and Tulving's subjects who were changed from weak to strong cues did badly relative to the other groups receiving strong cues at retrieval for one of two reasons both of which are consistent with the generate-recognize models. Either they knew the cues had been changed but not how, so they did not use them; or they assumed the cues had not been changed and so neglected words which were strong associates of them.

The general conclusion which follows from Santa and Lamwers' findings is that subjects can effectively use unencoded semantic relationships to guide retrieval provided they are not deceived into using unhelpful strategies. The effectiveness of such unencoded, or *extrinsic*, cues is neatly demonstrated in an ingenious experiment by Jones (1982). His subjects were shown a list of what appeared to be unrelated cue-target pairs (e.g. sleep–ORANGE) and then given cued recall. Before recall, though, some subjects were told that reversing the letters of each cue word would give a new cue related to the target (e.g. *sleep* gives *peels*). Such cues of course, were not encoded at presentation and any advantage these subjects might have would suggest the use of an 'indirect' retrieval route through semantic memory, this being equivalent to the generate stage of Kintsch's original two-stage model. In fact Jones found that the informed subjects recalled nearly three times as many target words as the uninformed subjects!

Taking the various findings we have discussed here it seems best to adopt a compromise view of retrieval and allow *at least* two routes. One route is the direct route advocated by Tulving in which encoded cues give direct access to the corresponding place on the episodic record – the process of ecphory. The other route is via the semantic network, this being equivalent to the generate stage of the generate-recognize models of recall.

Recollection

'Who was at the party you went to last week?' A little introspection by the reader may well suggest that when people go about answering questions such as this there is initially an attempt to mentally reinstate the context of the party. This may involve the general 'atmosphere', e.g. whether it was a formal or carefree situation, and this in turn might provoke a recall of conversations or activities together with the participants. In addition, the temporal course of the evening may act as a framework for remembering particular events and the people involved in them. Possibly, also, imagining each room and searching for faces therein may be undertaken. Whatever the methods employed there may well be a definiteness about remembering – most, if not all, of the retrieved characters may seem to 'belong' to the party context or may lead to the recall of further details in such a way as to confirm their belonging. For example, having recently been asked the above question the author was able to reason thus about one person: 'I know John was there because I saw him talking to Bill and I remember thinking at the time that they must be talking about locusts – they are the only two people I know who are remotely interested in locusts!'

Williams and Hollan (1981) were interested in the way individuals go about the task of remembering when asked questions such as the one above and they investigated it by asking subjects to recall the names of their classmates of up to 20 years ago. They also asked the subjects to record their strategies during the attempts. The protocols, which were generally in accord with what is suggested above might happen when asked who was present at the party, revealed what the authors called the *retrieval cycle*. First, there was an attempt to mentally recapture the temporal and geographical *context* of the schooldays. Second, a *search* for children and their names was carried out by, for example, examining images of classrooms, working around the neighbourhood identifying children in particular houses, or examining groups of children who had taken part in common activities. Sometimes the children and their names would seem to leap out of memory effortlessly while others would need considerable effort to retrieve them, requiring one approach then another. During the third stage of the cycle the retrieved information was *verified* by one or more means including judging whether it cued other information which could, in turn, be verified.

Baddeley (1982a) recounts that on one occasion when recalling the name of an acquaintance, he used a complex sequence of cognitive operations which broadly conforms with Williams and Hollan's retrieval cycle. In that paper and elsewhere (e.g. 1982b), Baddeley uses the term *recollection* to refer to the *active*, conscious components of remembering. He sees recollection as providing the basis for a broad framework to assist in understanding a wide range of recall and recognition phenomena. The emphasis which conscious memory processes receive in Baddeley's framework stands in contrast to the paucity of it in the generate-recognize models we have discussed here, and the complete lack of it in the episodic ecphory theory. Indeed, Baddeley (1982b) notes that it is interesting that Tulving, who is one of the strongest advocates of the view that *learning* depends on active organization by the subject, has emphasized an essentially passive interpretation of retrieval. However, to be fair, it must be noted that all these models do not exclude conscious aspects of remembering (see, e.g., Tulving, 1976), but nor do they deal with them explicitly. In contrast, Baddeley insists there is a need to give specific consideration to the possibility that subjects consciously generate information associated with the encoding context in the hope of encountering effective retrieval cues for the required items. According to this line of thinking it is not sufficient merely to envisage some *automatic* search taking place along a predetermined route initiated by a cue such as 'last list'. Also, it must be accepted that 'extrinsic' cues (see the last section) can be effective no matter whether they are provided by the experimenter or generated internally by the subject. Furthermore, as we noted in Chapter 1, metamemory skills such as memory monitoring are important aspects of retrieval. Subjects can often decide when further efforts at recall will be productive and this may well apply to individual retrieval routes: possibly they can judge if a particular route will prove fruitful, or if some other route should be explored.

In addition to the conscious generation of retrieval cues Baddeley also includes within the concept of recollection the process of evaluating any potential responses the subject may become aware of. This position, of course, is in stark contrast to the episodic ecphory model which explicitly denies that any editing process at all is required in recall. Furthermore, the concept of recollection encourages a flexible view of memory processes and so allows decisions concerning candidates for response (no matter how they reach consciousness) to draw on a wide range of cognitive skills and to utilize various types of information. Thus, the basis of a decision may vary according to the circumstances of encoding and the nature of the test. And there is no reason why the decision processes involved in recall and recognition tests should have any fixed relationship with each other. Accordingly, it is possible to agree with G. Mandler (1980) that items may be recognized as 'targets' because they 'lead back' to the encoding context or because they merely seem 'familiar'. Interestingly, Mandler suggested that a feeling of familiarity may result from the priming of perceptual or other processes by the initial presentation: subjects can be aware that 'old' items are easier to perceive or comprehend than they would be if they had not been presented recently. A rather different sort of effortful decision-making was

indicated by Santa and Lamwers (1974) when criticizing
Thomson and Tulving's study of encoding specificity.
Essentially, they were expressing the belief that subjects were
capable of complex and deliberate reasoning about retrieved
items based on how they thought the experimenter had
manipulated the task. And finally, Brown, Lewis and Monk
(1977) proposed that subjects are capable of consciously
assessing what they term 'negative recognition'. That is, they
are able to reason, 'This word is so unusual that if it had
been presented in the list I would definitely remember it.'

Tulving (see, e.g., 1982) has now accepted the need to
incorporate the concept of recollection into his model of
recall and recognition. His *synergistic ecphory model of retrieval*,
like his earlier *episodic ecphory model*, insists that retrieval is
achieved by ecphory. The inclusion of *synergistic* in the name
of this model serves to emphasize that ecphory results from
the conjunction of information in the cue and information in
the episodic trace. The results of this conjunction are referred
to as *ecphoric information* (the reader who goes to the original
sources should note that redefinition of some terms occurs
between Tulving's 1976 paper and his 1982 paper). In
contrast to the earlier model there is now an emphasis on
passing ecphoric information on to *recollective experience*. This
recollective experience is then *converted* into overt behaviour.
Tulving continues to maintain that the ecphoric process is
not open to conscious experience – it is automatic. But the
involvement of recollective experience in the *conversion* of
ecphoric information allows the overt responses to reflect the
subject's knowledge of the task and other aspects of decision-
making discussed above.

Tulving still proposes that recall and recognition are
identical with respect to ecphory, but they differ with respect
to the conversion of ecphoric information and recollective
experience into memory performance. Thus, the earlier
insistence that recall and recognition are fundamentally
identical has been abandoned. It is now accepted that recall
and recognition tests make different demands so that the
episodic information may be adequate for one but not for the
other. For example, the *conversion threshold*, that is, the
minimum amount of ecphoric information, for a correct

recognition judgment may be lower than the conversion threshold for recalling the name of the target. This may well appear to be the old threshold model of recall and recognition resurrected after its death at the hands of generate-recognize models, but this is not so. Tulving points out that his conversion threshold refers to the adequate level of *ecphoric* information, not of *trace* information. The difference is crucial because the former takes account of the cue-trace relationship, the latter does not.

Summary

This chapter has emphasized the importance of retrieval processes in remembering. The successful use of particular retrieval cues where other cues have failed provides the basis for the distinction between availability and accessibility of information in memory. However, the provision of cues may inhibit rather than facilitate retrieval and two situations in which this occurs were discussed early in the chapter. The inhibiting effect of intra-list cues on the remaining list items has been discussed in terms of cue overload and output interference and these, in turn, may be seen as expressions of the retrieval system's limited capacity. The provision of cues at retrieval may also inhibit performance when those cues were not present at encoding. This situation forms the basis of the encoding specificity hypothesis which is important to Tulving's episodic ecphory theory.

Tulving's attack on the generic generate-recognize model has been impressive but the outcome is not definite. Certainly, *in principle*, these models have great difficulty accounting for context effects in recognition, for failures of strong associative cues to facilitate recall, and for failures to recognize recallable words. However, defenders of generate-recognize models, together with other critics of episodic ecphory theory, may point to possible artifactual sources of these three phenomena. Nevertheless, despite apparent constraints on the generality of the encoding specificity hypothesis on which it largely depends, the episodic ecphory theory has some distinct advantages. It allows all aspects of the experience associated with an episode to be incorporated in the memory trace; it insists that episodic memory is independent of semantic memory and so is able to deal with context effects in recognition with non-verbal items such as faces; and it takes account of the prevailing context of both the encoding and retrieval processes. However, this theory admits no flexibility in retrieval strategies and recent views involving the concept of recollection have served to highlight this deficiency. Tulving's incorporation of recollection into his synergistic ecphory model of retrieval is indicative of the growing belief that the strategic aspects of recognition and recall performance deserve a greater theoretical status than they have hitherto enjoyed.

7 Motivated forgetting

Several different accounts of forgetting have emerged in previous chapters. Notable, of course, is Tulving's encoding specificity principle, which is directed towards understanding the failure to acccess information available in memory. The cue-overload principle also stresses the distinction between forgetting due to loss of availability and forgetting due to loss of accessibility. Some of the work on iconic memory seems to imply that precategorical information decays, but may also be interfered with by visual masks. And the notion of interference has been useful in accounting for many other findings, including, for example, some of the effects of semantic or acoustic similarity on serial recall performance.

Forgetting is generally viewed as a shortcoming of the memory system because so much human activity involves accumulated knowledge; failure to remember often causes difficulties, therefore. However, forgetting appears to be a necessary requirement for the efficient working of certain aspects of memory. For example, the rehearsal buffer has a limited capacity and when it is full items must be displaced if other items are to be rehearsed. Indeed, it is important to realize that, whatever their merits and demerits, information processing models of memory depend on the notion of temporary stores from which information may be recoded into more permanent storage. And, of course, the temporary nature of such stores necessarily implies forgetting.

The need to forget one set of information in order to remember another set is vividly illustrated by Luria's (1968) account of the mnemonist S. This man could commit to memory large arrays or long sequences of words, numbers or letters and recall them accurately days or even years later. Unfortunately, so good was his retention that sometimes, during demonstrations of his skill, he would recall arrays from previous performances. Initially, he was unable to prevent these intrusions but eventually he found he could exert voluntary control over them. At a less exotic level the need to forget one thing in order to effectively remember another is illustrated by situations which may be conceptualized as requiring the *updating* of memory (Bjork, 1978; Bjork and Landauer, 1978). Suppose an acquaintance of yours, A, divorces his wife B and marries C. In order for you to subsequently recall that his current wife is C it is necessary to update the status attributed to the representations of B and C in memory. Thus, the forgetting involved here may be conceived of as removing the label 'A's wife' from B's representation.

Other situations where forgetting has obvious advantages occur when particular memories are painful or anxiety-provoking. In this chapter we shall consider *psychodynamic* forgetting, i.e. the active forgetting of memories of traumatic and embarrassing events, and of thoughts which conflict with the individual's moral principles. Also, we shall consider the ability of subjects to forget essentially neutral information when instructed to do so under hypnosis or in the waking state.

Psychopathological forgetting

By the end of the nineteenth century a number of influential clinicians including Freud in Austria, Janet in France and Prince in America had begun to take an interest in amnesias of psychopathological origin. In certain cases, patients exhibited an inability to remember specific events, or any events at all, occurring over a particular period of their lives. Often it became clear under examination that the forgotten material was distressing in some way and that it was not *unavailable* in memory because it would be accessible to awareness under special circumstances such as somnambulism or hypnosis. Freud (e.g. 1915/1957) believed such amnesias to be the result of a protective process which kept the distressing memories out of conscious awareness, and he referred to this process as *repression*. In contrast Janet (1904) viewed these amnesias as the result of a splitting up or dissociation of memories due to an inherent lack of the mental energy necessary to maintain the unity of personality. The differences between these two views will be discussed after some illustrations of psychodynamic forgetting have been considered.

Hysterical amnesia

Janet studied a number of patients suffering amnesia for events associated with specific traumas. One of these patients suffering what is termed *hysterical amnesia* was a girl Irene who had been greatly disturbed by her mother's slow and agonizing death. Subsequently she was unable to recall the events leading up to the death or the death itself. However, she began to experience 'fits' in which she would lose contact with reality and re-enact the events which took place when her mother died. The scene would also include an enactment of suicide by lying down in front of a train. Then after a while Irene would return to normal wakefulness and resume her life. Clearly, the memories associated with the traumatic event were available but were not normally consciously recallable. It was as though these memories were blocked from awareness, or dissociated from the remainder of the memory system in order to protect the conscious self against the pain which would be evoked by them.

Hysterical amnesia, as exhibited by Irene, must be distinguished from everyday techniques of forgetting which most people practise from time to time to avoid the recollection of embarrassing or painful memories. It is possible, for example, to deliberately direct attention away from such memories by thinking of something else. In these circumstances, however, the memory can be re-called at will. In hysterical amnesia this is not so, it being only under exceptional circumstances that recall is possible.

Fugues

Fugue states are so called because the individual takes flight from the reality with which he or she is unable to cope. Often in such a state the individual suffers complete amnesia for events of the past, wanders away from his usual surroundings, and adopts a new identity while being completely unaware of the changes which have taken place. During this period the person is often able to conduct himself in a reasonable manner, living what seems to others a normal existence. The durations of fugues vary considerably as the study by Abeles and Schilder (1935) showed. Of the 63 patients they studied, some 57 had fugues lasting less than one week with many of them lasting only one day.

The fugue state is dramatically illustrated by the case of Ansel Bourne reported by Hodgson (1892) and in which the fugue lasted for two months. Bourne disappeared from his home in Rhode Island, travelled to Pennsylvania, and kept a shop under the name of A.J. Brown. One morning, having gone to sleep as Brown, he woke up completely surprised at his surroundings, identifying himself as *Bourne* and having no recollection of his life as a storekeeper during the previous two months. Interestingly, William James (1890) was able to elicit memories of the fugue period under hypnotic suggestion but these memories were never accessible to the wakeful Bourne. Another striking case is that of the patient reported by Pratt (1977) whose fugue lasted for some 15 years. At the end of this period the patient, by his mother's deathbed, recalled his forgotten life with his wife and children.

There is little doubt that fugues usually occur in the absence of any identifiable organic damage and a high proportion of the precipitating situations involve family or financial crises. Thus, the function of the fugue state appears to be that it enables the individual to avoid stressful situations and memories by adopting a new role. As such, fugues may be a substitute for suicide (Stengel, 1941). Interestingly, however, the findings by Berrington, Liddell and Foulds (1956) that a high proportion of fugue patients have in the past suffered concussion or epileptic fits seems, at first sight, to indicate a physiological rather than a psychological origin. But, as Berrington *et al.* argue, it is possible that the amnesia which accompanies such trauma (see Chapter 8) suggests to the patient the strategy for coping with the later conflict situation when it occurs.

We have already noted that some patients emerge from the fugue state with the ability to recall earlier periods of their life. Others present themselves at hospitals or police stations with no recall of the past at all. Clearly, these latter patients are difficult to identify especially if they have been living alone, or very mobile, and so have not been reported missing by family or friends. The paper by Gudjonsson (1979) illustrates one possible means of coping with such a situation. Gudjonsson describes the case of a young woman who was unable to recall any personal details and about whom no information was obtained by public appeals. In an effort to reveal some of these details electrical conductivity of the subject's skin to various stimuli was recorded. It was found, for example, that the electrodermal activity changed more in response to the name of one month than to others when she was asked to recognize the month in which her birthday fell, even though she could not consciously identify it. Similar probing revealed where she had lived as a child and, together with other information, eventually led to her identification.

Multiple personalities

The multiple personality syndrome has been popularized by R.L. Stevenson with his characterization of the respectable Dr Jekyll and the uninhibited Mr Hyde. The situation depicted by Stevenson clearly embodies the main aspects of the syndrome, namely, one personality is an expression of the frustrated desires of the other, and often the existence of one personality (A) may be known to the other (B) while B is not known to A. The syndrome is not unlike the fugue state in that there is escape from an intolerable reality. But the presence of one-way, as opposed to two-way, amnesia and the alternation of the dominant or controlling personalities distinguishes the multiple personality syndrome from fugue. Martha G. described by Frankel (1976) provides an illustration of some aspects of the syndrome. Martha, who belonged to a strict religious sect which frowned upon smoking and drinking, was normally apathetic and complained of headaches and fatigue. After suffering a minor road accident she was unable to walk for reasons which were undoubtedly hysterical. She also complained of hearing a voice telling her to do things entirely out of keeping with her character. Martha stated that it was as if this voice wanted to take over control of her completely and when the therapist encouraged her to let it do so she writhed about and appeared to lose consciousness. After a short while she awoke and her personality was quite changed: now she was cheerful, lively and could walk normally. It was clear from discussion that the new 'person' who called herself Harriet knew all about Martha and resented her puritanical lifestyle, preferring night clubs to church. Eventually Harriet was persuaded to leave and Martha, on waking, had no recollection of her.

While Martha G. exhibited only two personalities other patients have been reported who have three or more. Usually in such cases the personalities have varying degrees of awareness of one another as in the recent cases of Sybil (Schreiber, 1974) and Eve (Thigpen and Cleckley, 1957). Also, one personality may seem to develop and have experiences at the same time that another personality dominates the individual and controls external behaviour. Prince (1924) reported such a case in which the patient exhibited three different personalities, B, C, and A. While A and C were amnesic for each other and B, B reported being fully aware of what the others experienced while they were dominant. It is interesting that in this state of *co-consciousness* the component personalities had quite different interests and literary tastes with B being very critical of the other two in these respects.

Despite the dramatic nature of the multiple personality, or perhaps because of it, a certain amount of caution is required before accepting descriptions of it at their face value. It should be realized that interpretation of the syndrome has depended somewhat heavily on the patients' accounts of what has been taking place. Furthermore, cases of multiple personality have been very rare and a number of writers, including Rapaport (1942) have noted that the syndrome has become less common throughout this century. They have also suggested that it may well require the collusion of the therapist for its appearance!

Some theoretical approaches
Pierre Janet (e.g. 1904) considered that hysterical amnesias and fugues, together with other neurotic complaints, reflect a splitting up or dissociation of the personality. According to his theoretical framework the individual's mental contents and processes are normally all integrated under the control of the *ego* which is responsible for awareness of mental activity and hence personal identity. In the completely integrated individual, Janet maintained, all mental contents are accessible to awareness, but in pathological states certain mental events become detached from the ego's control and so are no longer accessible to consciousness: they are *dissociated*. Dissociation, then, provides the means whereby specific portions of memory become inaccessible to awareness. The dissociated memories, however, have the power to produce pathological symptoms such as somnambulism and hallucinations of traumatic events, and because of this Janet viewed dissociation purely as pathological. Some individuals, he believed, are genetically predisposed to dissociation in that compared to others they have less of the mental energy required by the ego to maintain the unity of the personality. For these individuals trauma places too great an additional burden on the ego and dissociation occurs. In hysterical amnesia memories of the traumatic event are dissociated but the ego remains intact so that there is still effectively one personality. In the case of fugues, however, and especially in multiple personalities, we can see that the ego itself appears to suffer fragmentation with separate egos controlling separate personalities. Janet's theory is very mechanistic, relying, as it does, on the notion of psychic energy and leaving the individual entirely at the mercy of genetic predispositions.

Importantly, Janet maintained that one of the ego's normal functions is to bind together the components of mental activity against their tendency to split up. In contrast to Janet's theory Freud's account of the so-called dissociation phenomena emphasizes dynamic processes whose role is to defend the ego from conflict. According to Freud (e.g. 1915/1957), ideas which would cause suffering if they became conscious are rejected by the ego, i.e. they are *repressed*. Repression is a defence mechanism the function of which is to reject ideas and memories, and keep them out of consciousness. However, a number of questions arise from this general and simple definition and include those concerning whether repression is a conscious or unconscious process, and how it may be achieved. On the first point Freud seems to have accepted that it may be either conscious or unconscious depending on circumstances although later writers tend to insist that it is an unconscious process (see, e.g., Erdelyi and Goldberg, 1979, for discussion of this and other aspects of repression). As to the mechanisms of defending the ego, Freud mentioned a number of them in his writings. These include the *control of attention*; *projection*, in which the subject and object of a proposition are transposed (e.g. 'I love you' is allowed into consciousness as 'You love me'); and *reaction formation* in which the proposition is converted to its opposite (e.g. 'I love you' becomes 'I hate you').

According to Freud's view, then, hysterical amnesia and fugues may be seen to reflect the *strength* of the ego's defences rather than its weakness in not being able to bind together the components of personality as Janet proposed. Also, Freud was able to extend the usefulness of the repression concept beyond fugues and traumatic amnesia by insisting that conflict need not arise from the unpleasantness of ideas as Janet maintained. Rather, the ideas may be pleasurable, the conflict arising because they are deemed immoral as in the case of the patient who repressed the memory of the occasion on which his sister had seduced him (Freud, 1918/1955). Another important aspect of Freud's concept of repression is its ability to encompass certain failures of memory which cannot be considered abnormal. In his book *The Psychopathology of Everyday Life* Freud argues for the existence of motivated forgetting in normal individuals on the basis of a number of anecdotes. One of these involved a man who repeatedly forgot the name of an old acquaintance. It turned out that the man had good reason to repress the name because the acquaintance had recently married the woman whom *he* had hoped to wed. The importance of such everyday amnesias to the Freudian approach lies in their revelation that everyone, not only the neurotic patient, is influenced by unconscious processes and repressed ideas.

Experimental studies of repression
Freud put little value on any possible experimental validation of repression. For him, the clinical evidence was overwhelming: the recall of memories not recallable previously by patients was often followed by alleviation of the presenting symptoms. Freud's approach was unscientific in that, for example, no check was made to ensure that the symptoms would not have vanished without treatment, and the interpretation of symptoms in terms of repression was entirely *post hoc*. It is important, therefore, to note that experimental studies have had little success in demonstrating the presence of, or clarifying the nature of, repression. Discussions of such studies are available (e.g. Holmes, 1974; MacKinnon and Dukes, 1964) and some examples of the main approaches will suffice here to illustrate the problems which have arisen. Zeller's (1951) study of *induced anxiety* typifies one of these approaches.

Zeller's subjects initially learned a list of syllables and recalled them as a check that they were available in memory. In the experimental condition of interest here, subjects were required to perform a tapping task which they could not complete successfully. They were then made to feel anxious and inadequate by telling them that their performance indicated so low a level of mental ability that they would not succeed at college and would have difficulty performing any skilled job. On being asked to recall the syllables again they did worse than the control group who had not been subjected to failure nor made to feel anxious or inferior. After two days a recall test was given and the difference between the groups remained. This was followed by the tapping task and the experimental group was now allowed to succeed. They were also told that the previous result had been arranged by the investigator. Performance on the subsequent test for recall of the syllables was now not much different for the two groups.

These results have often been taken as evidence for repression, it being assumed that anxiety generated by failure on the tapping task generalizes to the syllables which were learned immediately beforehand, and that the invest- igator 'coming clean' about the initial results removes anxiety and hence repression. But other interpretations of these results and others like them (e.g. Penn, 1964) are possible as Erdelyi (see Erdelyi and Goldberg, 1979), D'Zurilla (1965) and Holmes (1972) have argued.

Erdelyi and Goldberg (1979) emphasize the need to distinguish between *memory* bias, where items are not accessible to recall, and *response* bias, where items are accessible but the subject is reluctant to give them as responses. It is possible, they note, that an experience of failure makes subjects more cautious in emitting responses which nevertheless have been accessed in memory and are present in consciousness. The same process is possible in clinical settings where the patient may be initially reluctant to openly admit certain recollections to the therapist.

D'Zurilla (1965) found that individuals who had been subjected to failure on a task reported *more* subsequent thoughts about the task than those individuals who had been told they were successful. This finding is, of course, contrary to what would be expected if repression were operating and suggests that differences in cognitive activity between Zeller's control and experimental groups either before or during the second recall test may have led to a temporary difference in accessibility of to-be-remembered items. Taking up this point, Holmes (1972) extended the general paradigm adopted by Zeller to include an ego-enhancing group (told they were successful) in addition to the ego-threatening and neutral feedback groups. Both the ego-threatened and ego- enhanced groups showed comparably poor recall immed- iately after feedback and comparable improvement after the investigator 'came clean'. Since ego-enhancement should not produce repression some other explanation of the reduced performance of both groups seems called for. Again it is possible that the subjects directed more attention to thoughts of the tapping task while trying to recall the syllables than did the group receiving neutral feedback, this temporarily lowering accessibility.

The study by Levinger and Clark (1961) in which they varied *stimulus emotionality* has often been taken to demonstrate repression and represents a different approach to Zeller's. Subjects in this study were required to produce an associative response to each of 60 stimulus words which varied from high emotionality (e.g. *fear*) to neutral (e.g. *window*). As was expected, the high emotionality words produced longer response latencies and greater galvanic skin responses than did the neutral words. In the second part of the experiment subjects were given the original list of stimulus words and asked to recall the responses they had given earlier. They recalled more responses to neutral than to emotional stimuli, this outcome being consistent with the idea that those responses associated with anxiety-provoking stimuli were repressed. Other explanations of the results are possible, however. One possibility is that emotional words generate more 'candidates' for associative responses than do neutral words and subjects have greater difficulty at recall deciding which one they had indeed given to a stimulus item.

Another explanation of Levinger and Clark's results is suggested by the findings of Kleinsmith and Kaplan (1964). In one of their experiments subjects read a short sequence of nonsense syllable-digit pairs and the galvanic skin response to each pair was recorded as a measure of physiological arousal. Recall of the appropriate digit in response to each of the syllables was then required and it was found that performance was best for those pairs which had produced low arousal. In the recall test one week later, however, the position was reversed; recall of digits from high arousal pairs had *improved* considerably while those from low arousal pairs showed a large decrement. Similar results have been obtained when the pairs are accompanied by various levels of arousal manipulated by presentation of white noise at different amplitudes (e.g. McClean, 1969).

Walker's *action decrement theory* (Walker, 1958) provides a plausible account of findings that the influence of arousal level varies with the retention interval although several authors have pointed out a number of problems for the theory in other respects (see, e.g., M.W. Eysenck, 1977).

According to Walker's theory a stimulus event initially gives rise to a relatively short-lived memory trace. During its life this trace may be consolidated into long-term memory but while this is happening certain physical processes in the brain preserve the trace against disruption by an inhibition of retrieval, or *action decrement*. The added assumption is made that high arousal levels facilitate the consolidation process but also produce greater action decrements. In this way items giving rise to, or accompanied by, high arousal levels should be less well recalled in the short term than those items accompanied by low levels, but the position should be reversed after long intervals when consolidation has been completed and the action decrement removed.

It is important to realize that Levinger and Clark employed a short-term test of memory – it followed the association test immediately. Thus, their finding that recall was better for the neutral (low arousal) words than for the high emotionality (high arousal) words is *consistent with* Walker's theory. But, of course, this finding on its own is not sufficient to distinguish between an arousal explanation and one in terms of repression or the number of competing associative 'candidates'. What is needed is evidence that the recall advantage to neutral words is reversed at long retention intervals because neither of the alternative explanations could seemingly account for that finding. Unfortunately Levinger and Clark did not include a delayed test but Parkin, Lewinsohn and Folkard (1982) did so. Their results showed the reversal in recall of responses to high emotionality and neutral words when the retention interval was increased from two minutes to seven days. It is difficult to see how the concept of repression can account for this finding because items which give rise to repression at one time should not show facilitation at another. Also, there is no obvious reason why the number of words available as possible associative responses should be more or less of a hindrance to recall of the original responses with changes in the retention interval. It seems clear, then, that Levinger and Clark's results are a particular example of a general phenomenon which appears when level of arousal is manipulated, even when the psychodynamic mechanisms of repression are not involved.

The work discussed in this part of the chapter illustrates the lack of success for attempts to study repression experimentally. Alternative interpretations of the results are possible and, in any case, it seems unlikely that the anxiety produced in the laboratory has mimicked the mechanisms of repression in the sense employed by Freud. This is so despite the flagrant disregard by some investigators of the ethical considerations which should govern the treatment of sub-jects. (Fortunately it is becoming more difficult to conduct an experiment such as Zeller's as awareness of these considera-tions grows.) The symptoms of traumatic amnesia and fugue states cannot be denied, but how are the interpretations based on dissociation or repression to be verified? If we accept, as Freud did, that experimental psychology is not equipped to deal with concepts such as repression then it must also be accepted that such concepts are likely to remain at a pretheoretical level.

Post-hypnotic amnesia

When a person has been deeply hypnotized he is able to experience a number of phenomena which do not occur in the waking state. These occur on instruction by the hypnotist and include regression to an earlier age with some corres-ponding changes in speech and drawing skills, feelings of weightlessness in an arm accompanied by apparently effortless levitation of the limb, and hallucinations in any of the sense modalities (see Bowers, 1976 and Hilgard, 1977 for reviews of hypnosis research).

Concern with the influence of hypnosis on memory performance has increased recently, largely because the technique is being used more frequently in the questioning of eyewitnesses by police forces all over the world. There have been many reports of eyewitnesses recalling additional useful information under hypnosis (e.g. Reiser and Nielson, 1980), these apparently testifying to the effectiveness of the technique. But such reports must be treated with great scepticism especially with respect to any claim that hypnosis *per se* is responsible for the hypermnesia (the hypnosis session invariably follows some other form of questioning and often takes place in a rather more conducive environment, e.g. a psychologist's office rather than a police station). It is especially important to note, therefore, that laboratory research on the use of hypnosis to improve recall has had mixed outcomes. Indeed, it seems likely that where improved recall has occurred it has often been at the cost of increased intrusions and fabrications (see, e.g., Dhanens and Lundy, 1975; Stalnaker and Riddle, 1932), this suggesting that hypnosis makes subjects less critical of their responses. This conclusion is supported by the general finding that recognition performance is not influenced, or may even be depressed, under hypnosis compared to the waking state when the forced-choice procedure is adopted, i.e. where any bias to respond *yes* or *no* is eliminated (Sanders and Simmons, 1983; Wagstaff, 1982). Orne (1979) has discussed the implication of such findings for the fair administration of justice.

Interesting though the possibility of enhanced memory under hypnosis might be, we must return to the principal theme of this chapter, namely, motivated forgetting. It is possible that a subject given instructions under hypnosis will carry them out after he has awakened even though he may not remember being told to do so. Amongst such post-hypnotic suggestions is amnesia for events taking place in the hypnotic period. This form of motivated forgetting is the main concern of this section but before dealing specifically with post-hypnotic amnesia it may be helpful to consider some broader aspects of hypnosis.

Hypnotic induction and scaling
Hypnosis can be induced by a number of methods. Indeed, the subject's readiness and ability to be hypnotized seem to be more important to successful induction than the method or the personal characteristics of the hypnotist. The first stage of induction usually involves relaxation and the production of what may loosely be described as 'partial sleep'. This may be done by encouraging muscle relaxation in combination with the use of a monotonous voice and eye

fixation, i.e. having the subject steadfastly gaze at a small object far enough above him to quickly tire the eye muscles. This process can conveniently be accompanied by suggestions of tiredness which, of course, are confirmed so initiating the link between the hypnotist's suggestions and the subject's experiences. The deepening of the hypnotic trance may proceed by exploitation of suggestions concerning body sensations which accompany relaxation and the encouragement of imagery to further divorce the subject from influences external to the hypnotic process.

In standardized tests the induction procedure incorporates items which allow hypnotic susceptibility to be assessed and compared with appropriate norms. The Stanford Hypnotic Susceptibility Scale Form C (Weitzenhoffer and Hilgard, 1962), for example, includes a 'hand lowering' item in which it is suggested that the arm, extended horizontally forwards, is dropping. About 92 per cent of subjects show a drop of more than 6 inches in response to the suggestion. Other items include hallucinating a mosquito (about 48 per cent of American subjects can do so), age regression in writing styles (about 43 per cent show regression to childish writing), and denial of the smell when ammonia is held close to the nose (19 per cent deny it). The scale also includes a test of post-hypnotic amnesia: before the subject is brought to a normal state of wakefulness the hypnotist suggests that he will forget everything that has taken place during the session until he is told he can remember. On being awakened a request to recall what happened is made and about 27 per cent of subjects recall 3 or fewer of the 11 items administered. After a short period the amnesia is cancelled by means of the reversal cue 'Now you can remember everything' and a further recall test given. Any increase in performance relative to the pre-cue test may be taken to indicate not only that the amnesia has been cancelled but that the initial failure to recall was due to the inaccessibility and not unavailability of the information in memory.

Theories of hypnosis
The modern study of hypnosis began with Mesmer (1734-1815) who put forward the theory that hypnotic phenomena

are induced by 'animal magnetism' originating in the hypnotist's hands. After Mesmer's magnetic theory had been discredited James Braid (1775-1860) in England did much to renew the scientific study of hypnosis and it was he who first appreciated the involvement of suggestion, i.e. the acceptance of ideas from others. The Nancy School under Bernheim (1837-1919) accepted that hypnotic phenomena are the result of increased suggestibility and that susceptibility to hypnosis is a widespread and normal characteristic. A different view was adopted by Charcot (1825-1893) who taught at the Salpêtrière where he influenced Sigmund Freud. The Salpêtrière School interpreted hypnotic susceptibility as pathological and indicative of a neurotic personality. But, of course, while a large proportion of neurotics may be highly susceptible to hypnosis this fact on its own does not deny that the trait is also common amongst normals. Indeed, as we have seen, norms of hypnotic susceptibility constructed in recent times confirm the position adopted by the Nancy School by showing a wide range of susceptibility amongst the population as a whole.

Hilgard (e.g. 1977) maintains that hypnosis involves a special *state* of awareness in which the subject has enhanced suggestibility. He postulates that the cognitive system has sub-systems within it, and that a central system directs these sub-systems and controls communication amongst them, and between them and consciousness. Hypnotic phenomena are accounted for by the dissociation of one part of the system from the remainder as is readily illustrated by the explanation of hypnotically induced analgesia. It is proposed that one part of the cognitive system registers pain and normally communicates it to consciousness. Analgesia is achieved by dissociating this part of the system and so blocking communication routes from it. According to Hilgard dissociations may occur in the waking condition but a distinct *hypnotic state* is reached when dissociations are particularly widespread. The reader will doubtless have appreciated the close resemblance between Hilgard's theory and the account of hysterical amnesia favoured by Janet which involved the notion of dissociation. Because of these similarities Hilgard's theory is referred to as *neo-dissociation theory*.

In contrast to *state* theories typified by that of Hilgard, *non-state* theories maintain that hypnotic phenomena do not arise from a cognitive or physiological state which is unique to hypnosis. Representative of those who have adopted this general approach are Sarbin and Coe (e.g. 1972) who, while acknowledging that hypnotic phenomena are real enough, emphasize that they involve processes which take place throughout our waking lives. They maintain that the hypnotized subject is acting out a role by doing what is expected of him, and that some people are more willing and able to adopt the role than others. This role-playing approach must be distinguished from the sceptical view of Barber (see, e.g., 1969) who disputes that hypnotic induction is necessary to produce behaviours traditionally known as 'hypnotic'. One of Barber's procedures for producing hypnotic-like behaviours involves the use of 'task motivational instructions', i.e. he merely tells subjects that unless they feel and act as he instructs they will have been wasting everyone's time, and falling short of his expectations of them. While Barber's demonstrations of conforming behaviour by wakeful subjects have done much to encourage a critical approach to the study of hypnosis they do not rule out the possibility that some behaviours can and do arise uniquely in the hypnotic state. As Marcuse (1959) points out, it is difficult to understand how hypnotic analgesia in surgery could be shammed. Taking a middle approach, Orne (e.g. 1972) has recognized that amongst any group of subjects some may be genuinely susceptible to hypnosis while others may simply simulate what they believe to be hypnotic behaviour in order to conform with the experimenter's wishes. Orne makes use of the fact that it is often possible to distinguish between the behaviour of 'genuine' subjects and simulators, as is aptly illustrated by what is known as 'trance logic'. If a deeply hypnotized subject is asked to 'see' an imaginary person sitting in a real chair he can often do so. But, when asked to describe the back of the chair he is able to do this also. It is quite possible for him to accept that the hallucination is real and at the same time accept that it is transparent. This trance logic usually escapes the simulator who, on being asked to describe the chair insists that it cannot be seen because the 'person' sitting on it is obscuring the view. While the possibility of simulating behaviour is a problem in hypnosis research it does appear that genuine hypnotic phenomena exist and need accounting for.

Suggested recall amnesia

We return now to the specific topic of primary concern in this section, namely, post-hypnotic amnesia. It is important to make an initial distinction between two classes of post-hypnotic amnesia. What may aptly be termed *spontaneous* amnesia refers to the loss of memory for events taking place during the hypnotic period even though no suggestion of amnesia was made by the hypnotist. Such amnesia may occur when a particularly deep trance has been achieved and, as Hull (1933) noted, it was once considered the most significant consequence of the hypnotic state (see also Spanos and Gottlieb, 1979). While spontaneous amnesia appears to have been common at one time very few individuals in modern times exhibit it to any great extent, hence research has been focused on *suggested* amnesia. We have already encountered a typical procedure for suggesting amnesia – that incorporated into the Stanford Hypnotic Suggestibility Scale: C. Suggestions for post-hypnotic amnesia can be applied to any information in memory and the following discussion is not limited to Stanford Hypnotic Suggestibility Scale items, therefore.

A number of questions arise about post-hypnotic amnesia, some of them being bound up with the nature of hypnosis generally. In particular, investigators have sought to determine if there is a genuine, albeit temporary, loss of accessibility and if so, how it comes about. Additionally it may be asked if studies of suggested amnesia can inform theories of memory in the waking state. This would be so if, for example, it were possible to 'functionally ablate' specific parts of the memory system by suggestion in much the same way as occurs involuntarily with damage to brain tissue (see Chapter 8).

It has been found that the amount of suggested post-hypnotic amnesia and the increase in recall following the release cue are related positively to the susceptibility of the subjects to hypnosis (see, e.g., Kilhstrom and Evans, 1979). In addition, amnesia and release from it do not occur for hypnotized subjects who have not been given the 'forget' instructions. The amnesia, therefore, depends critically on the suggestion that the subject will be unable to remember and is not attributable merely to some aspect of the induction procedure such as the emphasis on relaxation. Furthermore, Kilhstrom and Evans (1976) found that subjects who are highly susceptible to hypnosis show greater recovery of items following the release cue than do low susceptibility subjects even when the two groups are matched for recall scores in the amnesic period. Thus, the greater release effect found generally for high susceptibility subjects is not attributable merely to the fact that they do poorly on the prerelease test and so have a greater opportunity to show reminiscence.

Episodic and semantic memory
Kilhstrom (1980) has emphasized the theoretical advantages of distinguishing between the effects of suggested amnesia on episodic and semantic memories. Amnesic effects on semantic memory are illustrated by temporary specific aphasia for the meanings of the words *house* and *scissors* achieved by some 40 per cent of subjects in the Stanford Profile Scales of Hypnotic Susceptibility. In addition, temporary agnosia may be successfully suggested such that the subject is unable to demonstrate the use of scissors (see Hilgard, 1965).

Kilhstrom (1980) also demonstrated suggested recall amnesia specific to episodic memory in an extension of an earlier study by Williamson, Johnson and Eriksen (1965). In one of his experiments Kilhstrom hypnotized his subjects and had them learn a list of words to a criterion of two correct recalls thus ensuring that the items were available in memory. They were then told, 'You will not be able to remember that you learned any words while you were hypnotized until I say "Now you can remember everything".' After termination of the hypnotic period recall of the word list was requested and the attempt to do so was followed by a word association test in which, according to norms for waking subjects, the stimulus words evoked some of the list words with high probability. Although hypnotically susceptible subjects showed amnesia (and later reversibility) for the words when asked to recall the list they had learned, they had no difficulty giving them as responses in the word association test. Thus, the suggested amnesia in this instance influenced only episodic memory, semantic memory being apparently unaffected. A somewhat similar phenomenon known as *source amnesia* may be produced by telling a hypnotized subject some fact of which he was previously ignorant, such as the number of buildings in Stratford-upon-Avon. Administration of the instructions to forget all that has happened in the session often leaves the subject with knowledge of the fact but no idea of where he learned it.

The dissociation between the effects of suggested amnesia on episodic and semantic memory obtained by Kilhstrom rules out explanations of post-hypnotic amnesia based on the notions of repression or dissociation discussed in the previous part of this chapter because these predict that the critical items would not be produced at all, or produced only with great difficulty, in the word association test. Instead, as Kilhstrom and others have argued, post-hypnotic *recall* amnesia is most readily explained by the temporary loss of the episodic contextual cues which, according to the encoding specificity hypothesis, are necessary for retrieval. In Kilhstrom's view this loss of access is *genuine*, i.e. the subjects are unable to recall items under the influence of the amnesia suggestion, and this is entirely in accord with 'state' theories of hypnosis. But, the argument put by Kilhstrom to support this view is open to criticism because it relies largely on findings from a *semantic memory* task! While still under the amnesia suggestion Kilhstrom's (1980) subjects were requested to generate as many exemplars as possible from taxonomic categories represented in the 'amnesia' list. It was found that hypnotically insusceptible subjects clustered items from the list in their output while highly susceptible subjects randomly ordered list items and other exemplars. This finding purportedly shows the effect of the amnesia suggestion on the accessibility of category exemplars: insusceptible subjects were able to utilize the learned lists to generate exemplars, while these lists were *not accessible* to the susceptible subjects. But this finding of differences in clustering in the semantic task does not force the conclusion that the failure to access the learned list is *obligatory*, that is, outside the subject's voluntary control. It is feasible that susceptible subjects, under the influence of hypnotic sugges- tion, are able to voluntarily ignore the episodic information in memory! This point is elaborated below.

Organization in recall
Spanos (e.g. Spanos, Radtke-Bodorik and Stam, 1980) also interprets post-hypnotic amnesia in terms of episodic retrieval processes but, unlike Kilhstrom, he emphasizes that the loss of access reflects a *willingness* of the subject not to attend to the necessary retrieval cues rather than an *inability* to do so. Some of the evidence on which Spanos bases his view comes from studies which have concentrated on the organiz- ation present in recall protocols. In one such study (Spanos *et al.*, 1980) subjects were given hypnotic induction and then required to learn a list of categorized words to a criterion of two successive correct free recalls. They were then given an amnesia suggestion for the list and subsequently challenged to 'try and remember'. Later, in the waking condition, the amnesia was cancelled and another recall test given. Recall performance and the level of category clustering under the amnesia suggestion were both inversely related to hypnotic suggestibility (the measure of category clustering took account of the number of items recalled). Spanos *et al.* took the low level of clustering as indicating that subjects failed to make as much use of category names as retrieval cues during the amnesic period as they did before and after it, hence the low recall. Subjects' reports at the end of the session supported this view and suggested that they passively allowed their attention to be diverted from these cues: items which *were* recalled just 'came to mind' spontaneously. Spanos bases his view of the voluntary nature of this forgetting on several pieces of evidence. Among them is the finding that susceptible, hypnotized subjects do not exhibit amnesia if, before induction, they are encouraged to interpret

the challenge to recall as a *serious* request to try to remember (see Spanos and Radtke-Bodorik, 1980).

It is important to understand that Spanos and his colleagues believe that post-hypnotic amnesia arises from effects on the accessibility of items in memory; they do not arise from the deliberate withholding of items which have been accessed as could be achieved by unhypnotized subjects who attempt to please the experimenter by simulating hypnosis. But, while Spanos *et al.* (1979) found differences in the amount of clustering shown by simulators and hypnotized subjects, not everyone agrees that the two groups differ in this respect (e.g. Wagstaff, 1981). Because of this disagreement it may prove difficult to establish that there is a voluntary failure to attend to retrieval cues, rather than to output items which have been accessed, unless subjective reports are accepted as evidence. For these reasons, amongst others, there have been attempts to demonstrate hypnotic amnesia in circumstances where merely withholding items which have been accessed in memory cannot mimic genuine amnesia. Interference paradigms have been used to this end.

Neutralization of interference
If memories can be functionally ablated, or dissociated, then any interference with other items which they normally produce should be removed. The possibility of manipulating interference by suggested amnesia is important because it is difficult to see how the removal of interference can be faked, unlike recall amnesia.

Both retroactive and proactive interference designs have been employed to investigate the effects of suggestion for post-hypnotic amnesia. The basic retroactive design is depicted in Table 7.1 and involves two groups, one given amnesia suggestions, the other not. Both groups learn list 1 in the waking state, are then hypnotized and learn list 2. The amnesia group is instructed to forget list 2 until the release cue is given. Both groups are awakened and recall of list 1 is tested. At this point the amnesia group should recall more than the control group if list 2 has been functionally ablated and list 1 consequently not affected by retroactive interference. The release signal is then given and a further test for the recall of list 1 is made. Both groups should now be prone to retroactive interference from list 2 and their performance should not differ. The corresponding *proactive* design involves suggested amnesia for list 1. On the whole, results of studies employing such designs have led to the conclusion that the 'amnesia material' is *not* functionally ablated (e.g. Coe, Basden, Basden and Graham, 1976; Cooper, 1972).

Despite the failure to manipulate interference some authors have claimed that the effects of the amnesia suggestion may be revealed in other informative ways. For example, Coe *et al.* (1976) employed a retroactive interference paradigm in which recall of both list 1 and list 2 was required before and after the release signal. It was found that while recall of list 2 was reduced under the amnesia suggestion so also was list 1. This latter finding is, of course, contrary to the expectations based on the assumed removal of retroactive interference stemming from list 2. Accordingly the authors interpret this aspect of their results as being in agreement with neo-dissociation theory (Hilgard, 1977), i.e. the task demands of keeping list 2 out of awareness detract from performance on list 1. However, an alternative explanation of the results arises from the use, by Coe *et al.*, of words from the same taxonomic categories in the two lists. In order to understand this explanation assume that both list 1 and list 2 are at all times fully available and accessible to subjects given the amnesia suggestion. In order to recall list 1 but not list 2, as the instructions require, the amnesic subjects must be able to discriminate which list each item originated in. The use of the same categories in both lists should make such discrimination difficult and the only way to comply with the primary objective of not recalling list 2 would be to withhold any words where source was doubtful. These would, of course, include words from list 1. It seems, then, that studies employing interference techniques offer no firm grounds for concluding that suggestions for post-hypnotic amnesia lead to functional ablation of the 'amnesia' items.

The successful manipulation of interference effects would have provided good evidence for some unique effects of post-hypnotic suggestion. Also, it would have opened up the possibility of exploring the memory system by functionally dissociating specific components or contents in healthy individuals rather than relying on brain-damaged patients for such opportunities (see Chapter 8). However, the failure to manipulate interference effects seems to restrict the effects of suggestions for post-hypnotic amnesia to situations where subjects can influence performance by voluntary control of retrieval strategies, such as inattention to retrieval cues, or even by withholding items which have been accessed in memory. It is surprising, therefore, that little seems to have been done by way of exploring in detail the *extent* to which subjects can exercise voluntary control over memory processes in the suggested amnesia paradigm. Until this is done there may be little that studies of post-hypnotic amnesia can contribute to theories of memory in general. This situation is in contrast to the body of research carried out with non-hypnotized subjects and concerned with what may conveniently be termed 'directed forgetting'.

Directed forgetting

The essential feature of the directed forgetting paradigm is the provision of cues informing the subjects that they should forget certain items which have been presented to them and remember other items. In contrast to the situations discussed in the previous two sections the studies dealt with here involve subjects in their normal waking state, and materials which may be expected not to involve repression, i.e. defence of the ego. As in most experimental studies of memory the subjects' motives for carrying out the experimenter's instructions may reasonably be assumed to be a desire to contribute to the research. Also, there may be a small financial reward linked to performance.

There are several variants of the directed forgetting paradigm (see Bjork, 1972; Epstein, 1972, for comprehensive discussion). In what follows we will be concerned both with *intra-serial cueing* in which the cue or cues to forget or to remember are inserted into the list, and with *post-list cueing* in which the cues are given after the list has been presented. In one version of the intra-serial cueing procedure subjects are presented with a sequence of list-items all of which they have been told to try to learn in anticipation of a memory test. At some point in the sequence a cue is given to 'forget' the items which have already been presented and attempt to remember only the subsequent items. This *set-cueing* procedure, then, creates two sets of items, *forget* (F) items in the first part of the list and *remember* (R) items in the second part. Of particular interest in this type of study are the consequences of the F cue for memory of the following R items, and the effects on F items themselves. In another version of the intra-serial cueing procedure each item is followed by an R or an F cue before the next item is presented. This *item-by-item* cueing procedure allows the interval between each item and its subsequent cue to be specifically controlled.

One of the major problems with directed forgetting procedures can be that of convincing subjects that they really must treat the F cues seriously even though memory for items so cued will be tested later. This, of course, is no problem if only one sequence of items is tested. Where several lists are involved the use of financial incentives may convince the subjects that it is worthwhile to heed the F cues and give all their attention to R items. Alternatively, for example, the test of F items may be delayed until later stages of the experiment by which time subjects should be convinced that only R items will be tested (see Bjork, 1972, for discussion of this general problem).

In addition to providing evidence concerning whether or not it is possible to voluntarily delete information from storage, studies of directed forgetting have yielded results bearing on other theoretical issues. These include the extent to which subjects are able to control the processing of items and the consequences of different types of rehearsal for long-term storage. We begin by looking at evidence obtained with the set-cueing procedure and which concerns the possible deletion of information from memory storage.

Deletion or differentiation
If F-cued items are deleted from memory there should be an elimination of proactive interference arising from them. We

have already noted that attempts to demonstrate functional ablation by post-hypnotic suggestion in this way have proved unsuccessful. However, a number of studies have used the set-cueing procedure to investigate the influence of directed forgetting on proactive interference and these have proved informative in a number of ways (see, e.g., Bjork, 1972). One study by Reitman, Malin, Bjork and Higman (1973) will serve to illustrate several important findings which have arisen from these studies.

Reitman *et al.* presented subjects with lists of from 1 to 8 paired associates each consisting of a nonsense syllable and a word. In some lists there was a signal to forget the pairs which had been presented prior to that point and to concentrate only on the following pairs. At the end of every list one of the nonsense syllables was presented as a probe for recall of the corresponding word. For reasons which will become clear, if the list contained an F cue the probe was usually accompanied by an indication of whether the pair had been in a pre- or post-cue position. An important feature of the experiment was the joint manipulation of the serial position which was probed and the positioning of the cue within the lists. In this way it was possible to vary the number of both pre-signal (F) and post-signal (R) items which preceded and followed the probed item. Figure 7.1 illustrates this aspect of the experiment. Arrangements A and B show how the number of items in the F set preceding a probed R item may be varied while keeping the post-cue situations identical. Arrangements C and D show one way of varying the number of F items preceding a probed F item.

The results showed clearly that, by comparison with lists in which no F cue was included, instructions to forget early items led to an increase in recall of the R items. Also, there was no systematic variation in recall of R items as a function of the number of preceding F pairs. Both these findings are consistent with the deletion of F items from memory and the consequential removal of proactive interference. But other findings by Reitman *et al.* argue against this conclusion. When items from the F set were probed (and the subjects were informed that this was so), recall performance was substantial, this showing that F items were available in differentiating the F set from the R set. This *set differentiation* theory receives strong support from other aspects of the Reitman *et al.* results. First, performance on F items declined as a function of the number of F items preceding the probed position. This within-set build-up of proactive inhibition was also exhibited by R items – performance declined as a function of the number of preceding R items. Second, intrusion errors were largely within-set, e.g. an erroneous response to the probe of an R pair was much more likely to come from another R pair than from an F pair. Third, when subjects were tested on F pairs but not informed of this, performance was essentially zero as would be expected if the R set only was searched. According to Reitman *et al.*, then, when the F cue was given, subjects could ignore the F items and devote all their processing capacity to the R items. Hence the increase in recall of R items when the F cues were introduced. Although the F cues might have terminated the encoding of the preceding items, information about these items which was already in memory was not deleted but was in some way differentiated from information about R items.

Effects of cue delay
The set-cueing procedure, discussed above, encourages the subject to treat all items as R items from the moment they are presented until the F cue is given. It is clear from the findings of Reitman *et al.*, among others, that subjects can respond to the cue by concentrating encoding activities on R items and differentiating them from F items in memory. In contrast, with the item-by-item procedure the subject knows that every item will be followed by an F or R cue before the next item is presented. Hence, one possible strategy for coping with this task is to simply maintain an item by rote rehearsal over the pre-cue interval and carry out concurrent elaborative rehearsal of previously presented R items. This situation is depicted in Figure 7.2 where, following Craik and Lockhart (1972), the terms primary and secondary rehearsal respectively are used to refer to the maintenance of items in the rehearsal buffer in the absence of, or accompanied by, elaborative encoding. We saw in Chapter 4 that maintenance rehearsal alone has been shown to have little effect on recall

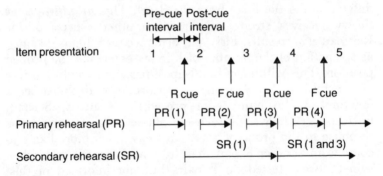

Figure 7.2: *The item-by-item cueing procedure*

from secondary memory. It follows from this that, under the strategy scheme depicted in Figure 7.2, recall of F items should not be appreciably affected by the length of the pre-cue interval because they would receive no secondary rehearsal. On the other hand, increased opportunities for secondary rehearsal of R items as the pre-cue interval is reduced, and the interval between cue and the next list item is increased, should lead to improved recall. These predictions were very largely confirmed by Wetzel and Hunt (1977).

In a later study Wetzel and his colleagues (Tzeng, Lee and Wetzel, 1979) applied what had already been learned about subjects' strategies in the item-by-item procedure to investigate the notion of automatic memory processes. They noted that previous research had shown that subjects are well able to judge which of two items was presented the more recently in a list whether or not they know in advance that such information will be tested. For this and other reasons it has been widely accepted that the encoding of temporal information in memory is an automatic process in the sense employed by Hasher and Zacks (1979; see Chapter 1). Tzeng *et al.* argued that if temporal coding is indeed automatic then following items by an F cue should not influence the ability to make temporal judgments about them. In fact they found that the ability to judge which of two items had occurred the more recently in a list was good for pairs of R-cued items but poor for pairs involving F-cued items. Thus, it seems that performance did not depend on the automatic laying down of a temporal code as a consequence of merely maintaining each item in short-term storage for the few seconds prior to the cue. Instead, Tzeng *et al.* argued, performance depended on the rehearsal and encoding together of R items through-out list presentation. As a consequence R items, but not F items, were continuously being encoded as 'prior to' the most recent item and this provided the basis for the judgments of order. The encoding of presentation order, then, may be seen to result from the *effortful* process of rehearsal. Nevertheless, subjects were not anticipating the test of order and in this respect at least it seems that performance did depend on the *automatic* encoding of order.

Post-list cueing
The effects of intra-serial F cues are largely accounted for by the dropping of F words from primary and secondary rehearsal and the more effective rehearsal of R words that this allows. It is perhaps more appropriate to label such cues as instructions to do no further processing of particular items rather than to 'forget'. But can 'forgetting' instructions be effective when they are directed at material which has already been learned? The answer seems to be *Yes* or *No* depending on how the instructions are given. Epstein (1972) discussed several studies in which subjects learned two sets of items which were clearly distinguishable by, for example, temporal grouping. The finding of these studies was that recall of set A was better when the post-list cues indicated that only set A, rather than both set A and set B, was to be recalled. Clearly, the explanation of this effect must lie at retrieval: because subjects did not know beforehand which cue would be given it is safe to assume that the conditions were not distinguished by different encoding strategies. Instead, as Epstein suggested, it is possible to account for the effect by assuming that the cue *only set A* enables a selective search of a limited region of memory storage to be carried out. In addition, this cue releases the subject from any obligation to 'hold on' to set B while set A is being tested. This allows all available processing capacity to be devoted to

completing the recall of set A.

Roediger and Tulving (1979) drew attention to what they considered an important aspect of the post-list cueing studies discussed above. The cues indicated what should be *remembered*; the items to be forgotten were indicated only by implication. Is there any reason to suppose that different results would have been obtained if the cue had indicated what was to be *excluded* from recall? Roediger and Tulving argued that there are reasons for so believing because the situation then is very similar to the part-list cueing paradigm introduced by Slamecka (1968) and discussed in the previous chapter. In that paradigm it has been found that providing some of the list items as cues, purportedly to facilitate recall of the remaining words, actually reduced recall of them. It is possible to view the part-list cues as being essentially F items in that they do not have to be recalled. Hence, by analogy, it would be expected that post-list cueing to *forget* set B rather than to *remember* only set A would lead to a decrement in recall of set A. This is what Roediger and Tulving found when they presented categorized lists and cued forgetting by, for example, category names. A possible explanation of this finding follows from one account of the part-list cueing effect which was discussed in Chapter 6 and which assumes that presenting a cue is equivalent to adding an item to the list. The situation in which the subject is told what *not* to recall is rather like telling him that at all costs he must not think of the word *elephant*. The very instructions make the task difficult!

Summary

In many circumstances forgetting is regarded as an undesirable aspect of memory which the individual makes considerable effort to prevent. The three types of situation considered in this chapter contrast with such circumstances in being characterized by motivation to forget rather than to remember.

The psychopathological conditions of traumatic amnesia, fugue and multiple personality are readily understood by the exclusion from consciousness of memories associated with grief, anxiety, frustrated desires or moral conflict. The notion that such forgetting results from splitting off certain memories from the rest seems reasonable at a descriptive level. But, Janet's idea that the dissociation of memories results from an inherent lack of psychic energy fails to capture the complexity of motives behind this kind of forgetting. In contrast, Freud's concept of repression stresses the dynamic nature of forgetting and the complicated unconscious and conscious forces which may be involved. However, there has been little success for attempts to investigate repression by experimental methods: interpretation of results is complicated by possible artifacts and by difficulties in mimicking repression in the laboratory. Indeed, Freud's concept of repression does not appear to lend itself to scientific test. Despite the difficulties in understanding at a fundamental level it is clear that certain psychopathological conditions do involve motivated forgetting.

Neither studies of post-hypnotic amnesia nor directed forgetting reveal any ability to wipe out information which is stored. The effects of suggested post-hypnotic amnesia for events in the hypnotic period may be understood by voluntary processes at retrieval, e.g. inattention to episodic retrieval cues. But it is difficult to exclude the possibility that some post-hypnotic amnesia results from deliberate withholding of items which have been retrieved from memory storage. Intra-serial cueing procedures employed within the directed forgetting paradigm, too, seem to produce no startling revelations for general memory theory. However, studies using these procedures do confirm that primary and secondary rehearsal have differential effects on recall. They also testify to the subjects' abilities to differentiate sets of items in memory, and to successfully manage concurrent selective primary and secondary rehearsal of specified items. Post-list cueing to forget may have beneficial or detrimental effects on recall of to-be-remembered items depending on whether the instructions specify directly what should be remembered or what should be forgotten.

8 Organic amnesias

The complexity of the human brain in terms of anatomical structures, physiological processes, and the interdependence amongst these structures and processes makes its functioning prone to many disruptions of organic origin. Thus, tumours, defects of the vascular system, penetration of the skull by missiles, surgical incisions and viral infections are among the forms of damage which may give rise to specific or widespread effects on cognitive and other functions depending on the locus and extent of the damage. The study of behavioural changes which result from the disruption of brain functions by injury or disease falls within the province of *neuropsychology*.

In a clinical setting, particular psychological symptoms may be associated with particular types of damage which have been identified by physical means such as X-rays, surgery, or at post-mortem examinations. In view of this, psychological symptoms may provide important information for purposes of diagnosis and prognosis. That is, psychological tests may conveniently provide guidance for later physical exploration and treatment. Also, by understanding the nature of the patient's psychological deficits it may be possible to facilitate recovery or enable him to compensate for them thus minimizing the effects on his everyday life.

Clinicians draw on studies of normal memory in several ways. Necessarily, of course, the assessment of memory deficits must be made in relation to the performance of normal subjects. Also, models of normal memory can help by indicating which aspects of memory are fundamentally important and how they may best be assessed. While understanding normal memory functioning is important to the diagnosis and treatment of abnormal memory states there is a reciprocal influence. Accidents and disease provide human conditions which are otherwise not available to the experimental psychologist and because of this neurological evidence can contribute uniquely to the development of models of normal memory. A point made in Chapter 1 may be usefully emphasized here: it is possible to construct models of normal memory without considering the anatomical structures and physiological processes which underlie memory functions. Similarly, the effects of brain damage can be considered profitably without becoming involved in the physical mechanisms of the brain, i.e. a functional approach may be adopted. A simple illustration should make this clear. Suppose we were committed to Atkinson and Shriffin's model (Chapter 5) so that we considered access to LTS can only be achieved via STS. Clearly, it would be difficult to maintain this view if patients were found whose STS appeared to be virtually non-existent and yet were able to perform tasks which depend on LTS with normal or near-normal levels of competence. As we shall see, such patients do exist.

In this chapter we shall consider some of the mutual benefits deriving from work with normal subjects and patients with abnormal memory functioning. These benefits will be illustrated by considering some evidence which is compatible with the theoretical distinctions between availability and accessibility, LTS and STS, episodic and semantic memories, and imaginal and verbal systems. Next, some attempts to understand the amnesic syndrome in terms of established memory models will be reviewed. In the third section of this chapter some of the findings on age differences in memory will be considered. The inclusion of age differences in this chapter is not intended to suggest that the changes in memory which occur with normal ageing are entirely organic in origin. Rather, its inclusion here was motivated merely by certain similarities, possibly only superficial, between age-related changes and the amnesic syndrome (see Craik, 1977).

Dissociation of memory functions

Availability and accessibility: transient amnesia

Transient loss of memory functions often occurs in patients who have suffered closed head injuries (i.e. when the skull has not been penetrated) which result in loss of consciousness. Such injuries often arise from blows to the head which produce tissue damage by violent movements of the brain within the skull. Toxic and metabolic factors, such as carbon monoxide poisoning and hypoglycaemia, together with certain infections, epileptic fits, and electroconvulsive therapy may also produce transient amnesic states when they lead to loss of consciousness (see Whitty, Stores and Lishman, 1977). On regaining consciousness patients may suffer a period in which memory fails for events occurring before the trauma (retrograde amnesia) and for events after it (anterograde amnesia).

The extent of the period of anterograde amnesia, during which patients are unable to remember new material, is dependent on the severity of the trauma. Events taking place during this period cannot be recalled or recognized even when the ability to recall those events initially affected by *retrograde* amnesia has been recovered and retrieval processes generally appear to be functioning again. Anterograde amnesia, therefore, is readily attributable to the failure to store information.

The extent of *retrograde* amnesia may initially include events over many years and, like anterograde amnesia, is dependent on the severity of the trauma. This was recognized by Ribot (1882) who maintained that resistance to disruption of memory traces by disease or injury varies directly with the age of the traces. Thus, the initial extent of retrograde amnesia may be taken as a rough indication of the severity of the trauma (see Russell, 1971; Whitty and Zangwill, 1977). Gradually, after regaining consciousness, patients recover the ability to recall information learned before the trauma, starting with earlier memories and progressing to more recent ones, although 'islands' of events may recover out of sequence. Clearly, the successful recall of information which could not be recalled earlier indicates an initial failure of *access* rather than a loss of *availability*.

Recovery from the retrograde aspects of the so-called transient amnesias is rarely complete; there is usually permanent amnesia covering a period immediately prior to the trauma. Typically this extends for up to several minutes and is generally attributed to a failure to encode events in this period into long-term memory. This view is supported by the observation of Lynch and Yarnell (1973). They approached American football players shortly after they had regained consciousness following mild concussion and asked them to recall the moves which led up to the trauma. Initial recall was good, but when asked again later there was retrograde amnesia covering a brief period even though the events in it had been recalled earlier. Presumably concussion had not affected short-term memory but had disrupted the establishment of more permanent memory traces.

It has often been assumed that permanent retrograde amnesia is produced by the interruption of neural processes which consolidate short-term traces into more durable form. According to this view the period of retrograde amnesia may be taken as an indication of the time required to complete the consolidation process, but it is not clear what this process might consist of. Physiological investigations have taken a number of directions and work with animal nervous systems has identified a number of biochemical changes, such as protein synthesis, which could underlie it. On the whole, however, this research is inconclusive with respect to identifying the process which, when disrupted, gives rise to retrograde amnesia in humans. Simon Green (forthcoming), in his volume in this series, gives an extensive account of the relevant physiological work so it is not pursued here.

At a cognitive level, explanation of the permanent period of retrograde amnesia must take account of the incidental nature of much everyday learning. Thus, for example, a car driver involved in an accident is likely not to have been actively attempting to remember the events at any part of the journey prior to the incident. This appears to rule out rehearsal, or any other intentional learning strategy, as the cognitive counterpart of neural consolidation. Instead, some more or less automatic, ongoing integration of episodic information with traces of earlier and later events would seem to be indicated. Interestingly, the period permanently covered by retrograde amnesia appears to be more dependent on what the patient was doing at the time than on the severity of the trauma (see, e.g., Barbizet, 1970). When attention is sharply focused on a task, when the events are particularly novel, or when demanding cognitive activity is involved, permanent retrograde amnesia may cover only a few seconds or be non-existent. Thus, it seems that the deeper the level of processing being carried out at the time of the trauma the less extensive is the retrograde amnesia, possibly because consolidation, integration of traces or whatever, is more rapid with deeper processing.

The account of 'permanent' retrograde amnesia in terms of consolidation relies heavily on the argument that because retrieval processes are working normally for other periods of both old and new learning they necessarily have access to any information which is available concerning the amnesic period. However, on the basis of work with rats Miller and Springer (1972, see also 1973) found that retrograde amnesia following electroconvulsive shock can be dissipated if the context of learning is sufficiently reinstated. This shows that retrieval processes are involved in the phenomenon of 'permanent' retrograde amnesia (see Green (forthcoming), for further discussion). The effect of acute alcoholic intoxication vividly illustrates the advantages of this interpretation rather than the disruption of memory traces, in certain circumstances at least. If alcohol is consumed rapidly, and it is the rate rather than the amount which is crucial, amnesia for the drinking period may be experienced the following day. This amnesia can often be overcome by consuming more alcohol, presumably thereby reinstating the original encoding context and so enhancing the accessibility of intact episodic traces (see Chapter 6 for discussion of state-dependent retrieval).

Short-term and long-term stores
Neuropsychological evidence for separate short-term and long-term stores is provided by patients exhibiting the *amnesic syndrome*. This is characterized by persistent anterograde

amnesia which may be accompanied by retrograde amnesia, and generally stems from damage to the medial portions of the temporal lobes. Depending on the extent and location of the damage, the amnesia may be accompanied by other cognitive deficits. Thus, the Korsakoff syndrome, which often has its origin in extensive damage caused by prolonged alcohol addiction, includes disorientation and little or no awareness of memory defects (see Zangwill, 1977, for a fuller description). When damage is more specific the amnesia may be relatively pure, that is the patient has little other cognitive deficit.

Milner (1968) provides a detailed account of a pure amnesic, HM, who underwent surgery in 1953 for the relief of epileptic seizures. Tissue was removed from the medial surface of both temporal lobes including portions of the hippocampus and amygdala, and as a consequence HM was left with severe retrograde and anterograde amnesia. Although the period covered by the retrograde amnesia shrank somewhat with the passing of time the anterograde amnesia persisted fully throughout the years of observation. Thus, HM could not learn a new address when his family moved, nor could he remember where he had left things. He would repeatedly complete the same jigsaw puzzle or engage in the same conversation with no recollection of the earlier occasions. Despite these problems his IQ score was actually increased after surgery indicating that his cognitive functions were adequate unless new learning was involved in a task. His ability to converse and to perform day-to-day tasks indicates that semantic memory and long-established skills were spared, this agreeing with Ribot's principle that learning laid down in early life is least susceptible to disruption. Furthermore, performance of these day-to-day tasks involves short-term memory and their survival in HM indicates that this aspect of memory was spared.

The informal description of the amnesic syndrome given above is confirmed by the results of controlled investigations of HM and other amnesic patients. While tests involving long-term episodic memory show deficits, amnesics have memory spans which fall within the normal range. The short-term memory performance of amnesics was explored in some detail by Baddeley and Warrington (1970) in a series of experiments. In one of these experiments they gave immediate and delayed tests to their normal and amnesic subjects, and calculated the primary memory (PM) and secondary memory (SM) components of recall. The amnesics quite clearly had very low SM scores but did not differ from normals on estimates of PM capacity.

The different effects of brain damage on the PM and SM components of recall reported by Baddeley and Warrington are in line with the conceptual distinction between short-term and long-term stores embodied in several theories of normal memory. But it is important to note that there is a general danger of inferential circularity if neuropsychological evidence of this sort is taken as confirming theories of normal memory. This is apparent in the instance described above where the calculations of the PM and SM components of recall are themselves based on assumptions which the neuropsychological evidence may then be used to confirm. It is conceivable, in the absence of other evidence, that the poor SM scores of amnesics in conjunction with normal PM scores may be explained by *one* factor such as an abnormal pattern of trace decay in a single store. Alternatively, immediate recall of items may place fewer demands on the general cognitive resources available than does delayed recall, and the limits placed on these resources by brain damage may be evidenced only when demand on them is great. Suppose, however, that patients can be found who have a minimal PM component of recall but an almost normal SM component. As Shallice (1979) argues, it would be difficult to explain the deficiencies of *both* groups of patients by shortcomings in a single process or component.

Shallice and Warrington identified a selective STS deficit in a patient who received damage to the posterior left hemisphere in the region of the parietal lobe, and other similar patients have subsequently been identified (see, e.g., Basso, Spinnler, Vallar and Zanobio, 1982). In one of the experiments reported by Shallice and Warrington (1970) their patient KF was tested on immediate free recall of 10 common nouns presented auditorily at a rate of 1 every 2 seconds. The results showed essentially a greatly impoverished PM component and a more normal SM component. Thus, KF demonstrated a dissociation between STS and LTS. As we have already noted, amnesic patients also demonstrate such a dissociation but with them it is LTS which is selectively impaired. Taken together, the two types of patient show a *double dissociation* of STS and LTS, this being extremely strong evidence for two separate memory components.

According to the Atkinson and Shiffrin model of short-term memory, items must pass through STS on their way to LTS. As Shallice and Warrington point out, this model is unable to account for KF's pattern of recall. If STS is not functioning then information could not be transferred to LTS and the secondary memory component of recall should be deficient also. It is, of course, possible to argue that STS is able to *store* information and pass it on to LTS even though *direct retrieval* from it is not possible. Shallice and Warrington argued against this interpretation on the grounds that the deficit is still apparent when dependence on retrieval is minimized by a recognition test. They went on to argue that information does not have to pass through STS to reach LTS, an alternative, parallel route being available via semantic memory.

It is tempting to interpret KF's deficit in terms of Baddeley and Hitch's working memory model because it, too, does not require input to LTS to pass through STS. Certainly KF's deficit in short-term memory performance (he had a digit span of 2) with his successful comprehension and long-term learning suggests that he had a normal central processor but greatly impaired articulatory rehearsal loop. This pattern of deficit, then, offers support for Baddeley and Hitch's contention that working memory is not synonymous with short-term storage as envisaged by Atkinson and Shiffrin. One possible objection to this interpretation, as Basso *et al.* (1982) note, is that the working memory model emphasizes that the recency effect generally and in immediate recall in particular is not an STS or articulatory rehearsal loop phenomenon. Rather it is better interpreted in terms of temporal discriminability or some such principle operating in LTS (see Chapter 4). But KF showed impaired recency which, on this basis, is at odds with his relatively good long-term memory performance. Nevertheless, the articulatory rehearsal loop seems to be implicated by the findings of Vallar and Baddeley (1984). They studied a patient similar to KF and found that she had strong indications of a defective rehearsal loop, i.e. she showed no effect of phonological similarity, word length, or articulatory suppression on immediate memory performance. But she did have a normal rate of articulation, indicating that the rehearsal loop was intact! Vallar and Baddeley dealt with this apparent paradox by suggesting that it was the phonological store which was defective and this discouraged the subject from using sub-vocal rehearsal.

Whatever theoretical position is adopted, it is not easy to deny that KF and others like him, when taken with patients exhibiting the amnesic syndrome, demonstrate a double dissociation between the long-term and short-term components of recall.

Episodic and semantic memory

The distinction between episodic and semantic memory made by Tulving (1972) is useful and, as was made clear in Chapter 6, is seen by some people as being theoretically important. It has not been easy, however, to obtain direct evidence for the distinction largely because the two systems are bound up together in episodes involving verbal materials. Neuropsychological evidence bearing on this distinction is especially important, therefore.

Selective impairment of semantic memory has been reported by Warrington (1975). She investigated three patients who, it was found, had intact memories for both recent and distant episodes but had difficulty with verbal knowledge. Interestingly for what follows in the next section, this deficit was restricted to concrete nouns. For example, one patient could only reply 'I've forgotten' or 'Don't know' when asked to define concrete nouns such as *blacksmith* or *carrot*. When asked for definitions of abstract words he could respond well. For example, his definition of *supplication* was 'making a serious request for help'.

Kinsbourne has repeatedly drawn attention to the dissociation between episodic and semantic memory apparent in the amnesic syndrome (see, e.g., Wood, Ebert and Kinsbourne, 1982). Many amnesic patients are able to understand language, are not impaired on vocabulary tests, and can perform adequately when asked to generate exemplars from taxonomic categories. But they can remember virtually nothing of an episodic nature. Kinsbourne *et al.* aptly illustrate their point by referring to patients who are able to give an adequate definition of a word, e.g. *flags*, but will fail to recall any personal experiences involving such objects. A similar dissociation between the two types of memory has been reported by Signoret and Lhermitte (1976) in a patient who had an intact knowledge system but an inability to remember any event since the onset of his illness. These patients who show specific impairment of episodic memory, taken with those reported by Warrington who show specific impairment of semantic memory, support the conceptual distinction proposed by Tulving.

Verbal and imaginal systems
Evidence for separate verbal and visual/imaginal systems, as proposed by Paivio (1971), comes from patients suffering unilateral damage to the temporal lobes. Many of these patients have suffered strokes, or have undergone surgical treatment for the relief of epilepsy or tumours. It has long been established that, for right-handed subjects, damage which is restricted to the left temporal lobe produces selective impairment of verbal ability including the learning and retention of verbal items (e.g. Milner and Teuber, 1968). Conversely, patients with right temporal lobe damage have been found to have intact verbal memory but deficits in delayed reproduction of geometric patterns and complex figures, and recognition of faces (e.g. Hécaen and Angelergues, 1962; Kimura, 1963). Recent evidence for the functional distinction between the hemispheres includes that obtained by Moscovitch (quoted by Paivio and te Linde, 1982). The subjects included some with unilateral lesions of the right temporal lobe and others with left temporal lesions. They were shown 16 pictures of objects which could be classified

by shape or by lexical category and then given a free recall test. The right temporal patients clustered their output according to lexical category as would be expected if their visual memory was defective, and the left temporals clustered according to shape suggesting a loss of semantic processing ability.

There is, then, consistent evidence that the temporal lobes play a vital role in episodic memory and that the left (dominant) hemisphere is specialized with respect to verbal abilities and the right (non-dominant) hemisphere is adapted to deal with non-verbal, visuo-spatial tasks. This differentiation between verbal and non-verbal functions has often been taken as support for the dual coding theory, notably by Paivio. But Richardson (1980; Chapter 9) maintains that while the differentiation between verbal and non-verbal systems is well-founded it does not support that aspect of the theory which maintains that imaginal and verbal codes are *additive* in their effects on memory for verbal items. That is, the theory predicts that damage to the right temporal lobe *will* interfere with verbal memory, but this is contrary to the evidence we have noted above. This situation seems to favour Richardson's view that the difference in memory performance between concrete and abstract words is not due to the influence of imaginal activity (see Chapter 5). In contrast, Paivio and te Linde (1982) claim support for dual coding theory by referring to experiments by Jones-Gotman where right temporal lesions were associated with a deficit in the use of imagery to facilitate verbal memory, the deficit being positively related to the size of the lesion. Doubtless this issue will continue to be pursued.

One interesting point which emerges from the work reviewed by Paivio and te Linde (1982) and by Richardson (1980) is that right temporal patients report the experience of imagery. It may seem surprising, then, that such patients show any sign at all of a decrement in the facilitation of verbal memory by imagery, or any deficit in visual memory. The resolution of this seeming paradox is provided by indications that the generation and control of imagery as experienced consciously depend on the posterior region of the right hemisphere, while the effective functioning of episodic memory is dependent on the medial portions of the temporal lobes and the hippocampus in particular. Indeed, damage to the posterior region of the right hemisphere sometimes demonstrates a close link between imagery and perception. A good example of this is provided by Bisiach and Luzzatti (1978), who describe two patients with such damage and who had loss of perception in the left visual field. When told to imagine they were standing at the edge of a familiar square and to describe the scene everything to the left was ignored. When asked to imagine they had crossed the square and were now looking in the opposite direction they described the buildings previously ignored and ignored those which had earlier been described.

Psychological interpretations of the amnesic syndrome

The main features of the amnesic syndrome have already been described in connection with the dissociation of memory functions. The most distinctive and consistent symptom is the marked anterograde amnesia, there being extremely impoverished long-term learning although short-term storage is largely intact. This anterograde amnesia may be accompanied by extensive retrograde amnesia for pre-morbid personal episodes but with a sparing of memory for events early in life and well-established motor, verbal and social skills. The amnesic syndrome has been intensively researched and a number of theories have been put forward to account for it in psychological terms. It is convenient here to consider two main groups of theories consisting of those which attribute the deficits to problems with encoding and those which attribute them to problems with retrieval. This classification is crude but it does reflect what appears to have been a general aim of accounting for the amnesic syndrome as parsimoniously as possible. Cermak's theory, which is considered first, clearly places the amnesics' deficit at the encoding stage. Warrington and Weiskrantz, whose theory is discussed next, maintain that interference at retrieval is responsible. Third, discussion concentrates on a group of related theories which go some way towards meeting objections to the first two.

Semantic encoding deficit

Possibly the earliest interpretation of chronic amnesia is based on the notion that memory traces must undergo a process of consolidation if they are to survive in the long term. According to this interpretation amnesics are unable to consolidate their memory traces to the same extent as normals. Clearly, a failure to consolidate traces would account for anterograde amnesia and, as Milner (1968), one of the proponents of consolidation, noted, may be conceptualized in information processing terms as a deficit in the transfer of information from an intact short-term store to long-term storage. Recent theories which maintain that the amnesics' deficit lies at encoding include those of Cermak (e.g. 1979) who believes amnesics suffer a general difficulty with encoding semantic information, and Baddeley (see, e.g., 1982a) who has identified a more circumscribed problem with imaginal encoding.

An apparent problem with any account of chronic amnesia based on an encoding deficit is the difficulty of dealing with the retrograde amnesia which may extend over many years prior to the onset of the precipitating circumstances. Because memory was functioning normally over that period there is no reason why events falling within it should not have been established in long-term memory. However, there are patients such as NA, who was studied by Squire and Slater (1978), with dense anterograde amnesia but little if any retrograde amnesia. Thus it may reasonably be argued that a general account of the amnesic syndrome need deal only with anterograde amnesia, an explanation of retrograde amnesia being sought separately.

Cermak (e.g. 1979, 1982) has carried out a great deal of research with the most common group of amnesics, namely, those with Korsakoff's psychosis resulting from alcoholism. He has adopted the levels of processing approach to the amnesic syndrome. Indeed, he was advocating it at about the same time Craik and Lockhart published their influential paper on 'levels' in 1972. In keeping with this approach Cermak claimed that amnesics are able to maintain items at a superficial level but have difficulty processing to a deep level. Amongst the evidence supporting this semantic deficit theory is the finding by Cermak and Moreines (1976). They had their patients listen to a list of words and indicate when a word was repeated, rhymed with a previous word, or belonged to the same semantic category as a previous word. The first two conditions but not the third can be performed merely by maintaining superficial codes in memory, hence amnesic patients should do worse than control subjects in detecting category repetitions but no worse in the item repetition or rhyming conditions. The findings were in line with these expectations. In another study Cermak, Butters and Gerrein (1973) found that amnesics benefited just as much as normals from the provision of rhyming cues at recall but were much less assisted by semantic cues.

Other evidence which has been used to support the semantic deficit theory comes from a study of release from proactive interference (PI) by Cermak, Butters and Moreines (1974). They took up Wickens's argument that this phenomenon is indicative of the way items are encoded in memory (see Chapter 4). They found that a shift from letters to digits produced release from PI with amnesic patients but not a shift from animals to vegetables or vice versa. Control subjects, of course, showed release with both types of item.

While the evidence outlined above does suggest that amnesics suffer from impoverished semantic encoding this view would receive more powerful support if it could be shown that the memory deficit can be much reduced by forcing patients to process items to a deep semantic level. Cermak and Reale (1978) examined this possibility by using the levels of processing paradigm. In one experiment each amnesic patient was given five trials, each consisting of the presentation of 12 target words followed by a recognition test in which 24 distractors were added to the targets. During list presentation each target word was associated with one of three types of orienting questions such as those used by Craik and Tulving (see Chapter 5), i.e. 'Does the word fit this sentence?', 'Does the word rhyme with —?', and 'Is the word printed in upper- or lower-case letters?'. The first important aspect of the results concerns the answers to the orienting questions and the times taken to give them. The amnesic patients could answer all the questions accurately and were not dramatically slower than a group of non-amnesic control patients. Thus, in these circumstances at least, semantic memory performance appeared unimpaired and processing was carried out at the required levels. Nevertheless, although amnesics did show some increase in recognition scores with 'sentence' questions relative to 'case' and 'rhyme' questions performance in all conditions was very much worse than that of normals. Thus, forcing the amnesics to process deeply did not markedly affect their memory loss. Similar findings have been obtained with a variety of list lengths, orienting questions and materials (e.g. Squire, 1982). So it seems difficult to attribute anything more than a small fraction of the amnesics' problems to a semantic encoding deficit.

If a semantic encoding deficit does not provide an explanation of the amnesic syndrome there remains the problem of explaining why, as noted above, Cermak *et al.* (1974) failed to obtain release from PI with amnesic patients. Consideration of this point raises several interesting issues and it is worth dealing with it in some detail.

There are several reasons why the evidence reported by Cermak *et al.* does not offer unequivocal support for the semantic encoding deficit theory. If there is no release from PI and this is taken to indicate that semantic attributes are not encoded, how is any drop in performance over successive trials to be explained? Furthermore, we have already noted in Chapter 4 that release from PI may be explained by difficulty at retrieval produced by cue overload rather than by interference with the storage of information. Thus, the Cermak *et al.* findings do not necessarily point to an encoding deficit, and this doubt is increased by Kinsbourne and Wood's demonstration that providing category names as cues *at recall* can produce release from PI with amnesic patients (see Kinsbourne and Wood, 1975). However, there is an even more powerful reason for not taking the Cermak *et al.* findings as indicating that the root problem in amnesia is a semantic encoding deficit. Some amnesic patients such as NA, mentioned above, *do* show release from PI (Squire, 1982). Other patients, notably with damage *specific* to the frontal lobes, fail to show release from PI but do not suffer amnesia (Moscovitch, 1982). Thus, it seems likely that Cermak's patients who were all suffering from long-term alcoholic intoxication with attendant widespread lesions had symptoms of frontal lobe damage superimposed on those of chronic amnesia which may be the outcome of fairly specific damage to medial portions of the temporal lobes, in particular to the hippocampus.

Interference at retrieval
According to Warrington and Weiskrantz (1970, 1973), amnesics have difficulty retrieving correct information from memory because other, irrelevant information interferes with the process. In normal subjects, so the theory maintains, this competing information would either be lost from storage or its influence inhibited. Thus, in one sense at least, amnesics are considered to suffer because they can remember too much rather than too little.

One set of evidence which supports the interference at retrieval theory comes from studies employing techniques which may be assumed to reduce competition between responses. According to the theory the amnesics' deficit should be reduced by such techniques. In one of their early studies Warrington and Weiskrantz (1970) tested retention of lists containing 8 words by four methods. Recognition, free recall and two types of cued recall were given to normal and amnesic subjects after a filled interval of one minute. In one of the cued recall tests the first 3 letters of the to-be-remembered words were provided. In the other, the cues consisted of fragmented words, i.e. each word appeared as though it was viewed through a patchwork grating so that only random fragments of it could be seen. Depending on the density of the grating the words are more or less easy to identify and so act as more or less useful cues. The amnesics did badly on both free recall and recognition tests but did just as well as normal subjects when either type of partial cue was given at recall.

Warrington and Weiskrantz interpreted their findings as showing that amnesics exhibit no deficit when retrieval cues enable the number of possible, and hence competing, responses to be reduced. They produced further support for this view by using 3-letter cues which, apart from each cueing one to-be-remembered word, varied in the numbers of English words which could be generated using them as the initial letters (Warrington and Weiskrantz, 1974). The amnesics' recall performance approached that of normals as the number of possible responses generated by each cue decreased.

It is easy to understand how partial cues at recall reduce the competition from irrelevant information by restricting the number of possible responses relative to free recall. But it is less easy to understand why the *yes-no* recognition procedure does not reduce such competition likewise. Warrington (1976) has argued that because retrieval processes in recognition and recall may differ it is feasible that amnesics suffer considerable interference with recognition even though it is reduced in recall by cueing. But, without specification of the ways in which retrieval processes differ in the two situations and of the associated differences in sources of interference, this argument is not entirely convincing.

Whatever the problems created by recognition perform- ance there is other evidence supporting the Warrington and Weiskrantz theory and which has been obtained with techniques which *reveal* rather than constrain competition at retrieval. Warrington and Weiskrantz (1974) conducted several experiments in which the cues used to aid recall were common to items from two lists. In one of these experiments amnesics and normals were required to recall lists containing words from several small taxonomic categories such as *yellow flower* and *shell fish*. List 1 contained one word from each category, e.g. *daffodil*, *crab*, while list 2 contained another word from each of the same categories, e.g. *primrose*, *prawn*. There was no difference in recall between amnesics and normals when list 1 was cued with the category names. But amnesics did somewhat worse than normals when the same cues were given for list 2 as would be expected if they were unable to forget or inhibit what had been learned from the first list. Other evidence in line with these findings has been obtained by Winocur and Weiskrantz (1976). They required amnesic and control subjects to learn a list of semantically related paired associates and later to learn a second list in which the original stimulus words were paired with new semantically related response words. The amnesics learned the first list as effectively as the controls but did much worse on the second list principally because their responses included a large number of intrusions from the first list.

It is perhaps somewhat ironic that some of the strongest arguments against the interference at retrieval theory have been made by Warrington and Weiskrantz themselves. In one of their studies (Warrington and Weiskrantz, 1978) they employed lists of words each of which shared the first 3 letters with only one other English word (e.g. *cycle*, *cyclone*). Retention was tested by cueing with the initial three letters and amnesic patients performed just as well as controls. Subjects were then presented with a list containing the other member of each word pair and again recall was cued with the initial 3 letters. In these circumstances the amnesics should be more prone to interference from the first list than the controls but in fact performance on the second list did not differ between them in the crucial part of the experiment. A second experiment also employed lists containing words which shared the initial 3 letters. Subjects were required to learn and recall list 1, learn list 2 and then recall *both* list 1 and list 2 items in response to the common partial cues but without indicating to which list they belonged. According to the interference at retrieval theory the list 2 responses should suffer greater inhibition and be less well recalled for amnesics than for controls but this was not found. It seems, then, that while the theory has much in its favour there are limits to its applicability and it seems best to seek some more general theory to account for the amnesic syndrome.

Context deficits and failures of recollection
Gaffan (1976) found that monkeys with lesions bearing resemblance to those suffered by amnesic patients had difficulty discriminating between items which had been encountered before in the experiment and others which were

unfamiliar in order to obtain rewards. This deficit was not merely part of a general inability to learn because when only familiar objects were used the monkeys could learn to associate particular ones with reward. On this basis Gaffan suggested that amnesic patients are unable to judge the familiarity of items at the time of test and so have difficulty making appropriate responses in both recall and recognition. While his experiments with monkeys are very ingenious, evidence collected with patients points strongly against Gaffan's suggested account of the amnesic syndrome. Indeed, such evidence indicates that amnesics are able to judge whether items are familiar or not but unable to decide which specific context they appeared in. For example, Huppert and Piercy (1976) first of all familiarized amnesic and non-amnesic patients with 80 pictures. The following day everyone was shown half these familiar pictures together with 40 new ones which had not been seen before. These 80 pictures comprised the targets in a *yes-no* recognition test while the distractors were either familiar, having been shown the previous day, or unfamiliar, not having been seen before. Thus, the task was simply to recognize which pictures had been presented a few minutes previously. The amnesics performed poorly compared to the controls and made a disproportionately large number of false positive responses to familiar distractors (i.e. those shown the day before) compared to new distractors. Accordingly, Huppert and Piercy concluded that these patients were extremely poor at deciding which context the items had appeared in. This conclusion was supported by findings that when asked merely 'Have you seen the picture before?' the amnesics made few errors presumably because the answer did not depend upon specific contextual information.

In a further examination of the contextual deficit theory Huppert and Piercy (1978) required amnesic and control subjects to decide on which of two days they had seen each picture and how many times it had been presented on that occasion. Controls were well able to decide both how recently and how frequently each picture had occurred but amnesics confused recency and frequency, i.e. they tended to give similar judgments to pictures presented three times on

Day 1 and those presented once on Day 2. This finding supports the idea that the amnesics had difficulty discriminating between particular occurrences of items and suggests that they based their judgments on something such as 'trace strength' in which recency and frequency are crudely combined.

Several authors have made proposals similar to that of Huppert and Piercy. Notable amongst them is Wickelgren (1979) who has argued for two basic learning mechanisms dealing with the formation of what he terms horizontal and vertical associations. The formation of horizontal associations is seen as a phylogenetically primitive process which underlies classical conditioning and which by analogy with Huppert and Piercy's proposal is responsible for the formation of the rather crude 'trace strength'. The more advanced process which forms vertical associations is mediated by the hippocampus, is by analogy responsible for the encoding of contextual information, and is defective in amnesics. But whatever the specific mechanisms involved in particular theories it is possible to argue, as Stern (1981) has done, that the idea of a context deficit provides the basis for what are currently the most attractive accounts of amnesia because it can embrace a large number of phenomena. For example, Stern maintains that the failure of amnesics to show much improvement with enforced semantic processing is more easily explained by a failure to encode contextual information than by Cermak's *semantic* encoding deficit. Stern also suggests that while decrements in recall of the second of two lists can be explained by both context deficit and interference at retrieval theories the former theory is best able to account for the equivalent levels of recall when both list 1 and list 2 items are required with no reference to the source. Most interesting, though, is the way the context deficit theory deals with the near-normal performance of amnesics when recall is cued by initial letters or by fragmented words. It does so by emphasizing that, unlike more conventional recall and recognition tests, the 'priming' of responses to such partial cues need not depend on remembering the context in which the item was presented.

According to the suggestion made by Weiskrantz (1978)

and which has been pursued by Warrington and Weiskrantz (1982) and Baddeley (1982b), the failure of amnesics to utilize contextual information may be seen merely as one aspect of a more general deficit in *conscious recollection*. Normal subjects frequently report that in both everyday and laboratory situations they consciously engage in what may be termed problem-solving activities to generate plausible retrieval cues or to confirm or disconfirm that retrieved information is appropriate to the task at hand. These processes are what is meant by conscious recollection and as the study by Williams and Hollan (1981), described in Chapter 6, indicates the re-establishment of context is an important ingredient.

One great advantage of attributing the amnesic syndrome to a deficit in conscious recollection is that it is possible to acknowledge what amnesics *can* do in addition to what they cannot do. There is clear evidence that they benefit from previous experience on tasks such as maze-learning, completing jigsaw puzzles, and reconstructing sentences from shuffled words. The crucial feature of such tasks seems to be that improvement on them does not require any conscious appreciation of the previous experiences. Indeed, improvement may take place when patients fail to remember not only the context in which previous attempts took place but that they took place *at all*. This point was neatly demonstrated many years ago by Clarapède (1911) who shook hands with an amnesic patient while concealing a pin in his hand. The patient, having been pricked by the pin, was reluctant to shake hands on a later occasion but was unable to explain why. A recent illustration of the same point was provided by Jacoby and Witherspoon (1982). They employed a number of homophone pairs (e.g. *read* and *reed*) and asked normal subjects and amnesics questions to which the least common members of the pairs were answers (e.g. 'What is the part of the clarinet that vibrates?'). Subsequently, amnesic patients were very poor at recognizing the words they had given as answers when these were mixed with new distractors. But when later asked to spell the words amnesics showed just as much tendency as controls to give the responses to the earlier questions even though they were the least common members of each pair.

One or more amnesias?

A large amount of evidence concerning the amnesic syndrome has been collected. Despite this the psychological interpretation of the deficits suffered by amnesic patients in terms of general memory theory has not been conclusive. One of the difficulties here is that the amnesic classification contains several sub-groups including alcoholic Korsakoff patients. These have widespread brain damage and identification of a *primary* deficit in memory functions is made more difficult by accompanying *secondary* cognitive deficits of a general nature. Other sub-groups include surgical cases with clearly defined lesions and cases of vascular disorders and tumours who may be classified as *pure* amnesics because the deficits in episodic memory are not accompanied by more general, secondary, cognitive problems. Furthermore, it has become increasingly clear recently that patients classified as amnesic do not share detailed patterns of primary deficits in memory (e.g. Squire, 1982) while patients not classified as amnesic on the basis of both behavioural and neurological criteria may share memory deficits with amnesics (e.g. Moscovitch, 1982). Thus, there is increasing pressure for psychological accounts of amnesia to more adequately take into consideration the associations between *detailed* patterns of brain damage and specific patterns of memory deficits.

Of the theories discussed here the primary symptoms of amnesics seem best accounted for by those which involve context deficits either specifically identified as a failure to encode such information, as proposed by Huppert and Piercy, or as part of a more general failure of conscious recollection, as argued by Baddeley and others. Amongst the advantages of this general approach are its ability to embrace evidence that amnesics can learn and its emphasis of the distinction between automatic and voluntary memory processes.

Ageing

It is common for older people to complain about difficulties in learning new information and recalling past events and the names of long-standing acquaintances. These common observations reflect irritating and inconvenient memory failures in individuals who are generally healthy, normally oriented to reality, and who function adequately in society. As such, these dysfunctions must be distinguished from the gross loss of memory skills which is associated with senility. There is little that can be done to alleviate the general deterioration in cognitive functions which mark the senile state and which herald the approach of death. Nor are these symptoms surprising given the massive degeneration of brain tissues which is present in senile patients. However, age-related changes in cognition generally, and memory performance in particular, which occur up to the onset of senility are of theoretical and practical interest. Some of the changes in memory which take place from young adulthood to presenile old age are considered in this part. The next chapter is entirely devoted to developmental changes which occur up to about 15 years of age.

Some general points
There is much evidence, particularly from occupation-related studies, that ageing is accompanied by increased gaps in attention, a slowing of decision-making, and a general reduction in processing resources (see, e.g., Welford, 1958, 1977). However, as Birren and Renner (1977) point out, it would be wrong to believe that all cognitive skills increase up to some single optimal age and then decline. Certainly measures of general intelligence peak at about 35 years on average (Wechsler, 1958), but peak achievements in various professions occur at different ages. For example, highest individual achievements in chemistry and mathematics seem to occur at 30 years or earlier, in history and literature at 45 to 55 years, while excellence in the legal profession generally appears later still (see Birren and Renner, 1977). Clearly then, increases in certain skills may be associated with increasing age until quite late in life, especially if they must draw on accumulated knowledge. It is often possible for older people to offset particular processing limitations by drawing on experience, therefore.

Several problems complicate the study of age-related

changes in behaviour generally and in memory in particular. These problems include the definition of age itself. Because individuals mature at different rates, a group from a narrow chronological age range may consist of widely different *functional* ages (see Birren and Renner, 1977, who discuss a number of meaningful measures of age). This need not be a serious problem when widely different age groups are employed but most studies of age-related changes in memory have been based on chronological age without paying much attention to this issue.

Another problem concerns methodology. There are two basic methods available for research into ageing: longitudinal and cross-sectional. The longitudinal method, in which the same individual is studied repeatedly, has an obvious practical disadvantage where changes from young adulthood to old age are the object of investigation. The cross-sectional method compares the performance of groups of older and younger subjects tested over a single, short period of time. While this method has the advantage of convenience it suffers from a number of disadvantages. It is possible, for example, that any observed differences between groups on the dependent variable are peculiar to the particular generation from which the subjects are drawn. Thus, it is possible that observed differences in the attitudes towards foreigners expressed by old and young groups may not be associated with ageing generally but may simply reflect the fact that the older subjects had lived through a period of bitter international conflict not experienced by the younger group. The younger group, therefore, may not exhibit the same attitudes as the older group when they themselves are old. Similarly, little can be concluded about the ageing process if memory performance of a group of young undergraduates is compared with a group of elderly men who received no secondary education. While this is an extreme example it serves to draw attention to the impossibility of ensuring that matching subjects on all variables other than age has been achieved and of circumventing the problem by the usual experimental technique of randomly allocating subjects to groups so that any confounding is at a purely chance level. In essence, it is not possible to ensure that old subjects in a cross-sectional study would have performed similarly to the young subjects had they themselves been tested when young. These points should be borne in mind in what follows.

Age differences in short-term memory

Large age-related differences occur in short-term memory tasks which involve the division of attention among multiple sources of stimuli. One such situation is created by the dichotic listening paradigm in which pairs of items are presented simultaneously and dichotically, and the subject required to recall as many items as possible. It was established early on (see, e.g., Broadbent, 1958) that subjects usually report the items ear-by-ear rather than pair-by-pair if they are presented fairly rapidly, a possible implication being that items from the second channel reported must be held in some pre-attentional store while the first channel is reported. Differences in performance on this task over ages from about 20 to over 60 years were investigated by Inglis and Caird (1963). They presented three dichotic pairs of digits and instructed subjects merely to report what they heard. In line with other findings performance on the channel recalled first was better than on the second, but although there was no age decrement on the first channel recalled there was a large decrement on the second. These results are readily interpreted by assuming that the subjects decided in advance which channel they would recall first and focused their attention on it during presentation. Possibly, then, items on this channel were entered directly into verbal short-term storage and recalled from that store. Since there was no age decrement for the first channel recalled it seems that the abilities to encode in, and retrieve from, short-term verbal storage do not change with age. The contrasting age-related decrement found for the channel reported second is consistent with greater loss of information from pre-attentional storage with increasing age. Alternatively, older subjects may possibly be slower at switching attention between internal sources of information.

The disadvantage of older subjects in the recall of dichotically presented material is now well established although it now seems that the pattern of deficit is more complex than Inglis and Caird's results reveal (e.g. Clark and Knowles, 1973). Nevertheless, it does seem, as suggested above, that the capacity of the verbal short-term store changes little if at all with age. This conclusion agrees with findings from free recall studies in which subjects are presented with a single list of items on each trial. Such studies have shown that the primary memory component of immediate free recall shows little change with age while the secondary memory component shows a decrement for elderly subjects (Craik, 1968b; Raymond, 1971). Other tasks which contain a large short-term store component, such as memory span, also appear to show little change with age (e.g. Drachman and Leavitt, 1972). But the findings of Heron and Craik (1964) show that differences can be revealed if care is taken with the matching of old and young subjects. They first of all measured the memory span for Finnish digits which were unfamiliar to the English-speaking subjects and matched the two groups on this score. They then assessed memory span for English digits and found the old subjects to be inferior to the young ones. It seems, then, that the old subjects were just as good as the young ones at retaining meaningless sounds at a superficial level of processing but were less able to exploit any organizational opportunities presented by the meaningful stimuli. This is precisely in line with an age-related deficit in the secondary memory component of memory span and none in the primary memory component.

Age differences in long-term memory
Old people often claim that while they have difficulty remembering recent events their memory for remote events is good. It is possible to see some similarity between these claims and the symptoms of amnesic patients: both fit with Ribot's Law. However, such claims by old people are, of course, purely anecdotal and in any case are belied by their difficulty in recalling the names of long-familiar places and people. Warrington and Sanders (1971) set out to investigate the fate of old memories using items concerning public events and photographs of nationally prominent persons. The

choice of public events rather than private experiences was dictated by the difficulty of checking the accuracy of memories relating to the latter. Events taking place between 1930 and 1968, and pictures of people who were prominent during the period 1945 to 1968, were sampled. Subjects between the ages of 40 and 80 years were tested but, of course, the younger subjects could not be meaningfully tested on the earliest events. There was no evidence that remote memories were better preserved than recent ones. Also, there was a consistent age decrement across all periods tested and this was true for both recall and recognition tests. This suggests that storage loss rather than a retrieval deficit is associated with old age but the decrement on recall appeared greater than on recognition thus implicating retrieval to some extent, also. One interesting feature of the Warrington and Sanders study is the inclusion of a group of 16-year-olds who performed well on questions relating to recent events but very poorly on earlier events. From this it is possible to conclude that the failure to find differences between memory for early and later events in old subjects was not due to opportunities for relearning from broadcasting, books, etc.

There is some conflict in the results obtained with more conventional experimental paradigms as to whether age differences in memory performance arise in encoding or retrieval processes. Support for a retrieval deficit comes from Schonfield and Robertson (1966), for example. They presented subjects with 24 words and tested retention with free recall or a 4-alternative recognition test. Recall but not recognition showed an age-related decrement. Apart from problems with inferences based on comparisons of recall and recognition performance, doubts that this result may not reflect a general age difference in retrieval rather than storage are raised by findings that age decrements in recognition can appear, possibly, if the test is made difficult enough (e.g. Erber, 1974). Craik and Masani (1969) took another approach in order to separate the effectiveness of encoding and retrieval processes. They followed Tulving and Patkau (1962) and tested subjects on recall of sequences of words with different approximations to English text. Craik and Masani found that the number of adopted chunks (sequence of words in the output which corresponds with the input sequence) recalled differed between age groups while there was no difference in the number of words per chunk recalled. They argued from this that there was an age decrement in retrieval capacity but not in encoding. Hultsch (1975) also concluded that older subjects suffer a retrieval deficit. He tested memory for categorized word lists with free and cued recall and found that his older subjects benefited more from cueing than his younger subjects. However, in contrast to Craik and Masani, he also found an age difference in the number of words per category recalled, this indicating an encoding deficit.

Resource and strategy limitations
Taking the somewhat conflicting evidence from various sources, there appear to be grounds for accepting age-related changes in both encoding and retrieval processes. Are these changes the inevitable consequences of a reduction in the processing resources available to older subjects or do they arise from failure to use the available resources fully? Several authors (e.g. Craik, 1977; Eysenck, 1974; and Perlmutter, 1978) have approached this issue by employing the levels of processing paradigm to examine the consequences of enforced processing on memory performance (as we have seen, Cermak adopted a similar approach with amnesic patients). The study reported by Craik (1977) is particularly interesting because it assessed both recall and recognition performances under three incidental conditions (orthographic, phonemic and semantic), and one intentional condition (learn). There was an age decrement on recognition under *learn* instructions, as can be seen in Figure 8.1. This is readily attributed to a failure by the old subjects to spontaneously encode deeply because no age differences appear under the enforced coding conditions. In recall, however, old subjects suffered in both the *semantic* and *learn* conditions. Thus, Craik was able to argue that the recognition test established that encoding was adequate under enforced deep processing and the old subjects, therefore, must have suffered a retrieval deficit in recall. In

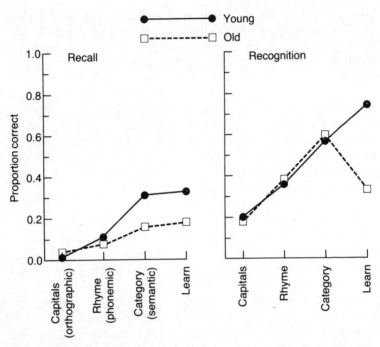

Figure 8.1: *Recall and recognition performance for old and young subjects following incidental and intentional learning procedures (adapted from Craik, 1977)*

brief, the old subjects failed to spontaneously adopt appropriate strategies at both encoding and retrieval.

Craik's findings, taken with those of other studies (e.g. Murphy, Sanders, Gabriesheski, and Schmitt, 1981), show that some age differences in memory may be reduced if older subjects are forced to use appropriate strategies while others may be reduced by the provision of retrieval cues. It would be wrong, though, to conclude from these findings that age-related decrements in memory performance are due solely to the failure of older subjects to employ strategies which would be effective if specifically encouraged. Indeed, given the wealth of evidence from studies of motor skills, decision-making and other aspect of performance, that there is an age-related decrease in cognitive resources, it would be surprising if there were no *obligatory* limitations on memory processes also. This point has been emphasized by Burke and Light (1981) who concluded from their review of the literature that age-related decrements are possibly present in processes which may be considered *automatic*, i.e. not at all dependent on the employment of *effortful* strategies. Burke and Light also concluded that on balance the existing evidence shows that age-related decrements may be *alleviated* but not *eliminated* by encouraging appropriate strategies in effortful tasks such as recall and recognition of word lists. Further evidence consistent with this conclusion includes failures to find differences between old and young subjects in either expressed knowledge of which mnemonic strategies are appropriate for particular situations or in ability to monitor the state of their memories and so predict performance (e.g. Lachman, Lachman and Thronesbery, 1979; Murphy *et al.*, 1981; Perlmutter, 1978).

Finally, it is worth noting a potential bias against older subjects in the choice of the items to be remembered. The point is neatly demonstrated by Barrett and Wright (1981), who had subjects recall word lists following incidental learning conditions. Old and young subjects were required to perform semantic orienting tasks which consisted of rating the words for pleasantness or for the size of their referents. The crucial aspect of the study was the construction of the lists from 'old' and 'young' words. 'Old' words were selected for their presumed familiarity to the old subjects and included *poultice*, *crony*, *fedora* and *bolster*. The 'young' words, presumed to be more familiar to the young subjects, included *Afro*, *denim*, *disco* and *frisbee*. Young subjects recalled more 'young' words than did old subjects, but 'old' words were recalled better by the old subjects. Barrett and Wright concluded that age-appropriate words have richer meanings for a subject and so were more elaborately processed in the orienting tasks. The consequential differences in trace elaboration readily account for the pattern of recall scores.

Summary

This chapter has not attempted to give a comprehensive account of the organic amnesias, nor to deal with the neural mechanisms involved. Instead, several psychological aspects of these dysfunctions were considered. The first section made the general point that one way in which neuropsychological evidence can contribute to theorizing about normal memory is by demonstrating dissociations or, more powerfully, double dissociations of memory functions. Evidence from studies' of traumatic amnesia was used to confirm the distinction between availability and accessibility of information in memory. Attention was then drawn to demonstrations of dissociation of function with respect to short-term storage and long-term storage, episodic and semantic memories, and verbal and visual memory systems.

Some attempts to understand the amnesic syndrome in terms of models of normal memory were discussed in the second section. Explanations which attribute this syndrome to an encoding deficit were discussed and Cermak's theory of a semantic encoding deficit was dealt with in detail. The interference theory of Warrington and Weiskrantz was discussed as the prominent example of theories which attribute the amnesics' problems to retrieval deficits. Possibly the most attractive theories of the amnesic syndrome are those involving the idea that a failure to utilize contextual information, or more generally to recollect, underlie the amnesics' problems. The need for psychological accounts of amnesia to take into consideration associations between detailed patterns of brain damage and specific patterns of memory deficit was noted.

Ageing was included here more because of certain similarities between the deficits associated with ageing and those of the amnesic syndrome rather than any direct evidence on the organic origin of presenile age-related differences. Evidence suggests that the functioning of verbal short-term storage changes little with age while tasks involving report of several input channels show changes which may reflect a general reduction in cognitive resources with increasing age. Deficits in both encoding in and retrieval from long-term storage are associated with increasing age. While, in some circumstances at least, these deficits can be reduced by encouraging appropriate strategies or providing cues, it seems unlikely that they are due merely to the failure of older subjects to spontaneously employ at the appropriate times strategies which are in their repertoire.

9 Development of memory

The scientific study of children's memory goes back to the early days of experimental psychology. Early investigations include those of Hunter (1917) who found that young children, having seen an object hidden in a particular location, would seek it out with declining success as the retention interval was increased. Kirkpatrick (1894) reported changes in free recall performance with age, and Jacobs (1887) investigated developmental changes in digit span (this increases steadily from about 4 digits at 4 to 5 years, through 5 digits at 6 to 8 years to 6 at 9 to 12 years, and about 7 at 13 years onwards). The close relationship between the development of memory and other cognitive processes was acknowledged by the inclusion of episodic memory items in tests of children's intelligence. The Stanford Binet test (Terman, 1916), for example, included tests of span together with other items such as placing an object under a box and asking the child to recognize an identical object from amongst a number of distractors. On the whole, it seems that early concern centred on the use of memory tests for diagnostic purposes rather than on understanding the changes which take place in memory. This emphasis has gradually changed and in recent years the number of experimental investigations concerned with the development of memory has been increasing rapidly.

As with the study of adult memory, various theoretical approaches have been adopted in order to understand memory development in children. Some theorists, such as Piaget and the Geneva school of developmentalists, have been concerned with the growth of cognitive processes and knowledge in general. Their interest in episodic memory has been subservient to these aims. Others, working within the tradition of information processing theory, have attempted a detailed analysis of the structures and strategies which change with growth. Yet another approach, acknowledging that children appear to learn unintentionally, has much in common with the levels of processing notion. This chapter considers these three approaches to the development of memory.

Piaget's theory

The stages of development

Piaget's developmental theory centres on the postulate that cognitive development proceeds through a series of stages (see Piaget, 1953). Although the age at which each stage begins and ends varies from child to child, the order is considered to be invariant. A brief description of these stages is necessary before considering the Piagetian view of memory. A full description is available in Flavell (1963).

During the sensori-motor stage (0-2 years) the child is able only to take account of immediate aspects of the environment, that is, what can be currently perceived and the actions he can perform. He is said to have only *figurative* knowledge. The pre-operational stage (2-7 years) starts when the child is no longer tied to his immediate actions and perceptions. The growth of memory becomes apparent: he is able to represent events and objects internally and hence can perform cognitive activity involving them when they are physically absent. At this stage there is a failure to conserve as demonstrated by the famous beaker experiments in which water is poured from a wide beaker into a narrow one and the child asked which beaker contains the most liquid. Before the concept of conservation is achieved the child is inappropriately governed by the height of the liquid. Also, and importantly for what comes below, the child at this stage has difficulty with *seriation*: if asked to construct a 'staircase' by arranging sticks of different lengths into a series of increasing size he will be unable to do so. There may also be difficulty in copying such a staircase, especially in the early years.

Difficulties with concepts such as seriation and conservation disappear at about the age of 7-8 years when the development of *concrete operations* (7-11 years) begins. During this stage the thinking processes can *operate* on the symbolic representations of concrete objects and events in a manner close to the patterns of actions and events in the real world. *Formal operations* (11 years onwards) are said to have developed when concrete operations are extended to ideas of *combination* and *independence*. Thinking is then no longer bound by concrete objects and events, and abstract thinking develops.

According to Piaget, cognitive development takes place by a series of *adaptations* involving changes in the cognitive *schemes* which form the basis of intelligence. The schemes embody generalized knowledge about things, and plans for dealing with the world. It is postulated that any input from the environment may be *assimilated by*, i.e. interpreted in terms of, the schemes. Hence, the schemes regulate perception. At the same time the schemes and their overall organization undergo *accommodation*. That is, they themselves change in response to the assimilation of new information. Eventually assimilation and accommodation proceed to the point where the changes in cognition appear to mark progression from one developmental stage to another.

Piaget's theory of memory

Piaget's principal interest has been in the growth of knowledge, i.e. the long-term storage of general information and its utilization. Piaget and Inhelder (1973) refer to the storage of schemes which contain such information, as memory in the *wider sense*. This corresponds to the knowledge structures or schemata of theorists such as Rumelhart and Ortony (1977) and Schank and Abelson (1977), and incorporates semantic memory in the rather restricted sense employed by Tulving (1972). Piagetian theory acknowledges the need to distinguish memory in this wider sense from memory for specific events, skills and objects. Piaget and

Inhelder refer to the latter as memory in the *strict sense* and it corresponds roughly to Tulving's episodic memory although, by including memory for specific skills and objects, it is somewhat broader in the phenomena it covers. Thus, amongst other things, memory in the strict sense forms the basis for recognizing objects and people as familiar, and for the recall of episodic events.

A further aspect of memory in the strict sense is the distinction between figurative and operational memory. Figurative memory involves no assimilation process: it contains a more or less direct representation of the stimulus and is able to contain specific aspects of it which cannot be assimilated by the schemes at their current stage of development. Figurative traces are presumed to be short-lived and so bear comparison with the notions of short-term visual and auditory traces discussed in Chapters 2 and 3.

Usually, however, remembering in the strict sense is *operational*, i.e. the construction of memory traces involves transformation of the stimulus input via the process of assimilation. Because of this, the encoding of an episode is affected by the developmental stage of the schemes. But that is not all. Piaget and Inhelder insist that strict traces are automatically transformed in storage as the cognitive system develops. Likewise, the process of reconstruction from the trace takes place via the schemes and hence is controlled by their stage of development. It is not clear from the theory how the distinction between automatic transformation of traces and the control of the reconstruction process can be distinguished experimentally if they are both affected by the same factor. However, the theory predicts that memory for a specific event encoded and recalled at one developmental stage will show *progression*, i.e. become more advanced, if recalled again during the next stage.

Piaget and Inhelder (1973) report a number of experiments which test their theory of memory progression with respect to several cognitive operations including seriation, horizontality, and numerical and spatial relationships. The basic paradigm is illustrated by one of their experiments involving seriation and using 3- to 8-year-old children. Each child was shown a display of 10 wooden sticks arranged in

increasing size. As stated earlier, it is not until about 8 years
that children acquire the scheme for seriation, so for most of
the subjects the stimulus represented an advanced operational stage. After one week and again after eight months the
children were asked to draw what they had seen. No mention
was made of the nature of the stimulus nor, of course, was it
shown after the initial presentation. At the first test the 3- to
4-year-olds failed to reproduce any degree of seriation, the 5-
year-olds showed some evidence of organization, e.g. alter-
nating long and short sticks; but, at 8 years seriation was
present. Clearly, these results are consistent with the view
that the reproductions reflect the increasing presence of
seriation in the operational schemes from younger to older
groups. When tested again after eight months there was an
increase in the average amount of seriation in the reproductions for all age groups as would be expected if the schemes
had developed between the first and second tests.

Piaget and Inhelder's findings have been replicated many
times so there is little doubt about their reliability or
generality (see Liben, 1977, for a review of this work).
However, there is disagreement about how these findings
should be interpreted. A rather obvious shortcoming of
Piaget and Inhelder's work is their failure to eliminate the
possibility that performance on *any* stimulus array would
become more faithful with the passage of time. This could
come about if, as the child develops, the memory trace of the
stimulus remains undeveloped but retrieval skills and
attention to detail become more proficient. It is conceivable,
therefore, that if the original stimulus was a random array of
sticks reproduction would become more faithful in detail,
rather than more seriated, as the child develops. In contrast,
the theory of memory progression insists that both the
memory trace and its utilization are directly influenced by
the developmental stage of the schemes. Hence, the theory
predicts that if pre-operational children are shown a random
sequence of sticks their reproductions will exhibit increased
seriation as their schemes develop. If reproduction of
randomly arranged sticks were to become more faithful
rather than more seriated it would suggest that Piaget's
memory progression is merely an instance of the general

phenomenon of reminiscence, i.e. improvement of performance over time. There would then be no need to postulate the
influence of changes in memory in the wider sense (scheme
for seriation) on the storage of, and reconstruction from,
memory traces in the strict sense. Altemeyer, Fulton and
Berney (1969) examined this issue by presenting kindergarten children (aged about 5 years) with either a seriated or
random array of sticks. They found that almost the same
proportion of children in the two groups showed increased
seriation between the first test after one week and the second
test after six months. Thus, increased seriation is not
restricted to children who are shown seriated arrays and
Piaget and Inhelder's memory progression is not merely a
specific case of reminiscence.

Although the Altmeyer *et al.* results support Piaget's
contention that the development of the schemes has an effect
on the storage and retrieval of traces in the strict sense there
remains a problem. It is possible that as children get older
they seriate more even though they remember nothing about
the original ordering of the sticks. Altmeyer *et al.* point out
that the high proportion of children who drew sticks, in
whatever arrangement, rather than anything else, testifies
that the components of the stimulus not specifically concerned with seriation were well remembered. While this
shows that the original stimulus did influence the later
reproduction it is not convincing with respect to seriation. In
order to find some further data relevant to this issue we turn
to one of Liben's studies involving horizontality rather than
seriation.

Liben (1974) employed two stimuli similar to those shown
in Figure 9.1 each representing water in a tilted vessel. The
10-year-old subjects were transitional with respect to Figure
9.1(a), that is, they were about to acquire the operation of
horizontality. Until then they would produce the primitive
Figure 9.1(b) when asked to draw the water in an empty
tilted jar. The children were divided into two groups, each
being shown one of the stimuli and asked to reproduce it one
week later and again after six months. Both groups showed
increases in horizontally from the first to the second test but,
importantly, the proportion of children giving horizontal

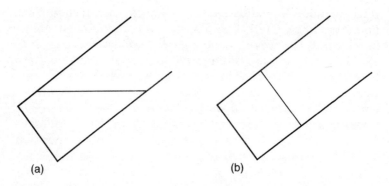

(a)   (b)

Figure 9.1:   *Operational and pre-operational drawings of water in a tilted vessel*

reproductions was less for the primitive stimulus group than for the advanced stimulus group. Clearly, the type of stimulus influenced the operational level reflected in the children's responses, thus supporting the view that memory in the strict sense does indeed interact with memory in the wider sense.

Non-operational explanations

In an extensive review of research on memory progression Liben (1977) has drawn attention to a number of non-operational explanations which have yet to be ruled out. These include the effects of repeated testing and the inclusion of recognition tests with those of recall. It is possible to eliminate increased drawing skills as an explanation because the ability to copy a seriated array in view develops faster than seriation in memory progression (see Piaget and Inhelder, 1973; Altmeyer *et al.*, 1969). The experiments described so far in this chapter have employed repeated testing of subjects. This design feature has certain advantages in that developmental changes do not occur at exactly the same age for all children. A within-subjects design ensures that the second test is conducted developmentally later than the first. It is possible, however, that repeated testing rather than cognitive development leads to changes in reproduction. Practice at retrieving from memory and drawing may give rise to improvement as may the greater familiarity with the experimenter and test situation.

A number of studies have been concerned with the effects of repeated testing but the results appear to conflict. For example, Dahlem (1969) presented 5-year-old subjects with a seriated array of sticks and asked for reproduction after a six-month interval. In addition, some of the subjects were tested immediately and again after one week. The groups did not differ on the degree of seriation in their reproductions at six months, thus indicating that repetition of testing had no effect. In contrast to this result, Finkel and Crowley (1973) found that prior testing did lead to an increase in seriation with a seriated array. As Liben (1977) points out, the differences in the results of these two studies may be largely explained by the inclusion of recognition tests by Finkel and Crowley: the repeated examination of distractors in these tests may have mediated the effects of repeated testing. Clearly, then, the use of repeated testing and the inclusion of recognition tests in many studies of memory progression make it difficult to assess tests of Piaget's theory. These issues have yet to be fully resolved.

Other approaches to memory development
There is, then, much evidence which is *consistent* with Piaget and Inhelder's theory that the storage and utilization of specific memory traces are directly influenced by the developmental stage of the schemes. But the requirements of a rigorous test of this theory are more complex than Piaget and Inhelder appear to have anticipated. Although others concerned with memory progression have included the necessary control groups receiving operationally primitive stimuli, there still remains the possibility that progression is artifactual.

One reason why Piaget's theory of memory in the strict sense is so difficult to test stems from the very general terms in which it is formulated. It is not surprising, therefore, that the more formal and detailed information processing approach has seemed an attractive alternative (see, e.g., Hagen, Jongeward and Kail, 1975). This approach has encouraged detailed consideration of developmental changes in memory structure and in control processes. A.L. Brown (1975) points out that while this approach seems appropriate where an intention to learn is essential for remembering, some other approach is necessary to deal with the apparently large amount of unintentional learning which takes place. The remainder of this chapter deals with these two aspects of memory development.

Incidental learning

Levels of processing and developmental theory
Developmental theories of cognition generally acknowledge that much of children's learning appears to take place without any intention to learn. Piaget acknowledged this by postulating that the processes of accommodation and assimilation are automatic: that is, much of what the child retains about past experiences, his knowledge of the world and language is assumed to be the *involuntary* consequences of his interactions with the environment. Russian psychologists, also, have emphasized the role of incidental learning in development (e.g. Smirnov, 1966/1973; Smirnov and Zinchenko, 1969; see also Meacham, 1977). Like Piaget, they have acknowledged the importance for memory of the involuntary consequences of cognitive activity, rather than intention to learn *per se*.

A.L. Brown (e.g. 1979) has drawn attention to the fact that three major principles which have guided recent developmental research and theorizing are incorporated in the levels of processing approach to memory (see Chapter 5). These principles are involuntary learning, the importance of cognitive activity rather than intention to learn *per se*, and what Brown (1975, 1979) calls *headfitting*. This last term refers to the processing limitations arising from the developmental level of the child's cognitive system, i.e. his knowledge structure or schemes. The term was chosen to acknowledge that a task can be successfully completed only if its demands are consistent with cognitive development, i.e. if it 'fits the child's head'. Similarly, the levels of processing approach to memory assumes that the depth to which information is processed depends on both the task demands and the ability of the subject to fulfil them. Also, the amount remembered is assumed to depend on the depth of processing achieved. Hence, what is remembered is determined by what is already known. Both the levels of processing approach and developmental theories, then, accept that 'the brain remembers what the brain does' (Jenkins, 1974b), and what 'the brain does' depends on the current structure of knowledge.

The similarities between the levels of processing approach and theories of cognitive development provide a point of contact between developmental and general memory research. However, the levels of processing approach, dealing as it does primarily with adult memory, has been able to ignore an aspect of memory which developmentalists should not neglect, namely, the way in which experiences influence knowledge. 'Levels of processing' is concerned with the recording of cognitive episodes in memory and the retrieval of episodic information from it. While the influence of semantic memory is seen as influential in these processes no provisions are explicitly made whereby episodic memory can influence semantic memory. And, of course, the same can be said of many other general approaches to, and theories of, memory. But as we have noted several times in earlier chapters, not everyone accepts a sharp distinction between episodic and semantic memory, and this includes proponents of the levels of processing approach (see Lockhart *et al.*, 1976). Naus and Halasz (1979) have felt it necessary to adopt that view in the developmental context. They conceive of the two types of memory as different aspects of the same system, differing in the degree of abstraction of information from the circumstances in which episodes occur. While this suggestion acknowledges the interdependence of Piaget's accommodation and assimilation it does not add significantly to our understanding of what accommodation involves, that is, it does not specify how changes in semantic memory are brought about. Unfortunately, as Brown (1979) and K.E. Nelson (1977) note, developmental theories in general have avoided the problem of accounting for *how* knowledge systems grow. They also observe that models of adult semantic memory too have difficulty dealing with the ways in which new information is added to existing knowledge structures.

Comparing intentional and incidental memory

Murphy and Brown (1975) presented pre-school children (under 5 years) with 16 pictures and required each child to categorize all of them on a taxonomic basis, judge them to be nice or nasty, or name the dominant colour in them. An unexpected recall test was given and, not surprisingly, the superficial colour-naming task yielded the lowest recall probability of 0.18 while the 'deeper' tasks gave probabilities of 0.41 and 0.38. Importantly, when other children of similar age were given instructions which stressed the need to learn the items for a later test the probability of recall was only 0.22. We have already noted in Chapter 5 that adult performance under intentional and 'deep' incidental conditions are very similar (Hyde and Jenkins, 1969) and that this probably arises because the strategies used by adults to deliberately facilitate remembering involve semantic processing. Murphy and Brown's results, then, suggest that pre-school children generally know very little about how or when to employ voluntary encoding processes in preparation for later tests of memory. This suggestion is supported by findings that, provided the task demands fit the heads of the youngest age group studied, there are no developmental trends in recall scores following orthographic, phonological or semantic orienting tasks (e.g. Geis and Hall, 1976). Also, tasks which apparently involve little voluntary encoding activity, such as *recognition* of pictures, show little change with age (Nelson, 1971). In contrast, as we will find in the next section, there are marked age-related changes in intentional memorizing.

The differences in developmental trends for incidental and intentional memorizing appear to reflect their different dependencies on voluntary strategies and so may enable age-related changes in strategic competence to be assessed. However, Hagen (1979) cautions against assuming too readily that so-called incidental learning paradigms are free of voluntary strategies. He refers to an experiment by

Sophian and Hagen in which children of pre-school and kindergarten ages performed an orienting task in which they sorted pictures of objects according to colour or taxonomic category. The unexpected memory tests included free recall and cued recall using colour names and category names as cues. Under free recall the older children recalled significantly more category-sort items, whereas for younger children this difference was not significant. In the cued recall conditions, however, *both* age groups recalled more category-sorted items with category cues than colour-sorted items with colour cues. Thus, the younger children apparently failed to benefit from the 'deeper' orienting task in free recall not because information was unavailable in memory but because they did not know how to use internally generated cues to facilitate access to the same extent as did the older children. Hence so-called incidental paradigms may involve voluntary processes at retrieval and the comparison of developmental trends in intentional and incidental learning may not provide the clear-cut index of strategic competence that some authors have implied (see, e.g., Naus and Halasz, 1979).

In any case the comparison of age trends in incidental and intentional learning on its own does not seem to allow *detailed* analysis of voluntary strategies. Such detailed analyses have taken place largely within those theoretical frameworks, such as information processing theory, which stress the distinction between structure and strategy. It is to these investigations that we now turn.

Intentional learning

Limitations of short-term storage
Studies of age-related changes in short-term memory performance under intentional learning conditions have shown that children do poorly, relative to adults, on most tests including memory span, probed recall and immediate free recall. These findings have often been interpreted in terms of multi-store models of short-term memory, such as that of Atkinson and Shiffrin, which maintain that performance on such tasks contains two components, one derived from the short-term

store (STS), the other from the long-term store (LTS). According to such models the children's poor short-term memory performance may arise from a limit on the capacity of STS, or lack of development of control processes which maintain items in STS or govern encoding in, and retrieval from LTS.

Several studies including that of Thurm and Glanzer (1971) have produced results suggesting that there are no developmental trends in structural aspects of memory such as the capacity of STS. In their study, Thurm and Glanzer presented 5- and 6-year-olds with 7 coloured drawings of common objects and obtained free recall of the object's names. The older children recalled more than the younger ones but there was little difference over the later serial positions. Although the STS and LTS components of recall were not formally assessed it seems from the data that STS capacity was similar for both groups.

Results such as those of Thurm and Glanzer, which fail to show age-related changes in memory structure, helped focus attention on developmental changes in control processes. Chi (1976) reviewed a number of short-term memory studies and concluded that developmental trends are due to the increasing ability to recode items into larger 'chunks' by optional processes, rather than the ability to retain more chunks. Case, Kurland and Goldberg (1982) have adopted a similar position. Essentially, like Atkinson and Shiffrin, they assume that the capacity of STS is divided amongst storage space and control processes, but they argue that the total capacity does not increase with age. What changes, they believe, is the processing efficiency so leaving more space available for storage.

Perhaps not surprisingly a number of recent studies have adopted the working memory model to help understand the development of memory. One such study is that of Nicolson (1981) in which short sequences of words were presented to 8-, 10-, and 12-year-olds. Every word in each list had the same number of syllables (1, 2, 3 or 4), and immediate recall was required. Following Baddeley *et al.* (1975; see Chapter 4) Nicholson also measured the rate at which the words could be read aloud. Not surprisingly, reading rate increased with age and decreased with the number of syllables but, importantly, when the number of words recalled is plotted against reading rate the points fall on a straight line (just as they did in the original Baddeley *et al.* study). Thus, Nicolson was able to suggest that the increase in memory span with age is due to the greater speed with which older children can articulate. In terms of the working memory model the older children are able to maintain more items in the articulatory rehearsal loop under the optional control of the central executive than are younger children.

Of course, the correlation between reading speed and recall does not constitute a causal relationship between the intentional use of rehearsal and performance. However, more direct evidence for such a relationship does exist and some of it is discussed in the next section. Before moving on, though, it is worth noting that developmental trends in the use of strategies such as rehearsal have been an extremely productive area of research. This is not surprising in view of the importance attached to control processes in adult memory. Work has been directed at discovering the types of strategies children use and the ages at which they first appear. Further interest has been focused on whether children of a specific age give poor performance because they do not have the skill to use a particular strategy, or simply do not appreciate when to use it. This work is discussed in the remainder of this chapter.

Production and mediation deficits
Flavell (1970) made an important contribution to the understanding of memory development by drawing together a body of previous work and emphasizing the distinction between two aspects of strategic competence. The first aspect concerns the child's spontaneous use of particular strategies for remembering: failure to spontaneously produce an appropriate strategy has been termed a *production deficit* by Flavell. The second aspect concerns the child's ability to make effective use of a particular strategy whether it was produced spontaneously or induced by the experimenter: failure to make use of an available strategy which could mediate remembering is referred to as a *mediation deficit*. Some

of Flavell's research involving the mediating strategy of rehearsal illustrates this distinction.

Falvell, Beach and Chinsky (1966) showed 5-, 7- and 10-year-olds a display of 7 pictures depicting objects which could be named easily by the youngest children. The experimenter pointed to a subset of the pictures one at a time and the child was required to point to them in the same order. In some of the conditions there was a 15-second delay before the test was given and during this interval the visor of the model space helmet worn by the subject was lowered. The visor prevented the child from seeing the pictures but enabled the experimenter to detect rehearsal of picture names by lipreading. Of the 20 subjects at each age two 5-year-olds, 12 7-year-olds, and 17 10-year-olds showed evidence of rehearsal. Thus, production of the rehearsal mediator increased with age, the younger children exhibiting a high incidence of production deficit.

Flavell *et al.* did not manipulate rehearsal as an experimental variable, hence their result on its own does not establish that rehearsal mediated recall. It is possible, for example, that good memorizers just happen to rehearse inconsequentially. The causal relationship was established by Keeney, Cannizzo and Flavell (1967) using 6-year-olds. This age is transitional for rehearsal, i.e. some children produce this mediator while others do not yet do so. Using a procedure similar to that of the earlier study, Keeney *et al.* replicated the finding that recall was higher for children who spontaneously rehearsed than for those who did not. They then took the non-producers (non-rehearsers) and encouraged them to rehearse. Not only were these children able to rehearse but their recall was then as good as that of the spontaneous rehearsers. This result establishes that the relationship between rehearsal and performance is causal and not merely correlational. It also shows that the original non-rehearsers had a production deficit but not a mediation deficit because they could make use of the mediating strategy once it was produced for them. Both these conclusions were confirmed when, at the end of the experiment, the task was completed again with no encouragement to rehearse. Over half the original non-producers stopped rehearsing with a consequent drop in performance.

A complication to the rather neat picture that emerges from Flavell's work has been introduced by Hitch and Halliday (1983). Like Flavell they concluded that there is no rehearsal of picture names by 5-year-olds but on the different grounds that they obtained no effect of word length, phonemic similarity, or concurrent vocalization, on recall. (Hitch's commitment to the working memory model is clear here!) In older children these variables all affected recall. But when the names were presented auditorily the effect of all the variables gave evidence of rehearsal in 5-year-olds. So, Hitch and Halliday concluded that children of 5 years and even younger do not have a production deficit for *rehearsal*. Rather they fail to encode picture names phonemically – a process considered to be optional in the working memory model. With auditory presentation such encoding is considered to be automatic. Thus there seems to be a production deficit in encoding rather than rehearsal. However, this conclusion must be seen against the findings of Keeney *et al.* that encouraging young children to *rehearse* improved recall. But, of course, such instructions doubtless carry with them the necessity to encode phonemically!

Organization

The rehearsal strategies studied by Flavell and his colleagues involve maintenance processes which may not on their own lead to long-term storage (see Chapter 4). To this end adults are able to exploit organization in the list or to create their own subjective organization when the list consists of 'unrelated' items. The development of organizational strategies has attracted much interest (see Lange, 1978, and Ornstein and Corsale, 1979, for reviews) and it is to this topic that we now turn.

Free recall of lists containing unrelated words or randomly arranged exemplars of several taxonomic categories increases with age. But there is little evidence of any corresponding increase in measures of subjective organization or category clustering until the age of about 11 years (see Ornstein and Corsale, 1979). One possible explanation of this situation is that the measures of output organization have not been sophisticated enough to reveal its presence. Indeed, the application of Friendly's proximity analysis (see Chapter 5) to developmental data does reveal some evidence of organization in 8-year-olds, but, nevertheless, the general picture remains one of little use of organization until late childhood.

Another possible explanation of the lack of organization in children's output is their lack of the necessary knowledge on which any organization must be based. But this account is not convincing in the face of evidence that children showing little evidence of organization in recall can, shortly afterwards, sort the material according to an adult scheme if given the appropriate encouragement (e.g. Liberty and Ornstein, 1973). This suggests that, to some extent at least, the failure to organize is due to a production rather than a mediation deficit, and several experimental results support this suggestion (e.g. Moely, Olson, Halwes, and Flavell, 1969; Worden, 1975). The Moely *et al.* study provides a good example of this type of experiment so it is worth describing it in a little detail.

Moely *et al.* used an ingenious technique to show that the failure of 5- to 9-year-olds to utilize the categorical structure of lists reflects a *production* rather than a *mediation* deficit. Subjects from each age range 5-6, 6-7 and 8-9 years were allocated to one of three groups, only two of which need concern us here. Both groups were presented with a haphazardly ordered display of cards containing pictures of objects from the categories *animals*, *furniture*, *vehicles* and *clothing*. The first, *uninstructed*, group was told they would be left alone for 2 minutes to memorize the items so they would be able to recall the names of the objects, and during this period they could move the cards if they wished. The second, *instructed*, group was induced to sort the cards into categories, name the resulting categories, and count the number of items in each. They were also told it might aid recall if they tried to remember the categories and the items in each. During the 2 minutes when the children were left alone they were observed through a one-way mirror. They were then asked to recall the items. The pre-recall observations showed that few of the uninstructed group sorted the cards into categories while many of the children of all ages in the instructed group did so. This difference in activity was reflected in the levels of performance and amount of clustering-by-category on the recall tests. Indeed, even at the lowest age those children in the instructed group who carried out extensive sorting and labelling activities produced more clustering and better recall than those who carried out little such activity. Thus, the failure of the uninstructed group to exploit the categorical nature of the list reflected a production and not a mediation deficit at all ages. This conclusion is reinforced by the results of a group of 11-year-olds who were run under the uninstructed conditions. These older subjects showed a very high incidence of spontaneous sorting and labelling in anticipation of the memory test.

Retrieval strategies
Young children's recall suffers from production deficits in retrieval as well as in encoding strategies. In Tulving's terminology they not only have fewer items available in memory than do older children, but these are less accessible as a result of failure to employ effective retrieval strategies. One set of evidence supporting this view comes from the study by Halperin (1974) in which the Tulving and Pearlstone (1966) paradigm was used. Children were required to free recall lists containing items from 9 taxonomic categories and were then given the category names as cues. The number of *categories* represented in free recall increased from 6 years to 12 years of age, but this age effect disappeared under cued recall. This shows that the older children were more skilled at gaining access to the items in memory when no cues are provided. The number of words recalled from each accessible category also increased with age and, according to Tulving and Pearlstone's (1966) logic, this may be taken to reflect the greater *encoding* skills of the older children, i.e. they had more items available. This is all as may be expected. However, some investigators have found that children recall more items from each category accessed with the aid of cues than without them in free recall (e.g. Kobasigawa, 1974). This contrasts with Tulving and Pearlstone's findings that the number of items retrieved is the same no matter how the category is accessed. A possible

explanation of this phenomenon is that the presence of cues guides the children's search of each category in memory so that instead of jumping haphazardly from one category to another they focus on each one in turn, exhausting the available items before moving on to the next. The presence of age differences in the control of such category searches is neatly demonstrated by the study of Salatas and Flavell.

Salatas and Flavell (1976) had groups of 6-, 9- and 21-year olds learn a list containing items drawn from the categories *toys*, *clothes* and *tools*, so they could recall all the items when given the category names as cues. They then asked for recall of all items from the list with certain properties such as 'would fit into a box measuring 30 × 20 × 13 centimetres'. The most effective way to perform this task is to search through the items in one category outputting the appropriate ones, and then move on to another category. If this is done then responses will cluster by category. Salatas and Flavell found that one out of the 36 6-year-olds, three out of the 32 9-year-olds and 21 out of the 32 21-year-olds showed such clustering. When directed to the category-by-category strategy by the experimenter, most 9-year-olds could carry it out but few of the 6-year-olds. Thus, the 9-year-olds suffered a production deficit while for the 6-year-olds the deficit was also of mediation.

Metamemory limitations
Why do production deficits in the absence of mediation deficits occur? If the child is able to make use of a mediator which is provided by someone else why does he not produce it spontaneously? A production deficit suggests a failure to appreciate that a particular strategy is appropriate for a specific task. In the extreme case the child may not be able to appreciate that *any* special effort is required. However, on the whole, young children do realize when some special mnemonic activity is called for, as the study by Acredolo, Pick and Olsen (1975) shows. Acredolo *et al.* took 4-year-olds on walks and exposed them to an episode such as the experimenter dropping a bunch of keys. Later, the children were asked to identify the place where it happened. Performance was much better if the children were warned

beforehand to remember the location, this indicating that the informed groups were aware that something special must be done to prepare for later recall. Even 3-year-olds adopt strategies such as pointing or looking at a location if asked to remember where a toy has been hidden (Wellman, Ritter and Flavell, 1975).

Knowing that a particular situation calls for special cognitive activity both in preparation for, and at retrieval, and being able to implement appropriate strategies, involves knowledge of the memory system. The subjects must know what it is best to do given the strengths and weaknesses of their own memory systems in relation to the task demands. We have already noted in Chapter 1 that Flavell (1971) introduced the term *metamemory* to refer to such knowledge. The way in which lack of metamemory can account for production deficiencies is well illustrated by the findings of Kennedy and Miller (1976). They carried out an experiment similar to that of Keeney *et al.* (1967) described earlier in this chapter. In it a group of children at the transitional age for rehearsal (6-7 years) was divided into those who rehearsed spontaneously when trying to remember a sequence of picture names and those who did not. The non-rehearsers were then given rehearsal training and, in addition, half of them were told, 'You did so much better when you whispered those words over and over. I guess whispering helped you remember the pictures better' (Kennedy and Miller, 1976, p. 567). Later, when no instructions to rehearse were given, more children in the 'feedback' group than in the 'no feedback' group continued to rehearse. Thus, because it expressed to the children the causal relationship between rehearsal and performance, the feedback can be seen as increasing metamemory and so removing the production deficit more effectively than merely providing the strategy.

In addition to the study of production deficits in rehearsal investigations of age-related changes in metamemory have included those concerned with knowledge of the effects of task variables, the children's awareness of their own memory ability, and their assessment of what is available and accessible in memory. Essentially, all these aspects of metamemory increase with age especially between the ages of

6 to 10 years. A few representative studies are mentioned below beginning with investigations of task variables. Speer and Flavell (1977) found that by the age of 6 years the majority of children realize that tests of recognition are easier than recall. By this age also there is an awareness that being able to name items such as pictures and objects is advantageous to remembering (Moynahan, 1973), and that familiar items are easier to remember than unfamiliar ones (Kreutzer, Leonard and Flavell, 1975). Kreutzer *et al.* also found that by 8 years children believed that paraphrase recall of stories is easier than verbatim recall.

Several studies have shown that an appreciation of the effects of retention interval develops after the age of 6 years. For example, Kreutzer *et al.* (1975) had children pretend that someone had just given them a telephone number to dial and asked if it would be best to dial immediately rather than after having a drink of water. The proportion of answers stating *immediately* rose from 60 per cent for 6-year-olds to 90 per cent for 9-year-olds. Rogoff, Newcombe and Kagan (1974), using a different procedure, confirmed that the effects of retention interval are not yet appreciated by 6 years. They left children free to decide for themselves how long they should study items in anticipation of a memory test after either a long or short interval. While 8-year-olds spent longer studying in anticipation of the longer interval 4- to 6- year-olds showed no such awareness of the task demands.

Another aspect of metamemory was investigated by Flavell, Friedrichs and Hoyt (1970) who showed that young children often have unrealistic estimates of their own mnemonic ability. In their study, children of various ages, and adults, were asked whether they would be able to remember sequences of from 1 to 10 pictures. Their actual memory spans for such sequences was than assessed. In line with general findings the actual spans increased steadily from 4 to 10 years, but younger children grossly over-estimated their ability while 10-year-olds were quite accurate. This unrealistic aspect of *mnemonic self-concept*, as Flavell and Wellman (1977) called it, may contribute to the lack of effort young children put into a memory task. Possibly, they believe that memorization will take place effortlessly!

The poor mnemonic self-concept of young children contrasts with their realistic estimates of how well they will perform on non-memory tasks such as jumping as far as possible (Markman, 1973). It seems likely that some of this difference is accounted for by the greater opportunity for feedback provided by physical activities because even 5-year-olds' predictions of memory span performance become more realistic if feedback is provided. Despite their over-optimistic views on their own abilities, young children believe that older children can remember more than younger ones (Kreutzer *et al.*, 1975). However, this belief is contributed to by generalization from the superiority of older children on more obvious skills rather than a direct knowledge of memory abilities.

Children's performance may suffer because they are poor at *monitoring* the state of their memory, e.g. judging the availability and accessibility of information in memory. Flavell, Friedrichs and Hoyt (1970) investigated the possibility that the inability to assess the state of memory storage leads children to terminate appropriate strategies prematurely. They assessed the memory spans for pictures of nameable objects for 4-, 7- and 10-year olds. They then presented span-length sequences of pictures to be learned, leaving the child to indicate when the whole sequence could be recalled correctly. The 7- and 10-year-olds recalled the sequences correctly thus showing they could assess the status of information in memory. The 4-year-olds, however, recalled only about a third of the sequences correctly. Since it had been established that the sequences were within the children's capabilities when the experimenter controlled the learning period, the learning process was presumably terminated prematurely because they overestimated what had been learned. Further evidence of a developmental trend in memory monitoring skills was provided by Wellman (1977) when he showed an age-related increase in the ability to judge whether the names of objects which could not be recalled could be recognized.

The concept of metamemory has assumed an important place in understanding memory development as it has in accounts of adult memory. However, as we noted in Chapter

1, a number of criticisms have been made against the adequacy of the way metamemory is currently conceived and the means by which it is assessed. These criticisms, discussed by Cavanaugh and Perlmutter (1982), include the frequent use of subjective reports which are, amongst other problems, open to influence by what subjects *feel* they should know or do, rather than what they *really* know about their memories. Thus, young children's premature foreclosure of learning may not be due to an inability to honestly assess their state of readiness but to a desire to appear 'grown up'. In addition, even when children are able to express what should be done to remember they may be unable to put such knowledge into practice when actually called upon to remember. It is possible that such inadequacies explain why memory performance and expressed metamemory are not always highly correlated. Nevertheless, the concept of metamemory does provide an attractive account of production deficits and it may be that more adequate means of assessing it will become available.

Summary

In this chapter we have considered three selected approaches to the development of memory, and we have done so with an emphasis on the changes in episodic rather than semantic memory skills. Piaget's developmental theory is concerned primarily with cognitive development, i.e. changes in the schemes which form the basis of intelligence. However, the postulated processes of accommodation and assimilation lead to specific predictions about changes in memory in the strict sense as development proceeds from one stage to another. While Piaget's theory is supported by observed changes in memory in the strict sense, as assessed by reproduction of stimuli at advanced and primitive operational levels, the extent to which these results are artifactual remains unclear.

Piaget's accommodation and assimilation are assumed to be automatic processes, thus reflecting the apparent involuntary nature of much of children's learning. There seems to be no satisfactory account of the mechanisms whereby episodic memory influences knowledge structures but the levels of processing approach to memory is able to deal equally well with the incidental acquisition of episodic memories by children and adults. Because episodic memory is conceived of as a record of cognitive activity it is necessarily influenced by the state of semantic memory. However, provided that the material fits the heads of the youngest age group there is little developmental trend in incidental learning in episodic memory. This is in marked contrast to trends found with deliberate memory situations thus suggesting that the distinction between voluntary and involuntary memory processes is an important one.

Studies of intentional learning and remembering show that age-related changes in short-term memory performance are best accounted for not by an increase in short-term storage capacity but by the efficient use of it through the employment of more effective strategies. The theoretical and experimental concern with developmental changes in voluntary strategies has been greatly influenced by Flavell's distinction between the child's inability to employ a particular strategy at all (a mediation deficit) and his failure to realize that the strategy is called for in particular circumstances (a production deficit). While the concept of metamemory, the individual's knowledge of his memory system, has been criticized on a number of grounds it goes a long way towards accounting for the presence of production deficits in the absence of mediation deficits.

Appendix

Corrected recognition scores

There are several ways of correcting recognition scores to take account of guessing and response bias. Two commonly used methods, borrowed from psychophysics, are based on *high threshold theory* and *signal detection theory*. Before describing them it will be helpful if some definitions are given.

In a recognition memory test subjects must try to distinguish *old* items, which have been presented earlier, from *new* items which have not been presented earlier. The subjects' responses to these types of item can be placed into a two-by-two matrix, thus:

		Response	
		new	*old*
Test item	*old*	miss	hit
	new	correct rejection	false positive

The terminology used in the table should be obvious. When an *old* item is correctly classified as 'old' a *hit* has been achieved. Failing to recognize an *old* item as such is termed a *miss*. Declaring that a *new* test item is indeed 'new' produces a *correct rejection*, while declaring that a *new* item is 'old' is termed a *false positive*.

High threshold method

The high threshold correction assumes that whenever an erroneous response is made (i.e. *miss* or *false positive*) the subject is guessing. That is, the subject is either *certain* the test item is *old* or *new*, or he has no information about it at all. Thus the probability of obtaining a *hit* (number of *hits* ÷ number of *old* test items) is made up of two components – the probability of making a 'true hit' (i.e. when certain) and the probability of guessing 'old' correctly. This may be expressed as follows:

p [obt. hit] = p [true hit] + p [correct guess for 'no
information' *old* items].

The probability of guessing 'old' correctly can be assessed by the probability of making a *false positive* (number of *false positives* ÷ number of *new* test items) because it is assumed that these are *all* guesses. So:

$$p \text{ [true hit]} = \frac{p \text{ [obt. hit]} - p \text{ [false positive]}}{1 - p \text{ [false positive]}}.$$

Signal detection theory

The assumption that subjects are either completely certain of their decisions or are merely guessing in a recognition test is a major shortcoming of the high threshold correction. This assumption intuitively seems wrong and there are good empirical grounds for rejecting it (see, e.g., Green and Swets, 1966). Signal detection theory makes no such all-or-none assumption about the subject's state of knowledge. Rather, it assumes that knowledge about an item lies on a continuum. The theory was developed to deal with situations in which observers must detect faint signals against a background of 'noise' as, for example, when picking out the presence of an 'aircraft' on the visual display screen of a radar system.

The application of the theory to recognition memory is straightforward: the *old* test items are analogous to target signals and the *new* items are analogous to noise. It is assumed that, *on the whole, old* items have associated with them greater *familiarity*, or some such information, indicating they have been more recently encountered than *new* items. (It is not necessary to resolve the precise nature of *familiarity* in order to understand the signal detection method of correcting recognition scores.) Another important assumption is that *old* and *new* items are normally distributed along the *familiarity* dimension. This situation is depicted in Figure A1 where X_n and X_o represent the mean levels of *familiarity* for *new* and *old* items respectively. The distributions of *new* and *old* items overlap. That is, some *new* items have greater levels of *familiarity* than some *old* items, and the extent of the overlap depends on the separation of X_n and X_o.

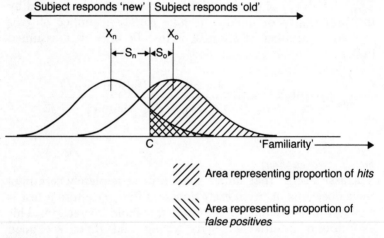

Figure A1:   *A representation of signal detection theory applied to recognition memory*

The signal detection method of correction assumes that the subject's task in a recognition memory test is to decide whether the level of *familiarity* associated with each test item is great enough to justify an 'old' response. To this end, the subject must establish a criterion point C along the *familiarity* dimension and respond 'old' to any item exceeding it, responding 'new' otherwise. If for any reason the subject is reluctant to respond 'old', C will be located towards the right-hand end of the familiarity axis. If, on the other hand, there is a greater readiness to respond 'old' than to respond 'new', C will be towards the left-hand end. It can be seen from Figure A1 how *hits* and *false positives* arise when *old* and *new* items respectively exceed C. It can also be seen that the position of C in Figure A1 reflects a bias towards caution i.e. against responding 'old'.

The difference between X_n and X_o reflects the subject's ability to distinguish between *old* and *new* items. As recognition performance improves, this difference increases.

Entering normal distribution tables with the probabilities of *hits* and *false positives* (these are represented by the areas under the curve to the right of C), it is possible to express the distances of C from X_o and X_n in terms of standard scores. The difference between X_o and X_n can then also be expressed in terms of standard scores ($S_o + S_n$ in Figure A1) and this provides the corrected recognition score d'. Other methods of obtaining d' include the use of tables provided by Elliott (1964) or of computer programs which work by drawing on stored representations of the normal distribution.

The application of signal detection theory to memory data, and some of its limitations, are discussed at length by Banks (1970).

Bibliography

Abeles, M. and Schilder, P. (1935), 'Psychogenic loss of personal identity', *Archives of Neurology and Psychiatry. Chicago, 34,* 587-604.

Acredolo, L.P., Pick, H.L. and Olsen, M.G. (1975), 'Environmental differentiation and familiarity as determinants of children's memory for spatial location', *Developmental Psychology, 11,* 495-501.

Altmeyer, R., Fulton, D. and Berney, K. (1969), 'Long-term memory improvement: confirmation of a finding by Piaget', *Child Development, 40,* 845-57.

Anderson, J.R. and Bower, G.H. (1972), 'Recognition and retrieval processes in free recall', *Psychological Review, 79,* 97-123.

Anderson, J.R. and Bower, G.H. (1973), *Human Associative Memory,* Washington DC: Winston.

Anderson, J.R. and Bower, G.H. (1974), 'A propositional theory of recognition memory', *Memory and Cognition, 2,* 406-12.

Anderson, J.R. and Ross, B.H. (1980), 'Evidence against a semantic-episodic distinction', *Journal of Experimental Psychology: Human Learning and Memory, 6,* 441-65.

Anisfeld, M. (1969), 'False recognition produced by semantic and phonetic relations under two presentation rates', *Psychonomic Science, 17,* 366-7.

Atkinson, R.C. and Shiffrin, R.M. (1968), 'Human memory: a proposed system and its control processes', in K.W. Spence and J.T. Spence (eds), *The Psychology of Learning and Motivation,* Vol. 2, New York: Academic Press.

Atkinson, R.C. and Shiffrin, R.M. (1971), 'The control of short-term memory', *Scientific American, 225,* 82-90.

Auble, P.M. and Franks, J.J. (1978), 'The effects of effort toward comprehension on recall', *Memory and Cognition, 6,* 20-5.

Averbach, E. and Sperling, G. (1961), 'Short-term storage of information in vision', in C. Cherry (ed.), *Information Theory: Proceedings of the Fourth London Symposium,* London: Butterworth.

Ayres, T.J., Jonides, J., Reitman, J.S., Egan, J.C. and Howard, D.A. (1979), 'Differing suffix effects for the same physical suffix', *Journal of Experimental Psychology: Human Learning and Memory*, 5, 315-21.

Baddeley, A.D. (1972), 'Retrieval rules and semantic coding in short-term memory', *Psychological Bulletin*, 78, 379-85.

Baddeley, A.D. (1978), 'The trouble with levels: a re-examination of Craik and Lockhart's framework for memory research', *Psychological Review*, 85, 139-52.

Baddeley, A.D. (1979), 'Working memory and reading', in P.A. Kolers, M.E. Wrolstad and H. Bouma (eds), *Processing of Visible Language*, New York: Plenum.

Baddeley, A.D. (1982a), 'Amnesia: a minimal model and interpretation', in L.S. Cermak (ed.), *Human Memory and Amnesia*, Hillsdale, New Jersey: Lawrence Erlbaum Associates.

Baddeley, A.D. (1982b), 'Domains of recollection', *Psychological Review*, 89, 708-29.

Baddeley, A.D. (1983), 'Working memory', *Philosophical Transactions of the Royal Society*, B302, 311-24.

Baddeley, A.D., Eldridge, M. and Lewis, V.J. (1981), 'The role of subvocalization in reading', *Quarterly Journal of Experimental Psychology*, 33A, 439-54.

Baddeley, A.D., Grant, S., Wight, E. and Thomson, N. (1975), 'Imagery and visual working memory', in P.M.A. Rabbitt and S. Dornic (eds), *Attention and Performance*, Vol. 5, London: Academic Press.

Baddeley, A.D. and Hitch, G. (1974), 'Working memory', in G.H. Bower (ed.), *The Psychology of Learning and Motivation*, Vol. 8, New York: Academic Press.

Baddeley, A.D. and Hitch, G. (1977), 'Recency re-examined', in S. Dornic (ed.), *Attention and Performance*, Vol. VI, London: Academic Press.

Baddeley, A.D. and Hull, A. (1979), 'Prefix and suffix effects: do they have a common basis?', *Journal of Verbal Learning and Verbal Behavior*, 18, 129-40.

Baddeley, A.D., Lewis, V. and Nimmo-Smith, I. (1978), 'When did you last . . .?', in M.M. Gruneberg, P. Morris and R.N. Sykes (eds), *Practical Aspects of Memory*, London: Academic Press.

Baddeley, A.D. and Lieberman, K. (1980), 'Spatial working memory', in R. Nickerson (ed.), *Attention and Performance*, Vol. 8, Hillsdale, New Jersey: Lawrence Erlbaum Associates.

Baddeley, A.D. and Patterson, K. (1971), 'The relation between long-term and short-term memory', *British Medical Bulletin*, 27, 237-42.

Baddeley, A.D., Thomson, N. and Buchanan, M. (1975), 'Word length and the structure of short-term memory', *Journal of Verbal Learning and Verbal Behaviour*, 14, 575-89.

Baddeley, A.D. and Warrington, E.K. (1970), 'Amnesia and the distinction between long- and short-term memory', *Journal of Verbal Learning and Verbal Behavior, 9*, 176-89.

Bahrick, H.P. (1970), 'Two-phase model for prompted recall', *Psychological Review, 77*, 215-22.

Balota, D.A. and Engle, R.W. (1981), 'Structural and strategic factors in the stimulus suffix effect', *Journal of Verbal Learning and Verbal Behavior, 20*, 346-57.

Balota, D.A. and Neely, J.H. (1980), 'Test-expectancy and word frequency effect in recall and recognition', *Journal of Experimental Psychology: Human Learning and Memory, 6*, 576-87.

Banks, W.P. (1970), 'Signal detection theory and human memory', *Psychological Bulletin, 74*, 81-99.

Barber, T.X. (1969), *Hypnosis: A Scientific Approach*, New York: Van Nostrand Reinhold.

Barbizet, J. (1970), *Human Memory and its Pathology*, San Francisco: Freeman.

Barrett, T.R. and Wright, M. (1981), 'Age-related facilitation in recall following semantic processing', *Journal of Gerontology, 36*, 194-9.

Bartlett, F.C. (1932), *Remembering*, Cambridge: Cambridge University Press.

Basso, A., Spinnler, H., Vallar, G. and Zanobio, M.E. (1982), 'Left hemisphere damage and selective impairment of auditory verbal short-term memory. A case study', *Neuropsychologia, 20*, 263-74.

Battig, W.F. and Bellezza, F.S. (1979), 'Organization and levels of processing', in C.R. Puff (ed.), *Memory Organization and Structure*, New York: Academic Press.

Bekerian, D.A. and Bowers, J.M. (1983), 'Eyewitness testimony: were we misled?', *Journal of Experimental Psychology: Learning, Memory, and Cognition, 9*, 139-45.

Berrington, W.P., Liddell, D.W. and Foulds, G.A. (1956), 'A re-evaluation of the fugue', *Journal of Mental Science, 102*, 280-6.

Betts, G.H. (1909), *The Distribution and Function of Mental Imagery*, Columbia, New York: Teachers College.

Birren, J.E. and Renner, V.J. (1977), 'Research on the psychology of aging: principles and experimentation', in J.E. Birren and K.W. Schaie (eds), *Handbook of the Psychology of Aging*, New York: Van Nostrand.

Bisiach, E. and Luzzatti, C. (1978), 'Unilateral neglect of representational space', *Cortex, 14*, 129-33.

Bjork, R.A. (1972), 'Theoretical implications of directed forgetting', in A.W. Melton and E. Martin (eds), *Coding Processes in Human Memory*, Washington, DC: V.H. Winston.

Bjork, R.A. (1978), 'The updating of human memory', in G.H. Bower (ed.), *The Psychology of Learning and Motivation*, Vol. 12, New York: Academic Press.

Bjork, R.A. and Landauer, T.K. (1978), 'On keeping one's memory current', in M.M. Gruneberg, P.E. Morris and R.N. Sykes (eds), *Practical Aspects of Memory*, London: Academic Press.

Bjork, R.A. and Whitten, W.B. (1974), 'Recency-sensitive retrieval processes in long-term free recall', *Cognitive Psychology*, 6, 173-89.

Block, N. (1981), *Imagery*, London: MIT Press.

Bousfield, W.A. (1953), 'The occurrence of clustering in the recall of randomly arranged associates', *Journal of General Psychology*, 49, 229-40.

Bousfield, W.A. and Sedgewick, C.H.W. (1944), 'An analysis of sequences of restricted associative responses', *Journal of General Psychology*, 30, 149-65.

Bower, G.H. (1970), 'Organizational factors in memory', *Cognitive Psychology*, 1, 18-46.

Bower, G.H. (1981), 'Mood and memory', *American Psychologist*, 36, 129-48.

Bower, G.H., Clark, M.C., Lesgold, A.M. and Winzenz, D. (1969), 'Hierarchical retrieval schemes in recall of categorized word lists', *Journal of Verbal Learning and Verbal Behavior*, 8, 323-43.

Bower, G.H. and Reitman, J.S. (1972), 'Mnemonic elaboration in multilist learning', *Journal of Verbal Learning and Verbal Behavior*, 11, 478-85.

Bowers, K.S. (1976), *Hypnosis for the Seriously Curious*, Monterey, Calif.: Brookes/Cole.

Braithwaite, R.B. (1962), 'Models in the empirical sciences', in E. Nagel, P. Suppes and A. Tarski (eds), *Logic, Methodology and Philosophy of Science: Proceedings of the 1960 International Congress*, Stanford, Calif.: Stanford University Press.

Bransford, J.D. (1979), *Human Cognition: Learning, Understanding and Remembering*, Belmont, Calif.: Wadsworth Publishing.

Bransford, J.D., Barclay, J.R. and Franks, J.J. (1972), 'Sentence memory: a constructive versus interpretive approach', *Cognitive Psychology*, 2, 331-50.

Bransford, J.D. and Johnson, M.K. (1973), 'Consideration of some problems of comprehension', in W.G. Chase (ed.), *Visual Information Processing*, New York: Academic Press.

Broadbent, D.E. (1958), *Perception and Communication*, London: Pergamon Press.

Broadbent, D.E. (1971), *Decision and Stress*, New York: Academic Press.

Broadbent, D.E., Vines, R. and Broadbent, M.H.P. (1978), 'Recency effects in memory as a function of modality of intervening events', *Psychological Research*, 40, 5-13.

Brown, A.L. (1975), 'The development of memory: knowing, knowing about knowing, and knowing how to know', in H.W. Reese (ed.),

Advances in Child Development and Behavior, Vol. 10, New York: Academic Press.

Brown, A.L. (1979), 'Theories of memory and the problem of development: activity, growth and knowledge', in L.S. Cermak and F.I.M. Craik (eds), *Levels of Processing in Human Memory*, Hillsdale, New Jersey: Lawrence Erlbaum Associates.

Brown, J. (1958), 'Some tests of the decay theory of immediate memory', *Quarterly Journal of Experimental Psychology*, *10*, 12-21.

Brown, J. (1964), 'Short-term memory', *British Medical Bulletin*, *20*, 8-11.

Brown, J. (1968), 'Reciprocal facilitation and impairment of free recall', *Psychonomic Science*, *10*, 41-2.

Brown, J., Lewis, V.J. and Monk, A.F. (1977), 'Memorability, word frequency and negative recognition', *Quarterly Journal of Experimental Psychology*, *29*, 461-74.

Brown, R. and Kulik, J. (1977), 'Flashbulb memories', *Cognition*, *5*, 73-99.

Brown, R. and McNeill, D. (1966), 'The "tip of the tongue" phenomenon', *Journal of Verbal Learning and Verbal Behavior*, *5*, 325-37.

Bruce, D. and Fagan, R.L. (1970), 'More on the recognition and free recall of organised lists', *Journal of Experimental Psychology*, *85*, 153-4.

Bruce, V. (1982), 'Changing faces: visual and non-visual coding processes in face recognition', *British Journal of Psychology*, *73*, 105-16.

Buckout, R. (1974), 'Now 2000 witnesses can be wrong', *Social Action and the Law*, *2*, 7.

Burke, D.M. and Light, L.L. (1981), 'Memory and aging: the role of retrieval processes', *Psychological Bulletin*, *90*, 513-46.

Campbell, R. and Dodd, B. (1980), 'Hearing by eye', *Quarterly Journal of Experimental Psychology*, *32*, 85-99.

Carey, S.T. and Lockhart, R.S. (1973), 'Encoding differences in recognition and recall', *Memory and Cognition*, *1*, 297-300.

Carmichael, L., Hogan, H.P. and Walters, A.A. (1932), 'An experimental study of the effect of language on the reproduction of visually perceived form', *Journal of Experimental Psychology*, *15*, 73-86.

Case, R., Kurland, M.D. and Goldberg, J. (1982), 'Operational efficiency and the growth of short-term memory span', *Journal of Experimental Child Psychology*, *33*, 386-404.

Cavanaugh, J.C. and Perlmutter, M. (1982), 'Metamemory: a critical examination', *Child Development*, *53*, 11-28.

Cermak, L.S. (1972), *Human Memory: Research and Theory*, New York: Ronald Press.

Cermak, L.S. (1979), 'Amnesia patients' level of processing', in L.S. Cermak and F.I.M. Craik (eds), *Levels of Processing in Human Memory*, Hillsdale, New Jersey: Lawrence Erlbaum Associates.

Cermak, L.S. (1982), 'The long and short of it in amnesia', in L.S. Cermak (ed.), *Human Memory and Amnesia*, Hillsdale, New Jersey: Lawrence

Erlbaum Associates.

Cermak, L.S., Butters, N. and Gerrein, J. (1973), 'The extent of the verbal encoding ability of Korsakoff patients', *Neuropsychologia*, *11*, 85-94.

Cermak, L.S., Butters, N. and Goodglass, H. (1971), 'The extent of memory loss in Korsakoff patients', *Neuropsychologia*, *9*, 309-15.

Cermak, L.S., Butters, N. and Moreines, J. (1974), 'Some analyses of the verbal encoding deficit of alcoholic Korsakoff patients', *Brain and Language*, *1*, 141-50.

Cermak, L.S. and Moreines, J. (1976), 'Verbal retention deficits in aphasic and amnesic patients', *Brain and Language*, *3*, 16-27.

Cermak, L.S. and Reale, L. (1978), 'Depth of processing and retention of words by alcoholic Korsakoff patients', *Journal of Experimental Psychology: Human Learning and Memory*, *4*, 165-74.

Chi, M.T.H. (1976), 'Short-term memory limitations in children: capacity or processing deficits?', *Memory and Cognition*, *4*, 559-72.

Chomsky, N. (1959), 'Review of Skinner's verbal behaviour', *Language*, *35*, 26-58.

Chopping, P.T. (1968), 'Holographic models of temporal recall', *Nature*, *217*, 781-2.

Clarapède, E. (1911), 'Recognition et moiite', *Archives Psychologiques*, *11*, 79-80.

Clark, L. and Knowles, J. (1973), 'Age differences in dichotic listening performance', *Journal of Gerontology*, *28*, 173-8.

Clifford, B.R. and Bull, R. (1978), *The Psychology of Person Identification*, London: Routledge & Kegan Paul.

Coe, W.C., Basden, B., Basden D. and Graham, C. (1976), 'Posthypnotic amnesia: suggestions of an active process in dissociative phenomena', *Journal of Abnormal Psychology*, *85*, 455-8.

Cofer, C.N., Bruce, D.R. and Reicher, G.M. (1966), 'Clustering in free recall as a function of certain methodological variations', *Journal of Experimental Psychology*, *71*, 858-66.

Collins, A.M. and Quillian, M.R. (1969), 'Retrieval time from semantic memory', *Journal of Verbal Learning and Verbal Behavior*, *8*, 240-7.

Coltheart, M. (1975), 'Iconic memory: a reply to Professor Holding', *Memory and Cognition*, *3*, 42-8.

Coltheart, M. (1980), 'Iconic memory and visible persistence', *Perception and Psychophysics*, *27*, 183-228.

Conrad, R. (1964), 'Acoustic confusion in immediate memory', *British Journal of Psychology*, *55*, 75-84.

Cooper, L.A. and Shepard, R.N. (1973), 'Chronometric studies of the rotation of mental images', in W.G. Chase (ed.), *Visual Information Processing*, New York: Academic Press.

Cooper, L.M. (1972), 'Hypnotic amnesia', in E. Fromme and R.E. Shor (eds), *Hypnosis: Research Developments and Perspectives*, Chicago: Aldine-Atherton.

Craik, F.I.M. (1968a), 'Two components in free recall', *Journal of Verbal Learning and Verbal Behavior*, 7, 996-1004.

Craik, F.I.M. (1968b), 'Short-term memory and the aging process', in G.A. Talland (ed.), *Human Aging and Behavior*, New York: Academic Press.

Craik, F.I.M. (1970), 'The fate of primary memory items in free recall', *Journal of Verbal Learning and Verbal Behavior*, 9, 143-8.

Craik, F.I.M. (1977), 'Age differences in human memory', in J.E. Birren and K.W. Schaie (eds), *Handbook of the Psychology of Aging*, New York: Van Nostrand Reinhold.

Craik, F.I.M. (1983), 'On the transfer of information from temporary to permanent memory', *Philosophical Transactions of the Royal Society, B, 302,* 341-59.

Craik, F.I.M. and Jacoby, L.L. (1979), 'Elaboration and distinctiveness in episodic memory', in L.G. Nilsson (ed.), *Perspectives on Memory Research: Essays in Honor of Uppsala University's 500th Anniversary*, Hillsdale, New Jersey: Lawrence Erlbaum Associates.

Craik, F.I.M. and Kirsner, K. (1974), 'The effect of speaker's voice on word recognition', *Quarterly Journal of Experimental Psychology*, 26, 274-84.

Craik, F.I.M. and Lockhart, R.S. (1972), 'Levels of processing: a framework for memory research', *Journal of Verbal Learning and Verbal Behavior*, 11, 671-84.

Craik, F.I.M. and Masani, P.A. (1969), 'Age and intelligence differences in coding and retrieval of word lists', *British Journal of Psychology*, 60, 315-19.

Craik, F.I.M. and Tulving, E. (1975), 'Depth of processing and the retention of words in episodic memory', *Journal of Experimental Psychology: General*, 104, 268-94.

Craik, F.I.M. and Watkins, M.J. (1973), 'The role of rehearsal in short-term memory', *Journal of Verbal Learning and Verbal Behavior*, 12, 599-607.

Crowder, R.G. (1967), 'Prefix effects in immediate memory', *Canadian Journal of Psychology*, 21, 450-61.

Crowder, R.G. (1969), 'Improved recall for digits with delayed cues', *Journal of Experimental Psychology*, 82, 258-62.

Crowder, R.G. (1972), 'Visual and auditory memory', in J.F. Cavanagh and I.G. Mattingly (eds), *Language by Eye and by Ear: The Relation between Speech and Learning to Read*, Cambridge, Mass.: MIT Press.

Crowder, R.G. (1976), *Principles of Learning and Memory*, Hillsdale, New Jersey: Lawrence Erlbaum Associates.

Crowder, R.G. (1978), 'Mechanisms of auditory backward masking in the stimulus suffix effect', *Psychological Review*, 85, 502-24.

Crowder, R.G. and Morton, J. (1969), 'Precategorical acoustic storage (PAS)', *Perception and Psychophysics*, 5, 365-73.

Crowder, R.G. and Raeburn, V.P. (1970), 'The stimulus suffix effect with reversed speech', *Journal of Verbal Learning and Verbal Behavior*, 9, 342-5.

Dahlem, N. (1969), 'Reconstructive memory in Kindergarten children revisited', *Psychonomic Science*, 17, 101-2.

Dark, V.J. and Loftus, G.R. (1976), 'The role of rehearsal in long-term memory', *Journal of Verbal Learning and Verbal Behavior*, 15, 479-90.

Darwin, C.J. and Baddeley, A.D. (1974), 'Acoustic memory and the perception of speech', *Cognitive Psychology*, 6, 41-60.

Darwin, C.J., Turvey, M.T. and Crowder, R.G. (1972), 'An auditory analogue of the Sperling partial report procedure: evidence for brief auditory storage', *Cognitive Psychology*, 3, 255-67.

Davies, G.M., Ellis, H.D. and Shepherd, J.W. (1977), 'Cue saliency in faces as assessed by the Photofit technique', *Perception*, 6, 262-9.

Davis, R., Sutherland, N.S. and Judd, B.R. (1961), 'Information content in recognition and recall', *Journal of Experimental Psychology*, 61, 422-9.

Daw, P.S. and Parkin, A.J. (1981), 'Observations on the efficiency of two different processing strategies for remembering faces', *Canadian Journal of Psychology*, 35, 351-5.

Deatherage, B.H. and Evans, T.R. (1969), 'Binaural masking: backward, forward and simultaneous effects', *Journal of the Acoustical Society of America*, 46, 362-71.

Dhanens, T.P. and Lundy, R.M. (1975), 'Hypnotic and waking suggestions and recall', *International Journal of Clinical and Experimental Hypnosis*, 23, 68-79.

Dillon, R.F. and Reid, L.S. (1969), 'Short-term memory as a function of information processing during the retention interval', *Journal of Experimental Psychology*, 81, 261-9.

Dowling, W.J. (1978), 'Scale and contour: two components of a theory of memory for melodies', *Psychological Review*, 85, 341-54.

Dowling, W.J. and Fujitani, D.S. (1971), 'Contour, interval, and pitch recognition in memory for melodies', *Journal of the Acoustical Society of America*, 49, 524-31.

Drachman, D.A. and Leavitt, J. (1972), 'Memory impairment in the aged: storage versus retrieval deficit', *Journal of Experimental Psychology*, 93, 302-8.

D'Zurilla, T. (1965), 'Recall efficiency and mediating cognitive events in "experimental repression" ', *Journal of Personality and Social Psychology*, 3, 253-6.

Ebbinghaus, H. (1913), *Memory* (H.A. Ruger and C.E. Bussenius, trans.), New York: Teachers College. (Originally published in 1885, reprinted by Dover, 1964.)

Efron, R. (1970), 'Effect of stimulus duration on perceptual onset and offset latencies', *Perception and Psychophysics*, 8, 231-4.

Eich, J.E. (1977), 'State-dependent retrieval of information in memory', in I.M. Birnbaum and E.S. Parker (eds), *Alcohol and Memory*, Hillsdale, New Jersey: Lawrence Erlbaum Associates.

Eich, J.M. (1982), 'A composite holographic associative recall model', *Psychological Review*, *89*, 627-61.

Elliott, P.B. (1964), 'Tables of d' ', in J.A. Swets (ed.), *Signal Detection and Recognition by Human Observers*, New York: Wiley.

Ellis, H., Shepherd, J. and Davies, G. (1975), 'An investigation of the use of the Photofit technique for recalling faces', *British Journal of Psychology*, *66*, 29-37.

Epstein, W. (1972), 'Mechanisms of directed forgetting', in G.H. Bower (ed.), *The Psychology of Learning and Motivation*, Vol. 6, New York: Academic Press.

Erber, J.T. (1974), 'Age differences in recognition memory', *Journal of Gerontology*, *29*, 177-81.

Erdelyi, M.J. and Goldberg, B. (1979), 'Let's not sweep repression under the rug: toward a cognitive psychology of repression', in J.F. Kihlstrom and F.J. Evans (eds), *Functional Disorders of Memory*, Hillsdale, New Jersey: Lawrence Erlbaum Associates.

Eriksen, C.W. and Johnson, H.J. (1964), 'Storage and decay characteristics of unattended auditory stimuli', *Journal of Experimental Psychology*, *68*, 28-36.

Eysenck, M.W. (1974), 'Age differences in incidental learning', *Developmental Psychology*, *10*, 936-41.

Eysenck, M.W. (1977), *Human Memory: Theory, Research and Individual Differences*, Oxford: Pergamon.

Eysenck, M.W. (1978), 'Levels of processing: a critique', *British Journal of Psychology*, *69*, 157-69.

Eysenck, M.W. and Eysenck, M.C. (1979), 'Processing depth, elaboration of encoding, memory stores, and expended processing capacity', *Journal of Experimental Psychology: Human Learning and Memory*, *5*, 472-84.

Fincke, R.A. (1980), 'Levels of equivalence in memory and perception', *Psychological Review*, *87*, 113-39.

Finkel, D. and Crowley, C. (1973), 'Improvement in children's long-term memory for seriated sticks: change in memory storage or coding rules?', paper presented at the biennial meeting of the Society for Research in Child Development, Philadelphia.

Flavell, J.H. (1963), *The Developmental Psychology of Jean Piaget*, New York: Van Nostrand Reinhold.

Flavell, J.H. (1970), 'Developmental studies of mediated memory', in H.W. Reece and L.P. Lipsitt (eds), *Advances in Child Development and Behavior*, Vol. 5, New York: Academic Press.

Flavell, J.H. (1971), 'First discussant's comments: what is memory development the development of?', *Human Development*, *14*, 272-8.

Flavell, J.H. (1981), 'Cognitive monitoring', in P. Dickson (ed.), *Children's Oral Communication Skills*, New York: Academic Press.

Flavell, J.H., Beach, D.H. and Chinsky, J.M. (1966), 'Spontaneous verbal rehearsal in a memory task as a function of age', *Child Development*, *37*, 283-99.

Flavell, J.H., Friedrichs, A.G. and Hoyt, J.D. (1970), 'Developmental changes in memorization processes', *Cognitive Psychology*, *1*, 324-40.

Flavell, J.H. and Wellman, H.M. (1977), 'Metamemory', in R.V. Kail, Jr, and J.W. Hagen (eds), *Perspectives on the Development of Memory and Cognition*, Hillsdale, New Jersey: Lawrence Erlbaum Associates.

Flexser, A.J. and Tulving, E. (1978), 'Retrieval independence in recognition and recall', *Psychological Review*, *85*, 153-71.

Frankel, F. (1976), *Hypnosis: Trance as a Coping Mechanism*, New York: Plenum Press.

Freud, S. (1955), 'From the history of an infantile neurosis', in J. Strachey (ed.), *The Standard Edition of the Complete Psychological Works of Sigmund Freud*, Vol. 17, London: Hogarth Press. (Originally published 1918.)

Freud, S. (1957), 'Repression', in J. Strachey (ed.), *The Standard Edition of the Complete Psychological Works of Sigmund Freud*, Vol. 14, London: Hogarth Press. (Originally published 1915.)

Friendly, M. (1979), 'Methods for finding graphic representations of associative memory structures', in C.R. Puff (ed.), *Memory Organization and Structure*, New York: Academic Press.

Gaffan, D. (1976), 'Recognition memory in animals', in J. Brown (ed.), *Recall and Recognition*, London: Wiley.

Galper, R.E. (1970), 'Recognition of faces in photographic negative', *Psychonomic Science*, *19*, 207-8.

Gardiner, J.M. (1983), 'On recency and echoic memory', *Philosophical Transactions of the Royal Society*, *B302*, 267-82.

Gardiner, J.M., Craik, F.I.M. and Birtwistle, J. (1972), 'Retrieval cues and release from proactive inhibition', *Journal of Verbal Learning and Verbal Behavior*, *11*, 778-83.

Gardiner, J.M., Gathercole, S.E. and Gregg, V.H. (1983), 'Further evidence of interference between lipreading and auditory recency', *Journal of Experimental Psychology: Learning, Memory and Cognition*, *9*, 328-33.

Gardiner, J.M. and Gregg, V.H. (1979), 'When auditory memory is not overwritten', *Journal of Verbal Learning and Verbal Behavior*, *18*, 705-19.

Gathercole, S.E., Gardiner, J.M. and Gregg, V.H. (1981), 'Effects of auditory and lip-spoken distraction on the modality effect in free recall', paper presented at the meeting of the Experimental Psychology Society, Oxford.

Gathercole, S.E., Gregg, V.H. and Gardiner, J.M. (1983), 'Influences of delayed distraction on the modality effect in free recall', *British Journal of Psychology*, *74*, 223-32.

Geis, M.F. and Hall, D.M. (1976), 'Encoding and incidental memory in children', *Journal of Experimental Child Psychology*, *22*, 58-66.

Glanzer, M. and Cunitz, A.R. (1966), 'Two storage mechanisms in free recall', *Journal of Verbal Learning and Verbal Behavior*, *5*, 351-60.

Glanzer, M., Koppenaal, L. and Nelson, R. (1972), 'Effects of relations between words on short-term storage and long-term storage', *Journal of Verbal Learning and Verbal Behavior*, *11*, 403-16.

Glanzer, M. and Razel, M. (1974), 'The size of the unit in short-term storage', *Journal of Verbal Learning and Verbal Behavior*, *13*, 114-31.

Glenberg, A.M., Bradley, M.M., Stevenson, J.A., Kraus, T.A., Tkachuk, M.J., Gretz, A.L., Fish, J.H. and Turpin, B.A.M. (1980), 'A two-process account of long-term serial position effects', *Journal of Experimental Psychology: Human Learning and Memory*, *8*, 355-69.

Glucksberg, S. and Cowan, G.N. (1970), 'Memory for non-attended auditory material', *Cognitive Psychology*, *1*, 149-56.

Godden, D.R. and Baddeley, A.D. (1975), 'Context-dependent memory in two natural environments: on land and underwater', *British Journal of Psychology*, *66*, 325-31.

Gomulicki, B.R. (1953), 'The development and present status of the trace theory of memory', *British Journal of Psychology: Monograph Supplement*, No. 29, 1-94.

Green, D.M. and Swets, J.A. (1966), *Signal Detection Theory and Psychophysics*, New York: Wiley.

Green, S. (forthcoming), *Introduction to Physiological Psychology*, London: Routledge & Kegan Paul.

Greenspoon, J. and Ranyard, R. (1957), 'Stimulus condition and retroactive inhibition', *Journal of Experimental Psychology*, *53*, 55-9.

Gregg, V.H. (1976), 'Word frequency, recognition and recall', in J. Brown (ed.), *Recall and Recognition*, London: Wiley.

Gregg, V.H. and Gardiner, J.M. (1984), 'Phonological similarity and enhanced auditory recency in longer-term free recall', *Quarterly Journal of Experimental Psychology*, *36A*, 13-27.

Gruneberg, M.M. and Sykes, R.N. (1969), 'Acoustic confusion in long-term memory', *Acta Psychologia*, *29*, 293-6.

Gudjonsson, G.H. (1979), 'The use of electrodermal responses in a case of amnesia (a case report)', *Medicine, Science and the Law*, *19*, 138-40.

Guilford, J.P. (1967), *The Nature of Human Intelligence*, New York: McGraw-Hill.

Guttman, N. and Julesz, B. (1963), 'Lower limits of auditory periodicity analysis', *Journal of the Acoustical Society of America*, *35*, 610.

Haber, R.N. and Haber, R.B. (1964), 'Eidetic imagery: I. Frequency', *Perceptual and Motor Skills*, *19*, 131-8.

Hagen, J.W. (1979), 'Development and models of memory: comments on the papers by Brown and Naus and Halasz', in L.S. Cermak and F.I.M. Craik (eds), *Levels of Processing in Human Memory*, Hillsdale, New Jersey: Lawrence Erlbaum Associates.

Hagen, J.W., Jongeward, R.H. and Kail, R.V. (1975), 'Cognitive perspectives on the development of memory', in H.W. Reese (ed.), *Advances in Child Development and Behavior*, Vol. 10, New York: Academic Press.

Halperin, M.S. (1974), 'Developmental changes in the recall and recognition of categorized word lists', *Child Development*, *45*, 144-51.

Hardyck, C.D. and Petrinovitch, L.R. (1970), 'Subvocal speech and comprehension level as a function of the difficulty level of reading material', *Journal of Verbal Learning and Verbal Behavior*, *9*, 647-52.

Harris, M. and Coltheart, M. (1986), *Language Processing*, London: Routledge & Kegan Paul.

Hart, J.T. (1965), 'Memory and the feeling-of-knowing experience', *Journal of Educational Psychology*, *56*, 208-16.

Hasher, L. and Zachs, R.T. (1979), 'Automatic and effortful processes in memory', *Journal of Experimental Psychology: General*, *108*, 356-88.

Hécaen, H. and Angelergues, R. (1962), 'Agnosia for faces (prosopagnosia)', *Archives of Neurology*, *1*, 92-100.

Hellyer, S. (1962), 'Supplementary report: frequency of stimulus presentation and short-term decrement in recall', *Journal of Experimental Psychology*, *64*, 650.

Heron, A. and Craik, F.I.M. (1964), 'Age differences in cumulative learning of meaningful and meaningless material', *Scandinavian Journal of Psychology*, *5*, 209-17.

Hilgard, E.R. (1965), *Hypnotic Susceptibility*, New York: Harcourt, Brace & World.

Hilgard, E.R. (1977), *Divided Consciousness: Multiple Controls in Human Thought and Action*, New York: Wiley-Interscience.

Hintzman, D.L. (1967), 'Articulatory coding in short-term memory', *Journal of Verbal Learning and Verbal Behavior*, *6*, 312-16.

Hintzman, D.L., Block, R.A. and Inskeep, N.R. (1972), 'Memory for mode of input', *Journal of Verbal Learning and Verbal Behavior*, *11*, 741-9.

Hintzman, D.L. and Summers, J.J. (1973), 'Long-term visual traces of visually presented words', *Bulletin of the Psychonomic Society*, *1*, 325-7.

Hitch, G.J. (1975), 'The role of attention in visual and auditory suffix effects', *Memory and Cognition*, *3*, 501-5.

Hitch, G.J. (1978), 'The role of short-term working memory in mental arithmetic', *Cognitive Psychology*, *10*, 302-23.

Hitch, G.J. and Halliday, M.S. (1983), 'Working memory in children', *Philosophical Transactions of the Royal Society of London, B302*, 325-40.

Hodgson, F. (1892), 'A case of double consciousness', *Proceedings of the Society for Psychical Research, 1*, 221-57.

Holding, D.M. (1975), 'Sensory storage revisited', *Memory and Cognition, 3*, 31-41.

Holmes, D.S. (1972), 'Repression or interference? A further investigation', *Journal of Personality and Social Psychology, 22*, 163-70.

Holmes, D.S. (1974), 'Investigations of repression: differential recall of material experimentally or naturally associated with ego threat', *Psychological Bulletin, 81*, 632-53.

Hudson, R.L. (1969), 'Category clustering for immediate and delayed recall as a function of recall cue dominance and response dominance variability', *Journal of Experimental Psychology, 82*, 575-7.

Hudson, R.L. and Austin, J.B. (1970), 'Effect of context and category name on the recall of categorized word lists', *Journal of Experimental Psychology, 86*, 43-7.

Hull, C.L. (1933), *Hypnosis and Suggestibility: An Experimental Approach*, New York: Appleton-Century.

Hultsch, D.F. (1975), 'Adult age differences in retrieval: trace-dependent and cue-dependent forgetting', *Developmental Psychology, 1*, 197-201.

Hunter, W.S. (1917), 'Delayed reaction in a child', *Psychological Review, 24*, 75-87.

Huppert, F.A. and Piercy, M. (1976), 'Recognition memory in amnesic patients: effect of temporal context and familiarity of material', *Cortex, 12*, 3-20.

Huppert, F.A. and Piercy, M. (1978), 'The role of trace strength in recency and frequency judgements by amnesic and control subjects', *Quarterly Journal of Experimental Psychology, 30*, 347-54.

Huttenlocher, J. (1968), 'Constructing spatial images: a strategy in reasoning', *Psychological Revue, 75*, 550-60.

Hyde, T.S. and Jenkins, J.J. (1969), 'Differential effects of incidental tasks on the organization of recall of a list of highly associated words', *Journal of Experimental Psychology, 82*, 472-81.

Hyde, T.S. and Jenkins, J.J. (1973), 'Recall for words as a function of semantic, graphic and syntactic orienting tasks', *Journal of Verbal Learning and Verbal Behavior, 12*, 471-80.

Inglis, J. and Caird, W.K. (1963), 'Age differences in successive responses to simultaneous stimulation', *Canadian Journal of Psychology, 17*, 98-105.

Jacobs, J. (1887), 'Experiments on "prehension" ', *Mind, 12*, 75-9.

Jacoby, L.L. (1974), 'The role of mental contiguity in memory: registration and retrieval effects', *Journal of Verbal Learning and Verbal Behavior, 13*, 483-96.

Jacoby, L.L. and Dallas, M. (1981), 'On the relationship between autobiographical memory and perceptual learning', *Journal of Experimental Psychology: General*, *110*, 306-40.

Jacoby, L.L. and Witherspoon, D. (1982), 'Remembering without awareness', *Canadian Journal of Psychology*, *36*, 300-24.

James, W. (1890), *Principles of Psychology*, New York: Holt.

Janet, P. (1904), *Neuroses et idées fixes*, (2nd edn), Paris: Felix Alcan.

Jenkins, J.J. (1974a), 'Can we have a theory of meaningful memory?', in R.L. Solso (ed.), *Theories of Cognitive Psychology: The Loyola Symposium*, New York: Lawrence Erlbaum Associates.

Jenkins, J.J. (1974b), 'Remember that old theory of memory? Well forget it!', *American Psychologist*, *29*, 785-95.

Jenkins, J.J. and Russell, W.A. (1952), 'Associative clustering during recall', *Journal of Abnormal and Social Psychology*, 47, 818-21.

Johnson, M.K., Bransford, J.D. and Solomon, S. (1973), 'Memory tacit implications of sentences', *Journal of Experimental Psychology*, *98*, 203-5.

Johnston, W.A. and Heinz, S.P. (1978), 'Flexibility and capacity demands of attention', *Journal of Experimental Psychology: General*, *107*, 420-35.

Jones, G.V. (1982), 'Tests of the dual-mechanism theory of recall', *Acta Psychologica*, *50*, 61-72.

Jorm, A.F. (1983), 'Specific reading retardation and working memory: a review', *British Journal of Psychology*, *74*, 311-42.

Kahneman, D. (1973), *Attention and Effort*, Englewood Cliffs, New Jersey: Prentice-Hall.

Keenan, J.M., MacWhinney, B. and Mayhew, D. (1977), 'Pragmatics in memory: a study of natural conversation', *Journal of Verbal Learning and Verbal Behavior*, *16*, 549-60.

Keeney, T.J., Cannizzo, S.R. and Flavell, J.H. (1967), 'Spontaneous and induced verbal rehearsal in a recall task', *Child Development*, *38*, 953-66.

Kennedy, B.A. and Miller, D.J. (1976), 'Persistent use of verbal rehearsal as a function of information about its value', *Child Development*, *47*, 566-9.

Keppel, G. and Underwood, B.J. (1962), 'Proactive inhibition in short-term retention of single items', *Journal of Verbal Learning and Verbal Behavior*, *1*, 153-61.

Kilhstrom, J.F. (1980), 'Posthypnotic amnesia for recently learned material: interactions with "episodic" and "semantic" memory', *Cognitive Psychology*, *12*, 227-51.

Kilhstrom, J.F. and Evans, F.J. (1976), 'Recovery of memory after posthypnotic amnesia', *Journal of Abnormal Psychology*, *85*, 564-9.

Kilhstrom, J.F. and Evans, F.J. (1979), 'Memory retrieval processes during posthypnotic amnesia', in J.F. Kilhstrom and F.J. Evans (eds), *Functional Disorders of Memory*, Hillsdale, New Jersey: Lawrence Erlbaum Associates.

Kimura, D. (1961), 'Cerebral dominance and the perception of verbal stimuli', *Canadian Journal of Psychology*, *15*, 166-71.

Kimura, D. (1963), 'Right-temporal lobe damage', *Archives of Neurology*, *8*, 264-71.

Kimura, D. (1964), 'Left-right differences in the perception of melodies', *Quarterly Journal of Experimental Psychology*, *14*, 355-8.

Kimura, D. (1967), 'Functional assymetry of the brain in dichotic listening', *Cortex*, *3*, 163-78.

Kinsbourne, M. and Wood, F. (1975), 'Short-term memory processes in the amnesic syndrome', in D. Deutsch and J.A. Deutsch (eds), *Short-term Memory*, New York: Academic Press.

Kintsch, W. (1970), 'Models for free recall and recognition', in D.A. Norman (ed.), *Models of Human Memory*, New York: Academic Press.

Kintsch, W. (1972), 'Abstract nouns: imagery versus lexical complexity', *Journal of Verbal Learning and Verbal Behavior*, *11*, 59-65.

Kintsch, W. (1974), *The Representation of Meaning in Memory*, Potomac, Maryland: Lawrence Erlbaum Associates.

Kintsch, W. (1976), 'Memory for prose', in C.N. Cofer (ed.), *The Structure of Human Memory*, San Francisco: Freeman.

Kintsch, W. and Buschke, H. (1969), 'Homophones and synonyms in short-term memory', *Journal of Experimental Psychology*, *80*, 403-7.

Kirkpatrick, E.A. (1894), 'An experimental study of memory', *Psychological Review*, *1*, 602-9.

Kirsner, K. (1973), 'An analysis of the visual component in recognition memory for verbal stimuli', *Memory and Cognition*, *1*, 449-53.

Kiss, G.R. (1975), 'An associative thesaurus of English: structural analysis of a large relevance network', in A. Kennedy and A. Wilkes (eds), *Studies in Long-term Memory*, London: Wiley.

Klatzky, R.L., Martin, G.L. and Kane, R.A. (1982), 'Semantic interpretation effects on memory for faces', *Memory and Cognition*, *10*, 195-206.

Klein, K. and Saltz, E. (1976), 'Specifying the mechanisms in a levels-of-processing approach to memory', *Journal of Experimental Psychology: Human Learning and Memory*, *2*, 671-9.

Kleinsmith, L.J. and Kaplan, S. (1964), 'Interaction of arousal and recall interval in nonsense syllable paired-associate learning', *Journal of Experimental Psychology*, *67*, 124-6.

Kobasigawa, A. (1974), 'Utilization of retrieval cues by children in recall', *Child Development*, *45*, 127-34.

Kolers, P.S. and Ostry, D.J. (1974), 'Time course of loss of information regarding pattern analysing operations', *Journal of Verbal Learning and Verbal Behavior*, *13*, 599-612.

Koriat, A. and Lieblich, I. (1974), 'What does a person in a TOT state know that a person in a 'Don't know' state doesn't know?', *Memory and*

Cognition, *2*, 647-55.

Kosslyn, S.M. (1980), *Image and Mind*, Cambridge, Mass.: Harvard University Press.

Kosslyn, S.M., Ball, T.M. and Reisser, B.J. (1978), 'Visual images preserve metric spatial information: evidence from studies of image scanning', *Journal of Experimental Psychology: Human Perception and Performance*, *4*, 47-60.

Kosslyn, S.M., Pinker, S., Smith, G.E. and Schwartz, S.P. (1981), 'On the demystification of mental imagery', in N. Block (ed.), *Imagery*, London: MIT Press.

Kreutzer, M.A., Leonard, C. and Flavell, J.H. (1975), 'An interview study of children's knowledge about memory', *Monographs of the Society for Research in Child Development*, *40* (1, serial No. 159).

Lachman, J.L., Lachman, R. and Thronesbery, C. (1979), 'Metamemory through the adult life span', *Developmental Psychology*, *15*, 543-51.

Lange, G. (1973), 'The development of conceptual and rote recall skills among school age children', *Journal of Experimental Child Psychology*, *15*, 394-407.

Lange, G. (1978), 'Organization-related processes in children's recall', in P.A. Ornstein (ed.), *Memory Development in Children*, Hillsdale, New Jersey: Lawrence Erlbaum Associates.

Lazar, G. and Buschke, H. (1972), 'Successive retrieval from permanent storage', *Psychonomic Science*, *29*, 388-90.

Legge, D. and Barber, P.J. (1976), *Information and Skill*, London: Methuen.

Levinger, G. and Clark, J. (1961), 'Emotional factors in the forgetting of word associations', *Journal of Abnormal and Social Psychology*, *62*, 99-105.

Levy, B.A. (1978), 'Speech processing during reading', in A.M. Lesgold, J.W. Pellegrino, J.W. Fokkema and R. Glaser (eds), *Cognitive Psychology and Instruction*, New York: Plenum Press.

Levy, B.A. (1981), 'Interactive processing during reading', in A.M. Lesgold and C. Perfetti (eds), *Interactive Processes in Reading*, Hillsdale, New Jersey: Lawrence Erlbaum Associates.

Levy, B.A. and Craik, F.I.M. (1975), 'The coordination of codes in short-term retention', *Quarterly Journal of Experimental Psychology*, *27*, 33-46.

Liben, L.S. (1974), 'Operative understanding of horizontality and its relation to long-term memory', *Child Development*, *45*, 416-24.

Liben, L.S. (1977), 'Memory in the context of cognitive development: the Piagetian approach', in R.V. Kail, Jr, and J.W. Hagen (eds), *Perspectives on the Development of Memory and Cognition*, Hillsdale, New Jersey: Lawrence Erlbaum Associates.

Liberty, C. and Ornstein, P.A. (1973), 'Age differences in organization and recall: the effects of training in categorization', *Journal of Experimental Child Psychology*, *15*, 169-86.

Light, L.L. and Berger, D.E. (1976), 'Are there long-term "literal copies" of visually-presented words?', *Journal of Experimental Psychology: Human Learning and Memory*, 2, 654-62.

Light, L.L. and Carter-Sobell, L. (1970), 'Effects of changed semantic context on recognition memory', *Journal of Verbal Learning and Verbal Behavior*, 9, 1-11.

Lindsay, P.H. and Norman, D.A. (1972), *Human Information Processing*, New York: Academic Press.

Lockhart, R.S., Craik, F.I.M. and Jacoby, L.L. (1976), 'Depth of processing, recognition and recall: some aspects of a general memory system', in J. Brown (ed.), *Recall and Recognition*, London: Wiley.

Loftus, E.F. (1979), *Eyewitness Testimony*, Cambridge, Mass.: Harvard University Press.

Loftus, E.F. (1983), 'Misfortunes of memory', *Philosophical Transactions of the Royal Society, London*, B302, 413-21.

Loftus, E.F. and Palmer, J.C. (1974), 'Reconstruction of automobile destruction: an example of the interaction between language and memory', *Journal of Verbal Learning and Verbal Behavior*, 13, 585-9.

Luria, A.R. (1968), *The Mind of a Mnemonist*, New York: Basic Books.

Lynch, S. and Yarnell, P.R. (1973), 'Retrograde amnesia: delayed forgetting after concussion', *American Journal of Psychology*, 86, 643-5.

McClean, P.D. (1969), 'Induced arousal and time of recall as determinants of paired-associate recall', *British Journal of Psychology*, 60, 57-62.

McCormack, P.D. (1972), 'Recognition memory: how complete a retrieval system?', *Canadian Journal of Psychology*, 26, 19-41.

McGehee, F. (1937), 'The reliability of the identification of the human voice', *Journal of General Psychology*, 17, 249-71.

McKelvie, S.J. (1983), 'Effects of lateral reversal on recognition memory for photographs of faces', *British Journal of Psychology*, 74, 291-407.

MacKinnon, D. and Dukes, W. (1964), 'Repression', in L. Postman (ed.), *Psychology in the Making*, New York: Knopf.

Mandler, G. (1967), 'Organization and memory', in K.W. Spence and J.T. Spence (eds), *The Psychology of Learning and Motivation*, Vol. 1, New York: Academic Press.

Mandler, G. (1980), 'Recognising: the judgement of previous occurrence', *Psychological Review*, 87, 252-71.

Mandler, G. and Pearlstone, Z. (1966), 'Free and constrained concept learning and subsequent recall', *Journal of Verbal Learning and Verbal Behavior*, 5, 126-31.

Mandler, J.M. and Johnson, N.S. (1976), 'Some of the thousands of words a picture is worth', *Journal of Experimental Psychology: Human Learning and Memory*, 2, 529-40.

Mandler, J.M. and Ritchey, G.H. (1977), 'Long-term memory for pictures', *Journal of Experimental Psychology: Human Learning and Memory*, *3*, 386-96.

Marcuse, F.L. (1959), *Hypnosis: Fact and Fiction*, London: Penguin Books.

Markman, E. (1973), 'Factors affecting the young child's ability to monitor his memory', unpublished doctoral dissertation, University of Pennsylvania.

Marks, D.F. (1973), 'Visual imagery differences in the recall of pictures', *British Journal of Psychology*, *64*, 17-24.

Marshall, J.C. (1977), 'Minds, machines and metaphors', *Social Studies of Science*, *7*, 475-88.

Martin, E. (1975), 'Generation-recognition theory and the encoding specificity principle', *Psychological Review*, *82*, 150-3.

Massaro, D.W. (1970), 'Preperceptual auditory images', *Journal of Experimental Psychology*, *85*, 411-17.

Massaro, D.W. (1972), 'Perceptual images, processing time, and perceptual units in auditory perception', *Psychological Review*, *79*, 124-45.

Matthews, M.L. (1978), 'Discrimination of Identikit construction of faces: evidence for a dual processing strategy', *Perception and Psychophysics*, *23*, 153-61.

Mayes, A.R., Meudell, P.R. and Neary, D. (1978), 'Must amnesia be caused by either encoding or retrieval disorders?', in M.M. Gruneberg, P.E. Morris and R.N. Sykes (eds), *Practical Aspects of Memory*, London: Academic Press.

Meacham, J.A. (1977), 'Soviet investigations of memory development', in R.V. Kail, Jr, and J.W. Hagen (eds), *Perspectives on the Development of Memory and Cognition*, Hillsdale, New Jersey: Lawrence Erlbaum Associates.

Medawar, P.B. (1969), *Induction and Intuition in Scientific Thought*, London: Methuen.

Melton, A.W. (1963), 'Implication of short-term memory for a general theory of memory', *Journal of Verbal Learning and Verbal Behavior*, *2*, 1-21.

Melton, A.W. (1970), 'The situation with respect to the spacing of repetitions and memory', *Journal of Verbal Learning and Verbal Behavior*, *9*, 596-606.

Merikle, P.M. (1980), 'Selection from visual persistence by perceptual groups and category membership', *Journal of Experimental Psychology: General*, *109*, 279-95.

Meudell, P.R., Northern, B., Snowden, J.S. and Neary, D. (1980), 'Long-term memory for famous voices in amnesic and normal subjects', *Neuropsychologia*, *18*, 133-9.

Miller, G.A. (1956), 'The magical number seven, plus or minus two: some limits of our capacity for processing information', *Psychological Review*, *63*, 81-7.

298   *Bibliography*

Miller, G.A., Galanter, E. and Pribram, K.H. (1960), *Plans and the Structure of Behavior*, New York: Holt, Rinehart & Winston.

Miller, R.R. and Springer, A.D. (1972), 'Temporal course of amnesia in rats after electroconvulsive shock', *Physiology and Behavior*, *8*, 645-51.

Miller, R.R. and Springer, A.D. (1973), 'Amnesia, consolidation and retrieval', *Psychological Review*, *80*, 69-79.

Milner, B. (1968), 'Preface: material specific and general memory loss', *Neuropsychologia*, *6*, 175-9.

Milner, B. and Teuber, H.L. (1968), 'Alteration of perception and memory in man: reflections on methods', in L. Weiskrantz (ed.), *Analysis of Behavioral Change*, New York: Harper & Row.

Mitchell, D.B. and Richman, C.L. (1980), 'Confirmed reservations on mental travel', *Journal of Experimental Psychology: Human Perception and Performance*, *6*, 58-66.

Moely, B.E., Olson, F.A., Halwes, T.G. and Flavell, J.M. (1969), 'Production deficiency in young children's clustered recall', *Developmental Psychology*, *1*, 26-34.

Moray, N., Bates, A. and Barnett, T. (1965), 'Experiments on the four-eared man', *Journal of the Acoustical Society of America*, *38*, 196-201.

Morris, C.D., Bransford, J.D. and Franks, J.J. (1977), 'Level of processing versus transfer appropriate processing', *Journal of Verbal Learning and Verbal Behavior*, *16*, 519-33.

Morton, J. (1969), 'Interaction of information in word recognition', *Psychological Review*, *76*, 165-78.

Morton, J. (1970), 'A functional model for memory', in D.A. Norman (ed.), *Models of Human Memory*, New York: Academic Press.

Morton, J. (1976), 'Two mechanisms in the stimulus suffix effect', *Memory and Cognition*, *4*, 144-9.

Morton, J. and Chambers, S.M. (1976), 'Some evidence for "speech" as an acoustic feature', *British Journal of Psychology*, *67*, 31-45.

Morton, J., Crowder, R.G. and Prussin, H.A. (1971), 'Experiments with the stimulus suffix effect', *Journal of Experimental Psychology*, *91*, 169-90.

Morton, J. and Holloway, C.M. (1970), 'Absence of a cross-modal "suffix-effect" in short-term memory', *Quarterly Journal of Experimental Psychology*, *22*, 167-76.

Moscovitch, M. (1982), 'Multiple dissociations of functions in the amnesic syndrome', in L. Cermak (ed.), *Human Memory and Amnesia*, Hillsdale, New Jersey: Lawrence Erlbaum Associates.

Moscovitch, M. and Craik, F.I.M. (1976), 'Depth of processing, retrieval cues, and uniqueness of encoding as factors in recall', *Journal of Verbal Learning and Verbal Behavior*, *15*, 447-58.

Moynahan, E.D. (1973), 'The development of knowledge concerning the effect of categorization upon free recall', *Child Development*, *44*, 238-46.

Mueller, C.W. and Watkins, M.J. (1977), 'Inhibition from part-set cueing: a cue-overload interpretation', *Journal of Verbal Learning and Verbal Behavior, 16*, 699-710.

Murdock, B.B., Jr (1971), 'Short-term memory', in G. Bower (ed.), *The Psychology of Learning and Motivation*, Vol. 5, New York: Academic Press.

Murphy, M.D. and Brown, A.L. (1975), 'Incidental learning in pre-school children as a function of level of cognitive analysis', *Journal of Experimental Child Psychology, 19*, 509-23.

Murphy, M.D., Sanders, R.E., Gabriesheski, A.S. and Schmitt, F.A. (1981), 'Metamemory in the aged', *Journal of Gerontology, 36*, 185-93.

Murray, D.J. (1967), 'The role of speech responses in short-term memory', *Canadian Journal of Psychology, 21*, 263-76.

Naus, M.J. and Halasz, F.G. (1979), 'Developmental perspectives on cognitive processing and semantic memory structure', in L.S. Cermak and F.I.M. Craik (eds), *Levels of Processing in Human Memory*, Hillsdale, New Jersey: Lawrence Erlbaum Associates.

Neisser, U. (1967), *Cognitive Psychology*, New York: Appleton-Century-Crofts.

Neisser, U. (1976), *Cognition and Reality*, San Francisco: Freeman.

Neisser, U. (1982), *Memory Observed: Remembering in its Natural Contexts*, San Francisco: Freeman.

Nelson, D.L. (1979), 'Remembering pictures and words: appearance, significance, and name', in L.S. Cermak and F.I.M. Craik (eds), *Levels of Processing in Human Memory*, Hillsdale, New Jersey: Lawrence Erlbaum Associates.

Nelson, D.L., Walling, J.R. and McEvoy, C.L. (1979), 'Doubts about depth', *Journal of Experimental Psychology: Human Learning and Memory, 5*, 24-44.

Nelson, K.E. (1971), 'Memory development in children: evidence from non-verbal tasks', *Psychonomic Science, 25*, 346-8.

Nelson, K.E. (1977), 'Cognitive development and the acquisition of concepts', in R.C. Anderson, R.J. Spiro and W.E. Montague (eds), *Schooling and the Acquisition of Knowledge*, Hillsdale, New Jersey: Lawrence Erlbaum Associates.

Nelson, T.O., Metzler, J. and Reed, D. (1974), 'Role of details in the long-term recognition of pictures and verbal descriptions', *Journal of Experimental Psychology, 102*, 184-6.

Nicolson, R. (1981), 'The relationship between memory span and processing speed', in M.P. Friedman, J.P. Das and N. O'Connor (eds), *Intelligence and Learning*, New York: Plenum Press.

Noble, C.E. (1963), 'Meaningfulness and familiarity', in C.N. Cofer and B.S. Musgrave (eds), *Verbal Behavior and Learning*, New York: McGraw-Hill.

Orne, M.T. (1972), 'On the simulating subject as a quasi-control group in hypnosis research: what, how and why', in E. Fromm and R.E. Shor (eds), *Hypnosis: Research Developments and Perspectives*, New York: Aldine-Atherton.

Orne, M.T. (1979), 'The use and misuse of hypnosis in court', *International Journal of Clinical and Experimental Hypnosis*, 27, 311-41.

Ornstein, P.A. and Corsale, K. (1979), 'Organizatonal factors in children's memory', in C.R. Puff (ed.), *Memory Organization and Structure*, New York: Academic Press.

Ornstein, P.A. and Naus M.J. (1978), 'Rehearsal processes in children's memory', in P.A. Ornstein (ed.), *Memory Development in Children*, Hillsdale, New Jersey: Lawrence Erlbaum Associates.

Osgood, C.E. (1953), *Method and Theory in Experimental Psychology*, New York: Oxford University Press.

Pachella, R.G. (1974), 'The interpretation of reaction time in information processing research', in B.H. Kantowitz (ed.), *Human Information Processing: Tutorials in Performance and Cognition*, Hillsdale, New Jersey: Lawrence Erlbaum Associates.

Paivio, A. (1971), *Imagery and Verbal Processes*, New York: Holt, Rinehart & Winston.

Paivio, A. (1979), 'The relationship between verbal and perceptual codes', in E.C. Carterette and M.P. Friedman (eds), *Handbook of Perception, Vol. IX: Perceptual Processing*, New York: Academic Press.

Paivio, A. and Csapo, K. (1969), 'Concrete-image and verbal memory codes', *Journal of Experimental Psychology*, 80, 279-85.

Paivio, A. and Csapo, K. (1973), 'Picture superiority in free recall: imagery or dual coding?', *Cognitive Psychology*, 5, 176-206.

Paivio, A. and te Linde, J. (1982), 'Imagery, memory, and the brain', *Canadian Journal of Psychology*, 36, 243-72.

Parkin, A.J., Lewinsohn, J. and Folkard, S. (1982), 'The influence of emotion on immediate and delayed retention: Levinger and Clark reconsidered', *British Journal of Psychology*, 73, 389-93.

Parks, T.E., Kroll, N.E.A., Salzberg, P.M. and Parkinson, S.R. (1972), 'Persistence of visual memory as indicated by decision time in a matching task', *Journal of Experimental Psychology*, 92, 437-8.

Patterson, K.E. and Baddeley, A.D. (1977), 'When face recognition fails', *Journal of Experimental Psychology: Human Learning and Memory*, 3, 406-17.

Pellegrino, J.W. and Ingram, A.L. (1979), 'Processes, products, and measures of memory organization', in C.R. Puff (ed.), *Memory Organization and Structure*, New York: Academic Press.

Penn, N.E. (1964), 'Experimental improvements on an analogue of repression paradigm', *Psychological Record*, 14, 185-96.

Perky, C.W. (1910), 'An experimental study of imagination', *American*

Journal of Psychology, *21*, 422-52.

Perlmutter, M. (1978), 'What is memory aging the aging of?', *Developmental Psychology*, *14*, 330-45.

Peterson, L.R. and Peterson, M.J. (1959), 'Short-term retention of individual verbal items', *Journal of Experimental Psychology*, *58*, 193-8.

Phillips, W.A. (1983), 'Short-term visual memory', *Philosophical Transactions of the Royal Society*, *B302*, 295-309.

Phillips, W.A. and Christie, D.F. (1977), 'Components of visual memory', *Quarterly Journal of Experimental Psychology*, *29*, 117-33.

Piaget, J. (1953), *The Origin of Intelligence in the Child*, London: Routledge & Kegan Paul.

Piaget, J. and Inhelder, B. (1973), *Memory and Intelligence*, London: Routledge & Kegan Paul.

Pinker, S. (1980), 'Mental imagery and the third dimension', *Journal of Experimental Psychology: General*, *109*, 354-71.

Popper, K.R. (1959), *The Logic of Scientific Discovery*, London: Hutchinson.

Posner, M.I., Boies, S.J., Eichelman, W.H. and Taylor, R.L. (1969), 'Retention of visual and name codes of single letters', *Journal of Experimental Psychology Monograph*, *79*, (1, part 2).

Posner, M.I. and Rossman, E. (1965), 'Effect of size and location of informational transforms upon short-term retention', *Journal of Experimental Psychology*, *70*, 496-505.

Posner, M.I. and Snyder, C.R.R. (1975), 'Attention and cognitive control', in R.L. Solso (ed.), *Information Processing and Cognition: The Loyola Symposium*, Hillsdale, New Jersey: Lawrence Erlbaum Associates.

Postman, L. (1964), 'Short-term memory and incidental learning', in A.W. Melton (ed.), *Categories of Human Learning*, New York: Academic Press.

Postman, L. (1972), 'A pragmatic view of organization theory', in E. Tulving and W. Donaldson (eds), *Organization of Memory*, New York: Academic Press.

Pratt, R.T.C. (1977), 'Psychogenic loss of memory', in C.W.M. Whitty and O.L. Zangwill (eds), *Amnesia*, London: Butterworth.

Prince, M. (1924), *The Unconscious*, New York: Macmillan.

Puff, R.C. (1979), 'Memory organization research and theory: the state of the art', in R.C. Puff (ed.), *Memory Organization and Structure*, New York: Academic Press.

Pylyshyn, Z.W. (1973), 'What the mind's eye tells the mind's brain: a critique of mental imagery', *Psychological Bulletin*, *80*, 1-24.

Rapaport, O. (1942), *Emotions and Memory*, Baltimore: Williams & Wilkins.

Raymond, B. (1969), 'Short-term storage and long-term storage in free recall', *Journal of Verbal Learning and Verbal Behavior*, *8*, 567-74.

Raymond, B. (1971), 'Free recall among the aged', *Psychological Reports*, *29*, 1179-82.

Reder, L.M., Anderson, J.R. and Bjork, R.A. (1974), 'A semantic interpretation of encoding specificity', *Journal of Experimental Psychology*, *102*, 648-56.

Reiser, M. and Nielson, M. (1980), 'Investigative hypnosis: a developing speciality', *American Journal of Clinical Hypnosis*, *23*, 75-84.

Reitman, J.S. (1974), 'Without surreptitious rehearsal, information in short-term memory decays', *Journal of Verbal Learning and Verbal Behavior*, *13*, 365-77.

Reitman, W. (1970), 'What does it take to remember?', in D.A. Norman (ed.), *Models of Human Memory*, New York: Academic Press.

Reitman, W., Malin, J.T., Bjork, R.A. and Higman, B. (1973), 'Strategy control and directed forgetting', *Journal of Verbal Learning and Verbal Behavior*, *12*, 140-9.

Ribot, T. (1882), *Diseases of Memory*, London: Kegan, Paul, Trench & Co.

Richardson, A. (1969), *Mental Imagery*, New York: Springer.

Richardson, J.T.E. (1979), 'Mental imagery, human memory, and the effects of closed head injury', *British Journal of Social and Clinical Psychology*, *18*, 319-27.

Richardson, J.T.E. (1980), *Mental Imagery and Human Memory*, London: Macmillan.

Richardson, J.T.E. and Baddeley, A.D. (1975), 'The effect of articulatory suppression in free recall', *Journal of Verbal Learning and Verbal Behavior*, *14*, 623-9.

Rock, I. (1974), 'The perception of disoriented figures', *Scientific American*, *230*, 78-85.

Roediger, H.L. (1973), 'Inhibition in recall from cueing with recall targets', *Journal of Verbal Learning and Verbal Behavior*, *12*, 644-57.

Roediger, H.L. (1974), 'Inhibiting effects of recall', *Memory and Cognition*, *2*, 261-9.

Roediger, H.L. (1978), 'Recall as a self-limiting process', *Memory and Cognition*, *6*, 54-63.

Roediger, H.L. and Neely, J.H. (1982), 'Retrieval blocks in episodic and semantic memory', *Canadian Journal of Psychology*, *32*, 213-42.

Roediger, H.L., Stellen, C.C. and Tulving, E. (1977), 'Inhibition from part-list cues and rate of recall', *Journal of Experimental Psychology: Human Memory and Learning*, *3*, 174-88.

Roediger, H.L. and Tulving, E. (1979), 'Exclusion of learned material from recall as a postretrieval operation', *Journal of Verbal Learning and Verbal Behavior*, *18*, 601-15.

Rogoff, B., Newcombe, N. and Kagan, J. (1974), 'Planfulness and recognition memory', *Child Development*, *45*, 972-7.

Ross, J. and Lawrence, K.A. (1968), 'Some observations on memory artifice', *Psychonomic Science*, *13*, 107-8.

Rossi, E.L. and Rossi, S.I. (1965), 'Concept utilization, serial order and recall in nursery school children', *Child Development*, *36*, 771-8.

Rumelhart, D.E. and Ortony, A. (1977), 'The representation of knowledge in memory', in R.C. Anderson, R.J. Shapiro and W.E. Montague (eds), *Schooling and the Acquisition of Knowledge*, Hillsdale, New Jersey: Lawrence Erlbaum Associates.

Rundus, D. (1971), 'Analysis of rehearsal processes in free recall', *Journal of Experimental Psychology*, *89*, 63-77.

Rundus, D. (1973), 'Negative effects of using list items as recall cues', *Journal of Verbal Learning and Verbal Behavior*, *12*, 43-50.

Russell, W.R. (1971), *The Traumatic Amnesias*, London: Oxford University Press.

Sachs, J.S. (1967), 'Recognition memory for syntactic and semantic aspects of connected discourse', *Perception and Psychophysics*, *2*, 437-42.

Sakitt, B. (1975), 'Locus of short-term visual storage', *Science*, *190*, 1318-19.

Sakitt, B. (1976), 'Iconic memory', *Psychological Review*, *83*, 257-76.

Sakitt, B. and Appleman, I.B. (1978), 'The effects of memory load and the contrast of the rod signal and partial report superiority in a Sperling task', *Memory and Cognition*, *6*, 562-7.

Salamé, P. and Baddeley, A.D. (1982), 'Disruption of short-term memory by unattended speech: implications for the structure of working memory', *Journal of Verbal Learning and Verbal Behavior*, *21*, 150-64.

Salatas, H. and Flavell, J.H. (1976), 'Retrieval of recently learned information: development of strategies and control skills', *Child Development*, *47*, 941-8.

Salter, D. (1975), 'Maintaining recency despite a stimulus suffix', *Quarterly Journal of Experimental Psychology*, *27*, 433-43.

Salter, D. and Colley, J.G. (1977), 'The stimulus suffix: a paradoxical effect', *Memory and Cognition*, *5*, 257-62.

Sanders, G.S. and Simmons, W.L. (1983), 'Use of hypnosis to enhance eyewitness testimony: does it work?', *Journal of Applied Psychology*, *68*, 70-7.

Santa, J.L. and Lamwers, L.L. (1974), 'Encoding specificity: fact or artifact?', *Journal of Verbal Learning and Verbal Behavior*, *13*, 412-23.

Santa, J.L. and Lamwers, L.L. (1976), 'Where does the confusion lie? Comments on the Wiseman and Tulving paper', *Journal of Verbal Learning and Verbal Behavior*, *15*, 53-7.

Sarbin, T.R. and Coe, W.C. (1972), *Hypnosis: A Social Psychological Analysis of Influence and Communication*, New York: Holt, Rinehart & Winston.

Schank, R.C. and Abelson, R.P. (1977), *Scripts, Plans, Goals and Understanding: An Enquiry into Human Knowledge Structures*, Hillsdale, New Jersey: Lawrence Erlbaum Associates.

Schonfield, D. and Robertson, B. (1966), 'Memory storage and ageing',

Canadian Journal of Psychology, *20*, 228-36.

Schreiber, F.R. (1974), *Sybil*, New York: Warner Books.

Schulman, A.I. (1971), 'Recognition memory for targets from a scanned word list', *British Journal of Psychology*, *62*, 335-46.

Schulman, A.I. (1974), 'Memory for words recently classified', *Memory and Cognition*, *2*, 47-52.

Seamon, J.G., Stolz, J.A., Bass, D.H. and Chatinover, A.I. (1978), 'Recognition of facial features in immediate memory', *Bulletin of the Psychonomic Society*, *12*, 231-4.

Segal, S.J. and Fusella, V. (1970), 'Influence of imaged pictures and sounds on detection of visual and auditory signals', *Journal of Experimental Psychology*, *83*, 458-64.

Semon, R. (1909), *Die Mnemischen Empfindungen*, Leipzig: William Engelman.

Shallice, T. (1975), 'On the contents of primary memory', in P.M.A. Rabbitt and S. Dornic (eds), *Attention and Performance*, Vol. 5, London: Academic Press.

Shallice, T. (1979), 'Neuropsychological research and the fractionation of memory systems', in L.-G. Nilsson (ed.), *Perspectives on Memory Research*, Hillsdale, New Jersey: Lawrence Erlbaum Associates.

Shallice, T. and Warrington, E.K. (1970), 'Independent functioning of the verbal memory stores: a neuropsychological study', *Quarterly Journal of Experimental Psychology*, *22*, 261-73.

Shand, M.A. and Klima, E.S. (1981), 'Nonauditory suffix effects in congenitally deaf signers of American sign language', *Journal of Experimental Psychology: Human Learning and Memory*, *7*, 464-74.

Shankweiller, D.P. and Studdart-Kennedy, M. (1967), 'Identification of consonants and vowels presented to the left and right ears', *Quarterly Journal of Experimental Psychology*, *19*, 59-63.

Sheehan, P.W. (1967), 'A shortened form of Betts' Questionnaire Upon Mental Imagery', *Journal of Clinical Psychology*, *23*, 386-9.

Shepard, R.N. (1961), 'Application of a trace model to the retention of information in a recognition task', *Psychometrika*, *26*, 185-203.

Shepard, R.N. (1967), 'Recognition memory for words, sentences and pictures', *Journal of Verbal Learning and Verbal Behavior*, *6*, 156-63.

Shepard, R.N. and Chipman, S. (1970), 'Second-order isomorphism of internal representations: shapes of states', *Cognitive Psychology*, *1*, 1-17.

Shepard, R.N. and Metzler, J. (1971), 'Mental rotation of three-dimensional objects', *Science*, *171*, 701-3.

Shiffrin, R.M. (1970), 'Memory search', in D.A. Norman (ed.), *Models of Human Memory*, New York: Academic Press.

Shiffrin, R.M. (1976), 'Capacity limitations in information processing, attention, and memory', in W.K. Estes (ed.), *Handbook of Learning and*

Cognitive Processes, Vol. 4, Hillsdale, New Jersey: Lawrence Erlbaum Associates.

Shiffrin, R.M. and Schneider, W. (1977), 'Controlled and automatic information processing: II. Perceptual learning, automatic attending, and a general theory', *Psychological Review*, *84*, 127-90.

Shulman, H.G. (1970), 'Encoding and retention of semantic and phonemic information in short-term memory', *Journal of Verbal Learning and Verbal Behavior*, *9*, 499-508.

Shulman, H.G. (1971), 'Similarity effects in short-term memory', *Psychological Bulletin*, *75*, 389-415.

Signoret, J.L. and Lhermitte, F. (1976), 'The amnesic syndrome and the encoding process', in M.R. Rosenzweig and E.L. Bennett (eds), *Neural Mechanisms of Learning and Memory*, Cambridge, Mass: MIT Press.

Simon, H.A. (1974), 'How big is a chunk?', *Science*, *183*, 482-8.

Skinner, B.F. (1963), 'Behaviorism at fifty', *Science*, *140*, 951-8.

Slamecka, N.J. (1968), 'An examination of trace storage in free recall', *Journal of Experimental Psychology*, *76*, 504-13.

Smirnov, A.A. (1973), *Problems of the Psychology of Memory* (translated by S.A. Corson), New York: Plenum Press. (Originally published 1966.)

Smirnov, A.A. and Zinchenko, P.I. (1969), 'Problems in the psychology of memory', in M. Cole and I. Maltzman (eds), *A Handbook of Contemporary Soviet Psychology*, New York: Basic Books.

Smith, E.E., Shoben, E.J. and Rips, L.J. (1974), 'Structure and process in semantic memory: a featural model for semantic decision', *Psychological Review*, *81*, 214-41.

Smith, S.M., Glenberg, A. and Bjork, R.A. (1978), 'Environmental context and human memory', *Memory and Cognition*, *6*, 342-53.

Snyder, M. and Uranowitz, S.W. (1978), 'Reconstructing the past: some cognitive consequences of person perception', *Journal of Personality and Social Psychology*, *36*, 941-50.

Solso, R.L. and McCarthy, J.E. (1981), 'Prototype formation of faces: a case of pseudo-memory', *British Journal of Psychology*, *72*, 499-503.

Spanos, N.P. and Gottlieb, J. (1979), 'Demonic possession, mesmerism and hysteria: a social psychological perspective in their historical interrelations', *Journal of Abnormal Psychology*, *88*, 527-46.

Spanos, N.P. and Radtke-Bodorik, H.L. (1980), 'Integrating hypnotic phenomena with cognitive psychology: an illustration using suggested amnesia', *Bulletin of the British Society of Experimental and Clinical Hypnosis*, No. 3, 4-7.

Spanos, N.P., Radtke-Bodorik, H.L. and Stam, H.J. (1980), 'Disorganised recall during suggested amnesia: fact not artifact', *Journal of Abnormal Psychology*, *89*, 1-19.

Speer, J.R. and Flavell, J.H. (1971), 'Young children's knowledge of the relative difficulty of recognition and recall memory tasks', unpublished manuscript, Stanford University, California.

Sperling, G. (1960), 'The information available in brief visual presentations', *Psychological Monographs*, *74*, whole no. 498.

Sperling, G. (1963), 'A model for visual memory tasks', *Human Factors*, *5*, 19-31.

Sperling, G. (1967), 'Successive approximations to a model for short-term memory', *Acta Psychologica*, *27*, 285-92.

Spoehr, K.T. and Corin, W.J. (1978), 'The stimulus suffix effect as a memory coding phenomenon', *Memory and Cognition*, *6*, 583-9.

Springer, S.P. (1971), 'Ear asymmetry in a dichotic listening task', *Perception and Psychophysics*, *10*, 239-41.

Squire, L.R. (1982), 'Comparison between forms of amnesia: some deficits are unique to Korsakoff's syndrome', *Journal of Experimental Psychology: Learning, Memory and Cognition*, *8*, 560-71.

Squire, L.R. and Slater, P.C. (1978), 'Anterograde and retrograde memory impairment in chronic amnesia', *Neuropsychologia*, *16*, 313-22.

Stalnaker, J.M. and Riddle, E.E. (1932), 'The effect of hypnosis on long-delayed recall', *Journal of General Psychology*, *6*, 429-40.

Standing, L., Conezio, J. and Haber, R.N. (1970), 'Perception and memory for pictures: single trial learning of 2560 visual stimuli', *Psychonomic Science*, *19*, 73-4.

Stein, B.S. (1978), 'Depth of processing re-examined: the effects of precision of encoding and test appropriateness', *Journal of Verbal Learning and Verbal Behavior*, *17*, 165-74.

Stengel, E. (1941), 'The aetiology of fugue states', *Journal of Mental Science*, *87*, 572-99.

Stern, L.D. (1981), 'A review of theories of human amnesia', *Memory and Cognition*, *9*, 247-62.

Sternberg, R.J. and Tulving, E. (1977), 'The measurement of subjective organization in free recall', *Psychological Bulletin*, *84*, 539-56.

Sternberg, S. (1975), 'Memory scanning: new findings and current controversies', *Quarterly Journal of Experimental Psychology*, *27*, 1-32.

Stromeyer, C.F. and Psotka, J. (1970), 'The detailed texture of eidetic images', *Nature*, *255*, 346-9.

Terman, L.M. (1916), *The Measurement of Intelligence*, Boston: Houghton.

Thigpen, C.H. and Cleckley, H.M. (1957), *The Three Faces of Eve*, New York: McGraw-Hill.

Thomson, D.M. and Tulving, E. (1970), 'Associative encoding and retrieval: weak and strong cues', *Journal of Experimental Psychology*, *86*, 255-62.

Thurm, A.T. and Glanzer, M. (1971), 'Free recall in children: long-term versus short-term store', *Psychonomic Science*, *23*, 175-6.

Treisman, A. (1964), 'Monitoring and storage of irrelevant messages in selective attention', *Journal of Verbal Learning and Verbal Behavior*, *3*, 449-59.

Treisman, A., Russell, R. and Green, J. (1975), 'Brief visual storage of shape and movement', in P.M.A. Rabbitt and S. Dornic (eds), *Attention and Performance*, Vol. 5, London: Academic Press.

Tresselt, M.E. and Mayzner, M.S. (1960), 'A study of incidental learning', *Journal of Psychology*, *50*, 339-47.

Tulving, E. (1962), 'Subjective organization in free recall of "unrelated" words', *Psychological Review*, *69*, 344-54.

Tulving, E. (1967), 'The effects of presentation and recall of material in free-recall learning', *Journal of Verbal Learning and Verbal Behavior*, *6*, 175-84.

Tulving, E. (1968), 'Theoretical issues in free recall', in T.R. Dixon and D.L. Horton (eds), *Verbal Behavior and General Behavior Theory*, Englewood Cliffs, New Jersey: Prentice-Hall.

Tulving, E. (1972), 'Episodic and semantic memory', in E. Tulving and W. Donaldson (eds), *Organization of Memory*, New York: Academic Press.

Tulving, E. (1974), 'Cue-dependent fogetting', *American Scientist*, *62*, 74-82.

Tulving, E. (1976), 'Ecphoric processes in recall and recognition', in J. Brown (ed.), *Recall and Recognition*, London: Wiley.

Tulving, E. (1982), 'Synergistic ecphory in recall and recognition', *Canadian Journal of Psychology*, *36*, 130-47.

Tulving, E. and Colatla, V. (1970), 'Free recall of trilingual lists', *Cognitive Psychology*, *1*, 86-98.

Tulving, E. and Osler, S. (1968), 'Effectiveness of retrieval cues in memory for words', *Journal of Experimental Psychology*, *77*, 593-601.

Tulving, E. and Patkau, J.E. (1962), 'Concurrent effects, contextual constraint and word frequency on immediate recall and learning of verbal material', *Canadian Journal of Psychology*, *16*, 83-95.

Tulving, E. and Pearlstone, Z. (1966), 'Availability versus accessibility of information in memory for words', *Journal of Verbal Learning and Verbal Behavior*, *5*, 381-91.

Tulving, E. and Thomson, D.M. (1971), 'Retrieval processes in recognition memory: effects of associative context', *Journal of Experimental Psychology*, *87*, 116-24.

Tulving, E. and Thomson, D.M. (1973), 'Encoding specificity and retrieval processes in episodic memory', *Psychological Review*, *80*, 352-73.

Turvey, M.T. (1973), 'On peripheral and central processes in vision: inferences from an information-processing analysis of masking with patterned stimuli', *Psychological Review*, *80*, 1-52.

Tversky, B.G. (1969), 'Pictorial and verbal encoding in a short-term memory task', *Perception and Psychophysics*, *6*, 225-33.

Tversky, B.G. (1973), 'Encoding processes in recognition and recall', *Cognitive Psychology*, *5*, 275-87.

Tzeng, O.J.L. (1973), 'Positive recency effect in a delayed free recall', *Journal of Verbal Learning and Verbal Behavior*, *12*, 436-9.

Tzeng, O.J.L., Lee, A.T. and Wetzel, C.D. (1979), 'Temporal coding in verbal information processing', *Journal of Experimental Psychology: Human Learning and Memory*, *5*, 52-64.

Vallar, G. and Baddeley, A.D. (1984), 'Fractionation of working memory: neuropsychological evidence for a phonological short-term store', *Journal of Verbal Learning and Verbal Behavior*, *23*, 151-61.

Vining, S.K. and Nelson, T.O. (1978), 'Some constraints on the generality and interpretation of the recognition of recallable words', *American Journal of Psychology*, *92*, 257-76.

Von Wright, J.M. (1968), 'Selection in immediate visual memory', *Quarterly Journal of Experimental Psychology*, *20*, 62-8.

Wagstaff, G.F. (1981), 'Suggested amnesia: compliance or inattention – encoding specificity', *Bulletin of the British Society of Experimental and Clinical Hypnosis No. 4*, 14-15.

Wagstaff, G.F. (1982), 'Hypnosis and recognition of a face', *Perceptual and Motor Skills*, *55*, 816-18.

Walker, E.L. (1958), 'Action decrement and its relation to learning', *Psychological Review*, *65*, 129-42.

Wallace, B. (1978), 'Restoration of eidetic imagery via hypnotic age regression: more evidence', *Journal of Abnormal Psychology*, *87*, 673-5.

Wallace, W.P. (1978), 'Recognition failure of recallable words and recognizable words', *Journal of Experimental Psychology: Human Learning and Memory*, *4*, 441-52.

Warrington, E.K. (1975), 'The selective impairment of semantic memory', *Quarterly Journal of Experimental Psychology*, *27*, 635-57.

Warrington, E.K. (1976), 'Recognition and recall in amnesia', in J. Brown (ed.), *Recall and Recognition*, London: Wiley.

Warrington, E.K. and Sanders, H.I. (1971), 'The fate of old memories', *Quarterly Journal of Experimental Psychology*, *23*, 432-42.

Warrington, E.K. and Shallice, T. (1972), 'Neuropsychological evidence of visual storage in short-term memory tasks', *Quarterly Journal of Experimental Psychology* , *24*, 30-40.

Warrington, E.K. and Weiskrantz, L. (1970), 'Amnesic syndrome: consolidation or retrieval?', *Nature*, *228*, 628-30.

Warrington, E.K. and Weiskrantz, L. (1973), 'An analysis of short-term and long-term memory defects in man', in J.A. Deutsch (ed.), *The Physiological Basis of Memory*, New York: Academic Press.

Warrington, E.K. and Weiskrantz, L. (1974), 'The effect of prior learning on subsequent retention in amnesic patients', *Neuropsychologia, 12,* 149-428.

Warrington, E.K. and Weiskrantz, L. (1978), 'Further analysis of the prior learning effect in amnesic patients', *Neuropsychologia, 16,* 169-77.

Warrington, E.K. and Weiskrantz, L. (1982), 'Amnesia: a disconnection syndrome?', *Neuropsychologia, 20,* 233-48.

Watkins, M.J. (1972), 'Locus of the modality effect in free recall', *Journal of Verbal Learning and Verbal Behavior, 11,* 644-8.

Watkins, M.J. (1974), 'The concept and measurement of primary memory', *Psychological Bulletin, 81,* 685-711.

Watkins, M.J. (1975), 'Inhibition in recall with extralist "cues" ', *Journal of Verbal Learning and Verbal Behavior, 14,* 294-303.

Watkins, M.J. (1977), 'The intricacy of the memory span', *Memory and Cognition, 5,* 529-34.

Watkins, M.J. (1979), 'Engrams as cuegrams and forgetting as cue overload: a cueing approach to the structure of memory', in C.R. Puff (ed.), *Memory Organization and Structure,* London: Academic Press.

Watkins, M.J. and Gardiner, J.M. (1980), 'An appreciation of generate-recognize theory of recall', *Journal of Verbal Learning and Verbal Behavior, 19,* 194-209.

Watkins, M.J., Ho, E. and Tulving, E. (1976), 'Context effects in recognition memory for faces', *Journal of Verbal Learning and Verbal Behavior, 15,* 505-17.

Watkins, M.J. and Todres, A.K. (1978), 'On the relation between recall and recognition', *Journal of Verbal Learning and Verbal Behavior, 17,* 621-33.

Watkins, M.J. and Watkins, O.C. (1974), 'Processing of recency items for free recall', *Journal of Experimental Psychology, 102,* 488-93.

Watkins, M.J., Watkins, O.C. and Crowder, R.G. (1974), 'The modality effect in free and serial recall as a function of phonological similarity', *Journal of Verbal Learning and Verbal Behavior, 13,* 430-47.

Watkins, O.C. and Watkins, M.J. (1975), 'Build-up of proactive inhibition as a cue-overload effect', *Journal of Experimental Psychology: Human Learning and Memory, 104,* 442-52.

Watkins, O.C. and Watkins M.J. (1980), 'The modality effect and echoic persistence', *Journal of Experimental Psychology: General, 109,* 251-78.

Watson, J.B. (1913), 'Psychology as the behaviorist views it', *Psychological Review, 20,* 158-77.

Waugh, N.C. and Norman, D.A. (1965), 'Primary memory', *Psychological Review, 72,* 89-104.

Wechsler, D. (1958), *The Measurement and Appraisal of Adult Intelligence,* 4th edn, Baltimore: Williams & Wilkins.

Weiskrantz, L. (1978), 'A comparison of hippocampal pathology in man and animals', in Ciba Foundation Symposium 58, *Functions of the Septo-*

hippocampal System, Amsterdam: Elsevier.

Weitzenhoffer, A.M. and Hilgard, E.R. (1962), *Stanford Hypnotic Susceptibility Scale, Form C*, Palo Alto, Calif.: Consulting Psychologist Press.

Welford, A.T. (1958), *Ageing and Human Skill*, London: Oxford University Press.

Welford, A.T. (1977), 'Motor performance', in J.E. Birren and K.W. Schaie (eds), *Handbook of the Psychology of Ageing*, New York: Van Nostrand.

Wellman, H.M. (1977), 'Tip of the tongue and feeling of knowing experiences: a developmental study of memory monitoring', *Child Development*, *48*, 13-21.

Wellman, H.M., Ritter, K. and Flavell, J.H. (1975), 'Deliberate memory behavior in the delayed reactions of very young children', *Developmental Psychology*, *11*, 780-7.

Wetzel, C.D. and Hunt, R.E. (1977), 'Cue delay and the role of rehearsal in directed forgetting', *Journal of Experimental Psychology: Human Learning and Memory*, *3*, 233-45.

White, B.W. (1960), 'Recognition of distorted melodies', *American Journal of Psychology*, *73*, 100-7.

Whitty, C.W.M., Stores, G. and Lishman, W.A. (1977), 'Amnesia in cerebral disease', in C.W.M. Whitty and O.L. Zangwill (eds), *Amnesia*, London: Butterworth (2nd edn).

Whitty, C.W.M. and Zangwill, O.L. (1977), 'Traumatic amnesia', in C.W.M. Whitty and O.L. Zangwill (eds), *Amnesia*, London: Butterworth (2nd edn).

Wickelgren, W.A. (1979), 'Chunking and consolidation: a theoretical synthesis of semantic networks, configuring in conditioning, S-R versus cognitive learning, normal forgetting, the amnesic syndrome and the hippocampal arousal system', *Psychological Review*, *86*, 44-60.

Wickens, D.D. (1972), 'Characteristics of word encoding', in A.W. Melton and E. Martin (eds), *Coding Processes in Human Memory*, Washington, D.C.: Winston.

Williams, M.D. and Hollan, J.D. (1981), 'The process of retrieval from very long-term memory', *Cognitive Science*, *5*, 87-119.

Williamson, J.A., Johnson, H.J. and Eriksen, C.W. (1965), 'Some characteristics of post-hypnotic amnesia', *Journal of Abnormal Psychology*, *70*, 123-31.

Winocur, G. and Weiskrantz, L. (1976), 'An investigation of paired-associate learning in amnesic patients', *Neuropsychologia*, *14*, 97-110.

Winograd, E. and Rivers-Bulkeley, N.T. (1977), 'Effects of changing context on remembering faces', *Journal of Experimental Psychology: Human Learning and Memory*, *3*, 397-405.

Wiseman, S. and Tulving, E. (1976), 'Encoding specificity: relation between recall superiority and recognition failure', *Journal of Experimental Psychology: Human Learning and Memory*, 2, 349-61.

Wood, F., Ebert, V. and Kinsbourne, M. (1982), 'The episodic-semantic memory distinction in memory and amnesia: clinical and experimental observations', in L.S. Cermak (ed.), *Human Memory and Amnesia*, Hillsdale, New Jersey: Lawrence Erlbaum Associates.

Woods, R.T. and Piercy, M. (1974), 'A similarity between amnesic memory and normal forgetting', *Neuropsychologia*, 12, 437-45.

Woodworth, R.S. (1938), *Experimental Psychology*, New York: Holt.

Worden, P.E. (1975), 'Effects of sorting on subsequent recall of unrelated items: a developmental study', *Child Development*, 46, 687-95.

Yarmey, A.D. (1979), *The Psychology of Eyewitness Testimony*, New York: Free Press.

Yates, F. (1966), *The Art of Memory*, London: Routledge & Kegan Paul.

Yin, R.K. (1968), 'Looking at upside-down faces', *Journal of Experimental Psychology*, 81, 141-5.

Yussen, S.R. and Levy, V.M., Jr (1975), 'Developmental changes in predicting one's own span of short-term memory', *Journal of Experimental Child Psychology*, 19, 502-8.

Zangwill, O.L. (1977), 'The amnesic syndrome', in C.W.M. Whitty and O.L. Zangwill (eds), *Amnesia*, London: Butterworth (2nd edn).

Zeller, A. (1951), 'An experimental analogue of repression: III. The effect of induced failure and success on memory measured by recall', *Journal of Experimental Psychology*, 42, 32-8.

Author index

Slater, P.C., 232
Smirnov, A.A., 142, 260
Smith, E.E., 25
Smith, G.E., 52, 55, 58
Smith, S.M., 162
Snowden, J.S., 88
Snyder, M., 20, 155
Solomon, S., 153
Solso, R.L., 48
Spanos, N.P., 204, 207-8
Speer, J.R., 272
Sperling, G., 31-5, 38-9
Spinnler, H., 226
Spoehr, K.T., 86
Springer, A.D., 224
Squire, L.R., 232, 234-5, 241
Stalnaker, J.M., 200
Stam, H.J., 207
Standing, L., 44
Stein, B.S., 149
Stengel, 190
Stern, 239
Sternberg, S., 18
Sternberg, R.J., 136
Stevenson, J.A., 123
Stolz, J.A., 49
Stores, G., 222
Stromeyer, C.F., 29
Summers, J.J., 42
Sutherland, N.S., 18
Sykes, R.N., 117

Taylor, R.L., 39, 105
Terman, L.M., 252
Teuber, H.L., 229
Thigpen, C.H., 192
Thomson, D.M., 173-4, 177-80
Thomson, N., 113-4, 131
Thronesbury, C., 249
Thurm, A.T., 264
Tkachuk, M.J., 123
Todres, A.K., 178
Treisman, A., 37, 142
Tresselt, M.E., 140
Tulving, E., 23-5, 102, 133, 136, 145, 147-8, 150, 159-163, 166, 170-82, 184-6, 218, 228, 233, 246, 254, 269
Turpin, B.A.M., 123
Turvey, M.T., 36-7, 65-70, 75
Tversky, B.G., 21, 43
Tzeng, O.J.L., 123, 216-7

Underwood, B.J., 106
Uranovitz, S.N., 155

Vallar, G., 226, 228
Vines, R., 83
Vining, S.K., 175
Von Wright, J.M., 38

Wagstaff, G.F., 200, 208
Walker, E.L., 197-8
Wallace, B., 30
Walling, J.R., 144, 149
Walters, A.A., 47
Warrington, E.K., 226-8, 231, 235-7, 240, 245-6
Watkins, M.J., 81, 83-4, 100-2, 105, 111, 113, 163, 165, 173, 178
Watkins, O.C., 81, 83-4, 100, 111
Watson, J.B., 3
Waugh, N.C., 92-4, 96-7, 99, 101, 103-4
Wechsler, D., 242
Weiskrantz, L., 237, 239-40
Weitzenhoffer, A.M., 201
Welford, A.T., 242
Wellman, H.M., 21, 271-3
Wetzel, C.D., 216
White, B.W., 89
Whitten, W.B., 122-4
Whitty, C.W.M., 222
Wickelgren, W.A., 239
Wickens, 109-110, 214
Wight, E., 131
Williams, M.D., 181-2, 240
Williamson, J.A., 205
Winocur, G., 237
Winograd, E., 50
Winzenz, D., 135
Wiseman, S., 179
Witherspoon, D., 240
Wood, F., 229, 234
Woods, R.T., 238-9
Woodworth, R.S., 47
Worden, P.E., 267
Wright, M., 249

Yarmey, A.D., 48
Yarnell, P.R., 223
Yates, F., 128
Yin, R.K., 50

Zachs, R.T., 20, 139, 216
Zangwill, O.L., 222, 225
Zanobio, M.E., 226
Zeller, A., 195
Zinchenko, P.I., 142, 260

Subject index